OWEN MURRAY  DAN

The karateka who was m... hand

Best Wishes
Owen Murray M.BE

OTHER BOOKS BY CLIVE LAYTON

Conversations with Karate Masters
Unmasking the Martial Artist
Mysteries of the Martial Arts
Mind Training for the Martial Arts
Training with Funakoshi
Karate Master: The Life & Times of Mitsusuke Harada
Shotokan Dawn: Vol. I
Shotokan Dawn: Vol. II
A Shotokan Karate Book of Facts: Vol. I
A Shotokan Karate Book of Facts: Vol. II
A Shotokan Karate Book of Facts: Vol. III
The Kanazawa Years
Reminiscences by Master Mitsusuke Harada
A Shotokan Karate Book of Dates
The Shotokan Karate Book of Quotes
Kanazawa, 10th Dan
Funakoshi on Okinawa
Shotokan Dawn Over Ireland
The Shotokan Dawn Supplement
Shotokan Horizon
You Don't Have to Dress to Kill
The Liverpool Red Triangle Karate Club
Masao Kawasoe, 8th Dan
Ronnie Watt, 8th Dan
Scotland's First Karate Club
Master Masao Kawasoe: The Foundations of Shotokan Karate Technique

OWEN MURRAY, M.B.E., 6th DAN

The karateka who was made whole by the loss of a hand

DR. CLIVE LAYTON

SURESAFE (NORTH EAST) LTD.

Riverside Lodge, Riverside Farm, South Hylton, Sunderland, SR4 0NQ, Great Britain

First Published in 2014
by
SURESAFE (NORTH EAST) LTD.
Riverside Lodge, Riverside Farm, South Hylton, Sunderland, SR4 0NQ,
Great Britain
Tel: +44 (0) 1915344287
www.suresafe.net
email: ellen@suresafe.net

Copyright © 2014 Clive Layton

All rights reserved. No part of this publication may be reproduced, stored in a retrieval system, or transmitted in any form or by any means, electronic, mechanical, photocopying, recording, or otherwise, without the prior written permission of the copyright owner.

The moral right of the author has been asserted.

First Edition

**British Library Cataloguing-in-Publication Data.
A catalogue record for this book is available from the British Library.**

ISBN 978 0 9930858 0 2

DEDICATION

TO

RACHEL, PANDORA & FRITHA

ACKNOWLEDGEMENTS

The author and publisher are grateful to the following people for their help during the preparation of this book: Rachel Layton; Pandora Layton; Jeff Barwick, 5th Dan KUGB; Margaret Barwick; Joan Johnson; Dave Hazard, 7th Dan, Chief Instructor of the Academy of Shotokan Karate; Frank Brennan, 7th Dan, Vice-Chairman KUGB; Allan Turner, 3rd Dan, Karate Union of Australia; Ellen Grewcock; Sam Grewcock; David Buckley; Ronnie Bestford, 3rd Dan BJA, 4th Dan AMA; Jeff Wilkinson, 3rd Dan KUGB; John Holdsworth, 6th Dan KUGB; Julie Nicolson, 6th Dan KUGB; Andy Sherry, 9th Dan, Chairman and Chief Instructor of the KUGB; Terry O'Neill, 8th Dan KUGB; Bob Poynton, 8th Dan, National Administration and Finance Officer of the KUGB; Graham Adams, 6th Dan KUGB; John Thompson, 4th Dan KUGB; Graham Noble; Christine Pullan, 7th Dan, Amateur Martial Association.

Photo Credits: ALLSPORT/John Gichigi: 139 (bottom); Jeff Barwick: 181, 182; Echo: 86; Focus Plus Photography: 185; Norma Harvey: 108, 141; Dave Hazard: ix; Rachel Layton: 241; Owen Murray: 16, 17, 19, 20, 22, 23, 27, 35-37, 43-45, 59, 62, 63, 65, 69, 70, 76, 78 (top), 82, 96, 97 (top), 101, 104, 107, 109, 113, 114, 118-120, 122, 123, 125, 131, 134, 135, 137, 139 (top), 143, 148, 149, 153-160, 162, 164-166, 169, 170, 174, 176-178, 184, 189, 196-198, 200, 204, 206, 207, 210, 211, 213-219, 221, 223-229; F. Scoltock: 97 (bottom); Andy Sherry: 115; George Towndrow: 92; B. Waites: 78 (bottom).

Publisher's Appeal: The publisher of this work has been unable to trace or contact a number of owners (original photographer or other) of photographs used in this book. Such uncredited persons will be duly acknowledged by the publisher in any future edition of this book upon notification of proof of entitlement.

Front cover: Murray performing *age-uke* with his prosthetic arm (1977) (courtesy of the *Sunday Sun*)

Back cover: Murray performing *gyaku-zuki* (1979-1984). Note the KUGB Great Britain badge. Courtesy of Remploy.

CONTENTS

Dedication   v

Foreword – Dave Hazard, 7th Dan   ix

Preface   xi

I – Seemingly, Just Another Day at the Factory   15

II – One Hundred Cigarettes and Ten Pints of Lager a Day   33

III – A False Limb – 'Is it a Problem for You?'   49

IV – European Gold ... 'I Wish I Could Remember!'   81

V – KUGB National Champions   129

VI – A Sierra Leone Experience   151

VII – An M.B.E. and the Death of a Hero   173

VIII – Sure Safe   203

References & Notes   231

Glossary   239

About the Author   241

DISCLAIMER

The author and publisher of this book will not be held responsible in any way for any injury or damage of any nature whatsoever, which may occur to readers, or others, as a direct or indirect result of the information and instructions contained within this book.

FOREWORD

When I heard Owen was having a book about his life in the martial arts written by Dr. Clive Layton, I was thrilled. I thought what a perfect partnership; one that would provide an accurate account of a man who has led a very full life.

The first thing that comes to mind when I think of Owen Murray, in or out of the *Dojo*, is Spirit. In the *Dojo* he always gives one hundred per cent commitment to all that he does.

Whilst technically sound, it is his Spirit and belief that puts him in front of most martial artists. That 'never say die' attitude can rarely be taught and comes from within.

Those who have met him on the mat, or anywhere else for that matter, if they hadn't known beforehand, then they would soon find out, is that Owen only has one way, and that is straight at you – you either meet him in the middle, which many have tried to do, at their cost, or try to back off, in which case you are chased like a rabbit. Owen doesn't do backwards. I once joked that he didn't know his car had a reverse gear and forward, at full speed, was all he knew.

You know where you stand with Owen, for he is straight-talking and to the point; there are no added frills – if he says it happened a particular way, then it did.

So, I am really looking forward to reading the published version of this book, as Owen has had a life in an environment that few could imagine, or would wish to enter.

Owen is a valued colleague and a man I am proud to call my friend.

Dave Hazard, 7th Dan
Chairman / Chief Instructor of the Academy of Shotokan Karate

PREFACE

The A17 begins just over the bridge spanning the tidal stretch of the Great Ouse and winds its way for sixty-five sometimes torturously slow miles from the medieval town of King's Lynn, through the flat, low lying, agriculturally rich lands of Lincolnshire, into Nottinghamshire. To relieve the monotony of the fen landscape, the villages driven through and passed by, became a source of etymological fascination, for some of the place names are formed partly from old Scandinavian personal names, such as Fosdyke (Fótr), Asgarby (Ásgeirr), Rauceby (Rauthr) and Caythorpe (Káti), or have other Scandinavian origins, such as Wigtoft (*'vik'* + *'toft'*), Coningsby (*'konungr'* + *'by'*) and Kirton (*kirkja*).[1] Algarkirk, was of particular historical interest, for, reading later, it was discovered that Algar, Earl of Mercia, fell in battle against the Danes near Threekingham in *c.* 870 A.D., some ten miles from the village that bears his name (*'kirk'* is Old Norse for 'church' {and Algar is, reputedly, buried on the site}). Clearly, the Vikings had battled, settled and farmed this marshy part of eastern England more than a millennium ago and many centuries before it was drained.

The A17 ends at Newark-on-Trent where it bisects the Roman Road, the Fosse Way. This market town on the Great North Road was on the coaching route from London to Edinburgh and it was at this point I headed north on the A1 to a mutually agreed rendezvous point, where Owen Murray – who had driven down from Tyne and Wear – had just arrived.

I had wanted to meet Owen for some time because all the reports I had of him suggested that his story would make a most interesting book. It was agreed at the three-hour long meeting that followed, that such a venture would be a worthy pursuit and the discussion was then directed as to how this might best be achieved. Once decided, we bid farewell and headed in opposite directions. Many hours of telephone conversations and countless emails were exchanged in the year that followed.

As in the case of similar biographical works by the author, such as, *Kanazawa 10th Dan*, *Masao Kawasoe 8th Dan*, and, *Ronnie Watt 8th*

Dan, this book is, largely, a constructed monologue approved by the subject, in that it accurately relays what was said but in a structured way. The purpose of this approach has been to give a sense of continuum, whilst at the same time reducing the 'distance' between the subject and reader that one necessarily finds in traditional biographies.

Whilst Owen's words dominate the text, it was considered pertinent to refer to other sources to provide additional material. These sources take five forms. Firstly, certain individuals were interviewed on specific aspects of Owen's life and this material not only augmented, but added to the depth of his story. Secondly, some contributors provided written recollections for the book from which the author has quoted. Seventeen individuals form these two groups. Thirdly, largely contemporaneous quotes were taken from a number of articles and reports and inserted where appropriate. Fourthly, a number of Owen's seniors were members of the British Karate Federation, the first karate organisation in Great Britain, founded in 1957. It was felt that by including BKF application form signing dates for such seniors, another level of context and perspective might be added. A seismic split within the BKF led to the founding of the Karate Union of Great Britain in 1966, which Owen joined in 1972 and is still a member of to this day. Fifthly, brief biographical information on certain *karateka*, especially Japanese directly relevant to Owen, is given in the text, as this was deemed too important to leave to a reference and note section.

Each chapter contains its own set of superscripts that refer to such references and notes. By including superscripts, rather than the material forming part of the main text, continual breaks in Owen's speech has been avoided. The feeling was that if relevant information exists, access should be made available, and it is left up to readers to decide whether they wish to take advantage of it or not. However, continually referring to superscripts whilst reading can get tiresome, so readers may care to finish a chapter completely and then refer to said superscripts whilst the content is still fresh in the mind.

Owen was, understandably, unsure of certain dates, and where the author has been unable to verify them from other sources, they have been presented as believed correct by the subject at the time of interviewing. Similarly, some facts and stories may be presented one or two years out of their exact temporal setting, but, once again, when covering a span of more than sixty years, in an eventful life, this is only to be expected. Both Owen and the author strove for accuracy throughout and any error is made in good faith.

PREFACE

Most readers will, one imagines, be established *karateka* (student(s) of karate), and thus familiar with most of the Japanese terms used throughout this book, for many are widely referred to in the *dojo* (training hall) on a daily basis. However, a significant number of readers will, no doubt, have only a limited knowledge of karate terminology, if any, and for these individuals a glossary is provided. All Japanese words not generally found in English concise dictionaries, excluding proper nouns of course, are italicised for easy reference.

Owen's life may be said to fall, conveniently, into eight distinct episodes that have been exploited to form the chapters in this work. Today, he lives on the banks of the River Wear at South Hylton, a primarily residential suburb of Sunderland, accessible by a single road, with his partner, Ellen, and her three sons, Sam, Andy and Scott.

This is the account of a tough, charismatic and resourceful man; someone we can all learn from. As Andy Sherry, 9th Dan, Chief Instructor of the Karate Union of Great Britain has said of Owen, 'His story is an inspirational one.'[2]

One cannot help but feel that Owen was born a thousand years or more too late, for he would surely have been very much at home, raised drinking horn in hand, with Fótr, Ásgeirr, Rauthr, Káti and fellow Vikings of the east coast, sharing stories of battle and daring-do in an age of adventure and heroes.

May, 2013

Clive Layton

I

SEEMINGLY, JUST ANOTHER DAY AT THE FACTORY

Owen Murray began his story so: "Maureen, my aunt – my father's sister to be precise – and I sat in old fashioned flowery-patterned covered armchairs, worn with use, around the coal fire in the back room of my grandmother's semi-detached house on the council estate at Farringdon, a suburb of Sunderland and about three miles from the city's centre. It was 6.30 a.m. on a cold Monday, 5th April, 1971. I recall there was a piano in the room with a photo of a well-dressed man hanging on the wall behind it. That was my great-grandfather, a Stewart. My grandmother, Margaret Murray [*née* Stewart], who I always called 'Ganny', a North-East of England term for 'granny' I suppose, had, as usual, been up at least an hour before and had cleaned out, re-set and lit the fire. She'd also cooked the bacon in my sandwich that I'd just finished. I'd been living at Ganny's for about a year. We nearly always had breakfast in the back room because the rest of the house, even the kitchen, was so cold. Ganny didn't have central heating. As I sat there, sipping the milky, sweet tea that I learned to loathe, I lit up my first cigarette of the day. To all intents and purposes, it was to be, seemingly, just another day at the factory.

"I lived with Ganny because I'd fallen out with my mother (Sarah {*née* Redman}) and father, after whom I was given the Christian name 'Owen' and the middle name 'Patrick'. They lived on the council estate at 4, Galashiels Square, Grindon, another suburb of Sunderland, about a mile-and-a-half from Farringdon. I was born on the 7th March, 1951 and spent my first year in Johnson Street, Sunderland, before moving to Grindon. I think Johnston Street was a rough road to live in at the time and my parents wanted out.

"My mother was one of eleven children, nine boys and two girls, and my father had two brothers and four sisters. My father was a real family man. He would come home straight from work and stay in. He'd never go out in the evenings to the pub or a working man's club with his mates, as was the common practice for men from his social

Owen Murray Snr. and Sarah (née Redman) on their wedding day (1950)

class. He didn't have any hobbies either, though I recall he made me an American fort at work, and once built an acoustic guitar which he sold to a music teacher, so it couldn't have been too bad. He worked as a wood machinist and sander and drank three or four pints of milk a day as it was supposed – I'm not sure how – to reduce the intake and subsequent effects of all the dust he was breathing in, despite wearing

Owen Murray Snr. and Sarah on their wedding day, surrounded by close family members (1950).

a mask. He was a nice man, a real grafter, though I remember the occasions he was laid off, unemployed, and couldn't find work were difficult times.

"One day, I came home from work and I criticized the dinner my mother had cooked and put in front of me. It was liver, a cheap cut with a lot of stringy bits, and I said that it was disgusting and that I wouldn't feed it to the ferrets I kept out back. When my father came home she told him what I'd said and, I suppose, he'd had a hard day too. For a passive man he reacted totally out of character. He suddenly flared up and pinned me to the wall by the throat. He told me that I should apologise and never talk to my mother like that again. I believe I spoke the truth, at least as I saw it, the liver was inedible and, fuelled with a strong sense of injustice, packed my bags and walked out at nineteen years of age. My sister, Sarah – who I refuse to have anything to do with now – was seven years old at the time. My mother died of leukaemia on the 29th August, 1981, aged fifty-five years. I think back, sometimes, to that day and I wish I hadn't said what I did, but I guess it was just about growing up.

"My mother and father were a truly devoted couple and when she died he fell to bits and had to come and live with me for a while. He took flowers to her grave every day, sometimes twice. It was heartbreaking to see. He died of a heart attack on the 14th October 1996, aged sixty-nine, and, so, that's when I like to think they were re-united.

"I must be honest and say that I don't know if I actually loved my parents and I didn't really miss them when they died. I have a lot of mixed feelings on the subject. I can't remember many good times together, which I suppose is really sad. As a boy, I recall only a few family trips out. For one, we made a bottle of liquorice water and jam sandwiches and walked to the Penshaw Monument – an early Victorian folly upon a hill which is, actually, a half-size replica of an Athenian temple – and back, totalling about eight miles in all. Another time we caught the bus to Chester-le-Street, also about eight miles away, where the famous Jarrow marchers made their first overnight stop in 1936 on their way to London. The town is also the home of Durham County Cricket Club, but it wasn't a First Class county team in those days. We visited Lumley Castle, a 14th century building and, supposedly, one of the most haunted buildings in the North-East, and had a picnic down by the riverside. I'd look up at this castle, which I found so impressive, so daunting, but we never went inside, though I would dearly have loved to have done so. Maybe it was the admission fee, I don't know. We went to Durham a couple of times too and I really enjoyed climbing the three hundred and twenty-five steps to the top of the cathedral tower and appreciating the view, watching the River Wear meander about me, but I was only allowed to go up the once. These were the highlights of going out with my parents – in my entire childhood, that was it. These trips were my holidays with them, so when I look back I have no memories of happy fulfilling trips away somewhere, like most people. We never went much outside the Sunderland area – Durham was the furthest – and I suppose I resent being cheated out of childhood memories.

"I did, however, manage to go away when I was eleven, to Middleton-in-Teeside, when I was in my final year at Broadway Junior School. We camped in a church hall and I remember going to the High Force waterfall, which drops over seventy feet, on the River Tees. That was a big adventure for me as I was over thirty miles from home, as the crow flies, and that's the furthest I'd ever been. Unfortunately, one boy's father died when we were there and he had to go home and that put a bit of a damper on things. I also went to the Lake District, in Cumbria, and stayed at Derwent Hill, on Derwent Water, when I attended Broadway Comprehensive School. I enjoyed that and tried

What childhood memories are made of – Owen at Durham Cathedral (*c.* 1958).

my hand at canoeing and map reading, the latter of which I wasn't very good at and, as proof of that fact, I managed to climb the wrong mountain! We also went up Catbells Peak, a popular but modest fell at nearly fifteen hundred feet, just outside Keswick. I was over the other side of the country and out from the city, though I was only about seventy-five miles from Sunderland as the crow flies, but that now became my new record for distance from Sunderland. Getting away from home seemed to be important in those days.

"As a child I rarely had bought sweets because they were seen as expensive and an unnecessary luxury. We'd cut rhubarb and strip the stalks, suck the ends and then dip them in sugar. We'd also get sticks of Spanish and insert them in hot water and sugar and make a kind of pop. Sometimes we'd be given a liquorice root to chew on.

"Anyway, after the disagreement with my parents I went to see my uncle, my father's elder brother, Harry, a former army boxing

School photograph of Owen at Broadwell Junior School. Owen is middle row, fourth from right.

champion, at his council house on Plains Farm. Harry also worked as a wood machinist and was a foreman too. He had been in the Durham Light Infantry but had suffered a nasty injury during training and never saw active service in the Second World War. As part of training, he was required to jump into a dugout and inadvertently landed on his rifle's magazine, which broke a rib that pierced a lung – so that was that. I stayed as a guest with Harry and his wife, Edna, for two days and really got on well with them. They didn't have children at the time; Harry and Patrick came along later.

"I recall that when I was young my uncle and aunt took me out from Ganny's on a Sunday when I was on holiday from school. We went on two buses. I can remember all the lights on the Durham Road dual carriageway and finding this so exciting. They lived beside Sunderland Aerodrome, now the Nissan factory, and a pub called the Three Horse Shoes, which is still there. Uncle Harry would go to this pub and bring back bags of crisps – the one's where you got a blue bag of salt that you'd shake over the crisps. Little memories like that make childhood, don't they?

"It was decided – I think my father and uncle (who, together, could bash out a tune on the piano at family gatherings) had had a chat – that it would be best all around if I went to live with my grandmother and thereby help her out with money by making a contribution to my board and keep. I earned about five pounds a week in those days and I gave her about one-third of my pay packet. Maureen, who was unmarried,

SEEMINGLY, JUST ANOTHER DAY AT THE FACTORY

also paid Ganny board and keep from her wages as an assembly worker at the local Pyrex factory. So, combined, the three of us managed to get by okay.

"Ganny was a typical grey-haired grandmother who fussed over me. She was tough though and had survived miscarriages, stillbirths and a disabled son. She was a widow by this time and had been so for seven years. My grandfather, whose name was also Harry, had been in the 8th Yorkshire Regiment in the First World War and had received a bullet wound for King and Country. He had medals, Pip, Squeak and Wilfred[1], and so he'd seen action against the Germans early on, in 1914 or 1915, but that didn't prevent the authorities from committing him to Durham Prison for picking up bits of coal that had fallen off the wagons from the sides of railway tracks. He was a very fast runner, and strong, and on many occasions he would out-run the police, but they got him in the end. I suppose that was at the time of the Great Depression, in the early 1930s, when times up North were really hard. Ironically, a railway track taking coal from the Silksworth Colliery to the docks at Sunderland passed right by the side of the house where my grandparents lived and I believe old Harry wasn't averse to continuing his nefarious activities after he came out of prison. It wasn't a case of making a quick buck, they needed it to survive. He worked as a dustman all his life and two weeks before his retirement he was diagnosed with advanced cancer. I believe he actually passed away on the day of his retirement. There has got to be a moral in that.

"When he died, at home, Harry was laid out in his suit in the back bedroom – a small, dark room – for a few days. I was only twelve years old, but I was allowed to go in, alone, and see him whenever I wanted to. Being a child, I didn't really understand what death was of course and I would go in two or three times a day out of curiosity and just stand and look at him lying there in his coffin, silent and motionless. The coffin lid was off and his face was covered with a white silk cloth, like a handkerchief. I wanted to lift it up and take a peek, but I was too scared. Eventually, I did pluck up enough courage and I saw his blanched face, eyes closed and snow white hair. I then reached out with trembling fingers and touched his face and it was icy cold. Another memory that has stayed, because it frightened me, was leaving the bedroom door ajar upon leaving on one occasion and someone calling, 'Shut the door. We must keep the cat out.' Those two short sentences played on my imagination, because I wondered, in graphic detail, what the cat might do to my grandfather's corpse.

"Another thing that worried me when I was young was my Uncle

Harry Murray, Owen's grandfather

Robert. He was my Ganny's disabled son, whom I've mentioned, and he had both Down's syndrome and epilepsy. I saw him have a fit once and that disturbed me greatly, so I would tell on him when he didn't take his medicine. He'd chase me around the garden, but I was never sure if he was playing or not and I didn't want him to catch me. He died aged thirty-three, when I was fifteen.

"When I went to live at Ganny's, I slept in the room my grandfather had been laid out in. It didn't worry me. Once you're dead, you're dead, so there was nothing to fear. But let me return to that fateful morning in the early spring of 1971.

"I left Ganny's house at 37, Allendale Square and walked some three hundred yards to catch the 7:15 a.m. bus into Sunderland. All the roads on the council estate at Farringdon, by convention, begin with the letter 'A'. If I ever missed the bus, I'd walk another two hundred yards to the bus stop on the Durham Road. I hopped on to the double-decker and climbed the stairs, took a seat and lit up another filtered Embassy cigarette, which would keep me company on the fifteen to twenty minute journey. The air upstairs in the bus was dense with tobacco smoke, my eyes stung and I had developed a bit of a smoker's cough, but I still continued puffing away. I'd been to the wedding of

SEEMINGLY, JUST ANOTHER DAY AT THE FACTORY

From left to right: Harry Murray Snr., Robert Murray, Harry Murray Jnr., Owen (reading comic) and Gannie.

two good friends of mine, John and Dot Humphries, on the Saturday before and I suppose I must have reflected on that. I wasn't to know then, that the wedding photographs taken two days previously were to have special meaning for me.

"Once off the bus, I walked another mile or so through the less than salubrious district of Hendon, where the worst stampede disaster in British history occurred in the summer of 1883, when one hundred and eighty-three young children were crushed to death rushing to find free toys in Victoria Hall. The Hall, destroyed in World War II by a German bomb, used to face Mowbray Park and I would walk across this open space. A poignant marble memorial of a grieving mother holding her dead child is to be found in the park. This once magnificent municipal area, built following a cholera epidemic during the early years of Queen Victorian's reign, had fallen on hard times – all the iron railings and other metal structures, including the bandstand and even the bridge, had been melted down in the Second World War to make weapons, for example. Now, it has been restored to its former glory and was voted the best park in Britain in 2008.

"Anyway, a walk across the park provided another opportunity to light up again. Then it was in through the main entrance of what was the modern building of Vedrapak. I turned right, pushed through the single door and clocked-in at around 7:50 a.m. If you were a minute late you'd lose quarter-of-an-hour's pay. I arrived in good time that morning so I headed for the works' canteen and lit up my fourth cigarette before starting work at 8.00 a.m. In those days you were allowed to smoke even though it was a paper printing factory. I would get in a round of smoking with my mates to be sociable, so even if I didn't want a fag I would take one because I was in a round and the 'crack' as we say up north, the friendly banter, was good. My grandfather had caught me with his empty pipe in his mouth when I was young and, as a lesson against taking up smoking, put some tobacco in the bowl and made me smoke all of it. It was absolutely disgusting, sickening, and it put me off pipe smoking for life. My father smoked Woodbine cigarettes, unfiltered, and with that role model and peer group pressure at school, I took readily to smoking behind the bike sheds. My mates and I used to open up dog ends that we'd find on the pavement and gutter, take out any remaining tobacco and roll our own fags. If we found a discarded cigarette that still had some life in it, we just used to put it between our lips and light up.

"My normal working hours were 8.00 a.m. to 5.00 p.m. with an hour for break, or 8.00 a.m. to 4.30 p.m. with half-an-hour's lunch. However, I would regularly work from 6.00 a.m. to 6.00 p.m. Mondays to Fridays, and 6.00 a.m. to midday on Saturdays and Sundays.

"The first few weeks at Vedrapack had actually been difficult for me. People won't believe it now, but at the time I was very shy and had virtually no confidence, to the extent that when I left my previous job at Dukes, a furniture maker and went to work at Vedrapack, I would walk back to my previous place of employment at lunch-times, a mile away, have my sandwiches there and then walk back, because I was too embarrassed to enter the canteen which was full of people I didn't know. My Uncle Harry worked at Dukes and he got me my first job after leaving school and I remained there for a year to a year-and-a-half. To be honest, I was just the skivvy. I'd set, light and maintain two pot-bellied stoves – like you get in the Westerns – take the 'bait list' as we called it – in other words take the workers' lunch orders – and generally help out carrying timber and the like. I actually enjoyed it, but the boss came up one day and said that the job I was doing was dead-end and suggested I speak to a friend of his, Tom Youlden, the manager at Vedrapak, where I could become an apprentice. So, they were good to me at Dukes and I had friends there. I remember a chap I used to get on with by the name of Mick O'Connor who worked in the cutting room. He used a circular saw, a very dangerous piece of machinery, and he'd lost fingers on it.

"Sometimes, if I was unable to go back to my previous place of work for lunch, I would lock myself into a cubicle in the toilets at Vedrapak and have my food there. I couldn't even go around the back and have a quiet cigarette by myself because the stench coming from the tripe factory next door as they boiled the entrails of cattle was stomach wrenching and made me want to reach.

"I seemed not to have been able to escape animal viscera. I was always hungry in those days and I remember, later, when I'd plucked up enough courage to enter the Vedrapak canteen, someone offered me a sandwich one lunch-time out of their lunchbox, which I gratefully scoffed down. It was only afterwards I found out that what I'd been eating was mashed sheep's brain.

"Apprentices were initiated in the 1960s and depending where you worked – shipyard, pit, building site, etc. – the initiation differed. For printing apprentices, ink and grease were mixed together and rubbed over your genitalia. I didn't fancy having that done and as a consequence things went badly wrong for me on my initiation. I tried to fight off my fellow workers during which time the leather tie I was wearing around my neck tightened in the struggle. Unfortunately, as frantic as I was, I could not loosen it and I began to choke. By the time my colleagues had cut the tie off me, I was close to being unconscious. It was a very frightening experience for me and my 'mates' were shaken up too, but I did get initiated. The apprentices in the workshop had their genitalia rubbed with grease and sawdust, which I would have preferred because printer's ink stains!

"I reckon about eighty staff worked in the factory. Vedrapak had some big customers – washing powder giants like Daz, Omo and Persil, and Ford, the car manufacturer. I suppose the factory was about the size of a football pitch, maybe larger, and it housed the lithographic, screen printing and finishing departments, plus stores and offices. It was a busy place, a noisy place, with printing machines, guillotines, gluing machines and stitching machines all in operation at the same time.

"I'd been told by the work's foreman, George Longhurst, that the boss's son, Tony Reed, intended showing some VIPs around that morning and that I had to set up four manual cutting presses to show us working at full capacity. Although I was indentured as a bookbinder, I actually worked as a cutter and creaser on a heavy machine. I was an apprentice to Dave Robson and a Scot, Graham Wynde, and I looked up to both of them. They were both really nice fellas who 'took me under their wings', so to speak, and they would often invite me to go out with them for a pint, play dominoes, that kind of thing. Graham's wife also worked at the factory. Thomas Reed, who printed the *Reeds Nautical Almanac*, a famous seafaring book first published in 1932 and still very much in production, being updated annually, owned Vedrapak and I set up the Crossland hand fed platens for women operators, as requested, and then went to my own cutting and creasing press, which was a Saragolia, a large Italian machine, some three feet wide, maybe six feet long and weighing about half a ton. It took some time to set-up these Crosslands, so much so in fact that I missed my mid morning tea break.

"Whereas the Crossland machines were manually operated with the women putting in card and then taking it out again by hand, the Saro, as it was called, automatically fed in three to four hundred pieces of card, depending on thickness, or seventeen hundred pieces of paper, by air suction, each load.

"I had worked on this machine about a year and I knew its quirks, for not being British it had features that were back to front and so I had to be really careful. On British machines, the red stop button always protruded and the green start button was always indented and sometimes covered with a flap which had to be lifted first. These were well thought-out safety precautions. The Saro had a stop/start lever and this was in reverse, in that you pushed it forward to stop and pulled it back to start.

"These machines would have a wooden die fitted. The dies would have, maybe, a hundred or more cutting blades protruding from the die to shape whatever you were cutting – on this particular day, tablet cartons for a pharmaceutical company. The card would feed on to a base and this would be lifted and pressed against the cutting edge leaving a cut out shape of the carton. The base would then drop and another sheet of card would be fed in. The die had six cartons contained within it, so the card was large and the machine heavy. On this particular day there was a problem with the feeding of the card. Under normal conditions, I could cut up to two thousand sheets per hour, though this would affect quality, but that day the card was catching slightly, so this necessitated some fine adjustment work to the bed of the machine. I used a Stanley knife and some sand paper to allow the card to crease properly. I stood at the side of the Saragolia

SEEMINGLY, JUST ANOTHER DAY AT THE FACTORY

Owen, not long before his accident, wearing his watch (*c.* 1970)

and at one point had my head inside to see what I was doing. In the act of sanding with my left hand, palm downwards, I knocked the start lever with my left elbow. The machine shot into motion and commenced to crush my hand and lower forearm into the die blades. I was working close to the fork of the machine where the base and top section were linked so my hand was caught in an instant and there was never any chance of me being able to withdraw it. The time was 11.20 a.m. precisely and I know that because the only thing that wasn't crushed to a pulp was the face of my watch, which I kept for decades but somehow lost when moving home.

"I suppose I must have yelled out, but I don't recall doing so. The image that stands out vividly in my mind, even to this day, was looking at my left upper arm which had swollen enormously as all the muscle, ligaments and tendons from the forearm had been squeezed upwards, in a blink of an eye. I suddenly had a bicep like Arnold Schwarzenegger. I found out later – such was the force of the displacement –

that my upper arm bone, the humerus, had sustained two breaks. I don't remember seeing any blood, but then my arm was still trapped in the machine, which by this time had jammed shut. I think Graham Whynde was first on the scene and he manually turned the flywheel on the side of the Saro. Initially, he turned it the wrong way for a couple of inches, but quickly realising his error he turned it the other way. I didn't feel anything when he did this – there was nothing to feel with. I remember my girlfriend at the time and wife to be, Joan Wilkinson [now Johnson], whom I'd met at Vedrapak and who had been operating a stitching machine nearby, hurried over."

Joan recalled: "Someone rushed up to me and said that Owen had had an accident. I went over to where he worked straight away but about ten feet from Owen, Graham Whynde stepped into my path and stopped me from going over to where Owen was working. He turned me away and took me to another part of the factory because he didn't want me to see what had happened."

Murray continued: "After about four minutes the press was opened and they told me not to look. I was informed, later, that one of my work colleagues who saw the injury had to go to the toilets to be sick. George Longhurst was there and so was George Stores, a fellow first-aider, who, ironically, worked on a jigsaw making the dies, and it was Stores who scrapped up what was left of my hand and lower forearm, attached or otherwise, into a bandage and made a sling for me. I then walked unaided to the canteen about fifteen metres away. I felt no pain, but I did feel extremely nauseous and I laid down on one of the tables. I knew I wouldn't be eating Ganny's lovely dinner – egg and chips fried crisp and dry that evening – because I wouldn't be going to Farringdon."

Joan continued: "Once Owen had been freed from the machine, he was taken to the canteen to wait for the ambulance and then Graham took me in there. It was then that Owen told me not to worry and that he had probably only lost a couple of fingers."

Murray continued: "Although my father and I had not spoken for some time, I asked Joan to go and tell my dad what had happened and for them both to meet me at the hospital. My dad thought the world of Joan – so did my mum – and he'd often buy her a box of chocolates or other little presents. I wanted Joan off the premises because I was worried about her."

Joan continued: "When they brought Owen in [to the canteen], he looked so grey. He asked me if I would go and tell his father – who worked about twenty minutes walk away – which I did. I think I waited in an office and Owen's dad came in and I explained that Owen had had an accident and that he might lose a couple of fingers, because that's what I'd been told. His father went to see the foreman, excused himself and off we went without delay."

Murray continued: "I would estimate that the ambulance arrived in under ten minutes and I climbed the stairs into it, unaided. It was in the ambulance, on the way to Newcastle Road Hospital, which is now called Monkwearmouth Hospital, about three or four miles away, that pain started to kick in. We got stuck in traffic over Wearmouth Bridge and I said to the ambulance men that they'd better put on their blue flashing emergency lamp as I'd lost my hand. Because I walked into the ambulance I don't think they believed me, but they did put the lamp on, though the journey seemed to take an eternity.

"When we drove up outside Accident and Emergency I was shaky on my feet, so they sat me in a wheelchair and wheeled me in. I sat next to a young girl, waiting by herself, and when a sister came to have a look at my injury, I said that she'd better not look at it here because it wasn't something for a youngster to see. By an astonishing co-incidence, which will become clear later, the sister's name was Margaret Barwick."

Margaret recalled the injury forty-one years on: "When they brought Owen in, around lunch-time, he looked very pale and so I got him up on a trolley. When I looked inside the sling, well, let me say that I had never seen anything like it. What was in front of me was completely unrecognisable, there was no recognition of form, and I couldn't even pick out anything that remotely resembled a finger. Everything had been crushed and mangled beyond recognition. I couldn't even make out the bones – even the thicker ones like the carpals and metacarpals had been pulped. The only way I can describe it is by saying that what had been his hand and lower forearm looked like lamb chops that a butcher had attacked with a cleaver, in a frenzied way. I worked in A & E for eleven years in total and that was the worst hand and lower forearm crush injury I saw. I took Owen into a ward and passed a message for a doctor to attend as soon as possible, as they were all operating at the time. I never heard Owen complain, not once, which was pretty remarkable given the circumstances. I thought he was an extremely tough and resilient individual."

Murray continued: "I was in real pain now and they injected me with morphine I suppose. The next thing I remember was lying on a bed with Joan and my father beside me. After walking to where my father worked, remarkably, the two of them couldn't get transport to come and see me and had to walk for about half-an-hour. I remember my father, who was a catholic, standing at the bottom of the bed saying three Hail Mary's for me. They were aware by now, because they had had a word with a nurse or doctor, that it was more than a couple of fingers and they told me that the doctors hoped to save the hand, but it was wishful thinking, for I knew how severe it really was. Put it this way, I'd bought myself a piano accordion and knew I'd wasted the five pounds I'd paid for it. I'd actually bought it from George Stores, who'd removed my hand from the cutter. I should have asked him for my money back!"

Joan recalled: "The ward was small, only four to six beds, and there was Owen lying down all bandaged up. He was very brave. He was resigned to losing his hand. He wasn't upset."

Murray continued: "I was, of course, in a state of shock, but what really disturbed me at this stage was what I'd wake up to if I was put under general anaesthetic. It was the fear of the unknown. As I was being wheeled to the operating theatre I asked if I could remain awake, but the answer was a firm 'No.' It was some time after 4:00 p.m. that I went down to surgery."

Joan continued: "Whilst Owen was being operated upon, his father and I split up and we caught separate buses back to our homes. I lived on the same estate as Owen's grandmother, though at the other end. We'd been told the visiting times in the evening and I walked over to Grindon, as planned, and Owen's father and mother accompanied me on the bus back to the hospital. We didn't know what to expect as no one had been able to ring us because none of us were on the telephone. I remember Owen's mother, a very nice, quiet, shy person, a harmless woman who had few friends outside the family, crying. His father, who was obviously very worried too, was a kind man and extremely generous – you should have seen the number of presents he bought people for Christmas. [Murray noted: 'You might end up with lots of presents to open, but usually they were rubbish ... but more was {seen as} better]. These presents weren't particularly expensive, but had all been chosen with great care. If he saw me in the street he'd buy me flowers – but he was, like Owen, very stubborn, and that's where the problem between the two of them lay – neither would back down. But we all sat there in silence and none of us could really believe what had happened."

Murray continued: "When I woke up after the operation I thought to myself, 'I wonder what's left?' I expected to see one hundred stitches, but when I was allowed to look, after about two or three days,

SEEMINGLY, JUST ANOTHER DAY AT THE FACTORY

I was quite chuffed really, because it was as neat a job as anyone could wish for. My hand and about half my forearm had been removed, but the end was neat and they had folded over the skin, like an envelope, and there were only eight or nine stitches. So, the photograph of the wedding I'd been thinking about on the bus that morning was the last time I was ever to be photographed with two hands. Dot, the new bride, worked on the factory floor at Vedrapak, but was, of course, away on her honeymoon when the accident happened."

Joan continued: "As soon as we saw Owen with his arms out of the bed, we knew he'd lost his hand and part of his arm. During his two weeks in hospital, he never complained once. He escaped the ward one evening and we went to a pub, The Grange, a few hundred yards up the road. I think he felt caged in on the ward. I suppose he was away for an hour, without leave, as it were. I used to take him Chinese meals as well, because he hated the hospital food."

Murray continued: "I found it very frustrating being in hospital. I used to look out of a window at girls walking past wearing the latest fashion, hot pants, and thinking to myself, 'What the hell am I doing in here?' An orderly would, when the weather was nice and sunny, wheel my bed outside into the hospital gardens so I could greet people who came to visit me. I also remember not being able to sleep and watching Akira Kurosawa's, *Seven Samurai*, on television, late at night. I had to turn the volume switch right down and go up really close to the screen to hear it, because I didn't want to wake any of the other patients. It made reading the subtitles a bit difficult though.

"The hospital staff kept trying to get me to lift my arm, do exercises with it, but I didn't really want to. I was just so very embarrassed about having one hand and a shortened arm that I didn't want anyone to see it so I kept it, hid it really, in a sling.

"When it was time to leave the hospital, I went straight back to Ganny's. We were quite close and she was distraught by what had happened to me. A few weeks passed and my father came around and explained that my mother was fretting and wanted me to go home so that she could look after me. I didn't have the heart to refuse them and so, even though I didn't want to go back – I needed my own space – I returned to the house and stayed there a couple of years until I got married. I kept my head down at home and had few problems. I used to walk to Joan's most evenings – a five mile round trip – so as to be out of the house when both my mother and father were there. So, given that I used to walk about ten miles during the time most people were at work, I was walking, in total, about fifteen miles a day. I liked to shoot in those days and my father, who disliked guns, relented, and actually bought me a shotgun which I still have to this day. He was keen on keeping the family name going and had a silver engraving of the Murray crest mounted on the stock. Maybe it was a 'sorry you lost your hand' present, I don't know.

"My Ganny went on to live to the ripe old age of eighty-nine (died 28th January 1986]. Aunt Maureen, in her mid forties by this time, married a nice chap by the name of John Brook the year following Ganny's passing and they lived in Ganny's house. Alas, John died in October 2012, aged ninety. He had been in the Merchant Navy during the war, on Arctic conveys, and Maureen was active in trying to get such service recognised.[2] On the good side, the Government agreed to the decoration of an Arctic Convey Star for such men; on the down side, John didn't live to see it, though, hopefully, it will be awarded posthumously, so that the family will have something to be proud of."

II

ONE HUNDRED CIGARETTES AND TEN PINTS OF LAGER A DAY

Murray continued: "The next nine months were hell for me to be honest, absolute hell. I had always been low in self-esteem, as I've said, and, looking back, I suppose I have to blame my parents mostly for that, but it wasn't intentional on their part. Because I was so low in self-confidence, once I'd lost my hand I just plummeted in that department. Let me give you a few examples of why I believe I had such a low view of myself, because if I'd had more self-confidence I think I would have coped better.

"When I started Broadway School, aged eleven-and-a-half, every new boy arrived for their first day of term wearing long trousers, bar two – Philip Benison, of German ancestry, who proudly wore a pair of leather lederhosen that his grandparents had sent him from Bavaria, and me. I felt really awkward. Imagine starting at a new school with all the other children and being singled out, especially by the older boys further up the school, and made fun of. Surely to God my parents had been sent a uniform list. When I got home that first day I pleaded with them to get me a pair of long trousers.

"'You've got a lifetime to wear long trousers son, so wear short trousers while you can', was all my father said and just brushed off my pleas. He didn't seem to be able to empathise at all.

"Maybe he was just being stubborn or mean; whether we genuinely couldn't afford a pair of trousers I cannot say. He wore trousers that were 'out the ark', fashionable in the 1930s and 1940s no doubt, which just fell straight to the floor with twenty-one inch bottoms, and they looked ridiculous in the Sixties. The family tended to buy good quality items and use them until they fell to bits and it may have been that way with his trousers and my shorts. I reminded them constantly over the months that followed that I needed long trousers, and, eventually, I got my way, but by that time the damage was done.

"Another thing was the hair-cut. My parents insisted on me getting a hair-cut that was different from every other boy in the school. That's not the sort of thing you want when you are trying to settle in and just wish to conform and not be noticed. Perhaps, through me, at a subconscious level, he was sticking two fingers up to a society where a man can work all hours that God gives and still have barely enough to live on.

"I cringe to this day when I think that my mother insisted on walking me to school. Times were different then and nobody's mum walked them to senior school. She was being over-protective. It was just so embarrassing and everyone called me a Mummy's Boy. What made matters worse was that she wore stockings that were not secured properly and they would work their way down her legs so that by the time we were outside the school gates they were around her ankles. It was not a pretty sight and just added to my daily nightmare.

"I couldn't just pray that people wouldn't look at us because everybody's attention was drawn our way as we walked along, for the old pram that we pushed with my sister in squeaked quite loudly and no matter where you went, people would turn to see where the noise was coming from.

"My mother had read this article in a woman's magazine about how fish netting trapped air in some mysterious way and that a vest could be made from it. She knitted me a fishing net vest and I shiver when I think of the times I had to expose this thing when changing for P.E. and games. My mother was a good knitter and knitted the family's jumpers and woolly hats. She once made me a Davey Crocket hat, so I was Davey Crocket for a few months.

"I was never much of a sportsman in those days, but I was invited to play in the school football team. I couldn't run particularly fast nor was I any good at dribbling, but if a striker was coming my way I could stop him in his tracks, usually by bringing him down. No one could get past me and that was my forte, so I played half-back. Well, needless to say, I was absolutely delighted when I saw my name up on the list and ran home to tell my mum and dad. I had an ancient pair of heavy leather football boots, so old in fact, that the toe end on each boot had actually curled up. It goes without saying that they were far from being comfortable. Anyway, to cut a long story short, my father forbade me from playing because I'd done something wrong – I can't remember what exactly – and that was that, and I never got the chance to play on that occasion, or any other.

"I didn't have a pair of athletics shorts and I told my parents I needed some. My mother produced an old pair of yellow shorts with a

ONE HUNDRED CIGARETTES AND TEN PINTS OF LAGER A DAY

Owen with his mother (*c.* 1961)

pink strip down one side that she'd procured from my father's sister's daughter, Patricia O'Brien, who we called Patsy and who died quite young, of cancer. I removed the pink strip, but imagine a boy at a tough school having to wear yellow shorts in those days. I just stuck out like a sore thumb and was the butt of every unkind joke you can think of.

"I remember being given a second-hand bike, as a present, by my parents. The only trouble was, it was a girl's bike. I think it may have

Owen with Wearmouth Bridge in the background (*c.*1961)

been Patsy's. The bike didn't have a crossbar of course, so I was the odd one out again.

"This type of thing really knocked the little confidence I had managed to create for myself. Because my parents were so insular, lived in their own world, I think they became slightly removed from reality and sometimes got their priorities muddled up. For example, whenever there was any money left over at the end of the week, instead of buying their son a pair of games' shorts, let's say, they'd buy tinned food instead. We had a large cupboard at home that was stacked with hundreds of tins of baked beans, peas, fruit and the like. It was as though they were stock piling in case World War III broke out. They could get very touchy about it and I remember Patsy got barred from coming around to the house because my mother caught us making fun of their hoard.

Owen with his mother and Patsy (*c.* 1962)

"I remember one Christmas dinner. Now, most people look forward to a lovely spread with roast turkey on that celebrated day, but not the Murray's of Galashiels Square, Grindon. What my sister and I sat down to that Christmas was a long tin lying in the centre of the table. The tin was unceremoniously opened up one end and my mother pulled out by the legs the carcass of a small, ragged-looking chicken covered in thick jelly. It would have been doing well to have weighed two-and-a-half pounds. I'll carry that image to my grave.

"Being mid winter, it got dark early. Our curtains in the house were too small and wouldn't close properly, falling some way short of one another. My parents had been given them and people walking past the house could see everything that was going on inside when the lights were on. There was no privacy whatsoever from the outside world and

I always felt, as I sat there in the lounge, that I was being spied upon by someone out there in the dark that I couldn't see. I didn't like that at all. We didn't have any money, so to compensate for lack of blankets on these freezing nights, I had my father's old army coat on the bed. Electric blankets were all the rage then, but I had a hot water bottle. It still did the trick though.

"Later in life, my parents would always re-use tea bags. They would dangle two or three old tea bags with one new one in a pot of tea.

"I must also blame my senior school for my lack of confidence. I'm not saying I was a genius, I failed the eleven-plus, but some people develop later. I did try quite hard – I liked English, geography and woodwork – but I never stood a chance. I remember this obese maths teacher. His belly and backside bulged out of his suit and his tie was always askew. He always looked untidy and was really an uncouth individual. How he ever became a teacher I shall never know. He used to sit in front of the class and pick his nose. Then he'd roll up the 'bogeys', as we called them, between his thumb and forefinger and line them up on his desk. He'd then aim them at pupils and flick them at us. He'd often sit there with his flies unbuttoned and you could actually see his testicles sometimes.

"When I was at the junior school, I remember seeing these mysterious pink things that would frequently appear in the corners of the playground. We used to kick them about. They were used condoms. This is the sort of schooling I recall. I suppose there may have been good times, happy times, but if there were then I don't remember them.

"My first street-fight was whilst at school. I was a prefect, so I really shouldn't have been involved in punch-ups, but we had this bully called 'Blackie' who wanted to show how good he was at fighting, so he offered to fight myself and a lad called Andy McNaught and we obliged him. I think there were about fourteen members of the McNaught family and they were all small people. The whole school emptied at 4 p.m. and we went to a place called Springwell Park. Unbeknown to me, Blackie had already jumped Andy McNaught, both of whom were behind me, and was starting to beat him up. So I turned around, ran back and pushed him off. Blackie immediately took his belt off and wrapped it around his right hand. This leather belt was studded with a large metal buckle and you could either wrap the belt around your hand and use it as knuckledusters or whirl the whole thing around with the buckle whistling in the air – both were dangerous weapons. I said that I would fight him, one to one, if he put the belt away and he agreed. I knocked him into a stream and when he got out he tried to kick me. I obviously had no self-defence skills and I blocked it with an open hand and dislocated a finger. We had a real ding-dong which I eventually won. I didn't have a clue what to do about my finger which was swelling up and changing colour as I looked at it, so I hurried back home. My mother wasn't in and my father was working overtime. The next door neighbour loaned me some money for the bus and I went to my dad's workplace.

"'Why are you bothering me at work with that?' he complained. 'Take yourself along to Accident and Emergency.'

"So I went to the hospital by myself and the doctor cut my ring off to allow the finger to expand without constriction. My father had bought me the ring with the Murray coat of arms on. Whilst that was my first taste of street fighting, it certainly wasn't to be my last.

"I read my secondary school reports recently. It was nearly always a case of 'could do better' or 'not working to full capacity.' Well, I suppose I could have applied myself more, but there was just no inspiration. I just lacked drive. My behaviour was satisfactory, my conduct was good, or very good and I wasn't disruptive or anything like that, just bored to tears and going through the motions. The last report I have is when I was nearly sixteen and it stated plainly that if I spent more time working and less time talking my results would, at forty-seven per cent, have been better, so perhaps it was time for me to leave.

"I did take eight CSE [Certificate of Secondary Education] subjects, but I didn't do particularly well in them.[1] I managed, however, to get a Grade 2 in English Oral, but I didn't achieve any Grade 1's, which would have been equivalent to a Grade E at GCE [General Certificate in Education]. It was a two-tiered system in those days that, today, is combined to make the GCSEs. I was sixteen when I left school and had the summer holiday and then it was straight into work.

"So, with a history of things I have described behind me, when I lost my hand the little confidence I possessed dropped to virtually zero. For example, I was terrified of crossing roads. I thought something else awful might happen to me and I'd literally walk miles to find a zebra crossing. If I wanted to cross a small road on my own, I'd stand by the curb for ages until I couldn't see a car in either direction, then I'd double-check, then I'd triple-check, and then, and only then, I'd walk across, repeatedly looking sidewards as I did so. When I came to the next road, I'd go through the same procedure, so even a relatively short walk could take me hours.

"The pain from the amputation was awful. I didn't take tablets because I didn't want to put anything like that into my system. So I fought the pain on a daily basis. It was a very personal battle. My brain still thought I had a left hand and I could often feel that I had one too. Those pains, which would catch me unawares, were very uncomfortable, because it felt as though there was a surge of energy with nowhere to go. Whilst it lessened with time, it went on for decades and the last one I felt was in 2007 – thirty-six years after my hand was removed.

"I smoked one hundred cigarettes a day. People say that's impossible, but it isn't when you're up all night with the pain. The smoking helped because it acted as a distraction. I also drank ten pints of lager and lime a day to try and numb my brain. Smoking and drinking like that meant, of course, that I was killing myself. I was in a bad way.

"I'd actually got into the habit of drinking from an early age and had developed a liking for whisky. It all started when I was about thirteen and a friend 'found' a bottle of whisky which he hid in his family's rhubarb patch in the garden. When we used to go swimming at the local baths, the water was freezing and afterwards, having volunteered to hide the whisky in my rolled up towel, we'd both have a sip. We'd buy some pasty or dip, which is a bun soaked in gravy, and eat and drink as we sat on the upstairs back seat of the bus on the way home. That was lovely. I acquired a taste for whisky and would, once I had my own supply, have a mouthful most nights out of bravado.

"So, I'd walk miles and miles each day. I would just leave the house, turn left or right and walk aimlessly for as much as ten miles, as I've said before. Sometimes I'd walk up to Sandhill and back again, or up to Grindon Mill, a pub, and back again. It helped with the agitation and strained nerves I was experiencing. I didn't want to go and see a doctor; this was a very personal fight as I was coming to terms with myself."

Joan recalled: "When Owen wasn't smoking or drinking, he was fidgeting. He'd fidget with his buttons, shoe laces and tie. He was very much on edge all the time, living on his nerves, and he could be quite difficult to be with. He didn't feel sorry for himself, but he was, understandably, short-tempered. After the stitches had been taken out, I plucked up enough courage to have a look at where they'd cut the hand off. Actually, I was quite surprised; the surgeon really had done a good job."

Murray continued: "I kept my arm in a sling for far longer than was good for me because I was embarrassed and I thought that everyone would look at me if they saw I only had one hand. I took to wearing a parker jacket that was still in fashion at the time. These were long and very baggy garments and I was able to hide my arm so that, walking about, I looked normal. I just couldn't sit still and, I suppose, I took it out on Joan – well you do, don't you, take it out on the ones you love? But she was, as we say, 'As sound as a pound', and remained true.

"Whilst my walks were a bit of a distraction for me, they also allowed me time to think. I actually found that thinking about my condition was quite a destructive process because I couldn't come up with any positive solutions to my predicament. 'Just what could a one-handed, unskilled man do?' Being a ferreting and shooting man and liking the outdoors, Joan and I had thought about emigrating to either Canada or Australia and eventually we decided upon the latter. I certainly had the urge to travel, to get out the North-East and see a bit of the world. At the time there was a massive recruitment drive for Australia, with subsidised or free travel and the same with accommodation. I had made enquiries before the accident and was told that we'd have to delay until my apprenticeship finished, which would have been about another two years. To be interviewed in England for a job was bad enough but having one hand and trying to impress an interviewer in a hotel conference room – where such interviews were held – and convincing him that I could work as well as any able-bodied man, would, I felt, have been impossible. If I'd been interviewing and someone like me walked in I wouldn't have taken a chance on him and I didn't expect anyone else to either. Deep down I suppose I knew I was as good as the next man, but to be able to prove that would be a difficult thing to do in such a setting, so I didn't try further with my application after losing my hand and the idea was just 'knocked on the head'.

"At the time I enjoyed rough shooting, as I've said. Joan and I had a cottage at Wear Head, some forty miles away, which cost us fifty pence a week to rent and we'd go there at weekends. In those days, farmers had to pay a form of council tax on all the buildings on their land, so they were let out to cover costs. Neither of us could drive, so we'd pack our luggage and sit on a bus to Durham, then change for Crook, change again to Wolsingham, change again to Stanhope and yet again to Wear Head. Once we arrived there, we had to walk two miles uphill carrying our luggage to the cottage. The cottage was pretty basic, having oil lighting, a wood fire and an outside toilet. After my accident, we couldn't get to the cottage because I couldn't carry any of the luggage and, anyway, I couldn't hold, let alone fire a shotgun. Sometime later, we moved to another cottage in Daddry Shield, on a direct bus route, which cost one pound per week.

"I was experiencing strange contradictory thoughts because whilst I knew I could still do most things, I just didn't feel I could face them. I felt inferior, not whole. I know life has to go on, but what was I to do? How could I provide for myself and a wife and family I'd hoped to have in the future? What would happen if my mother and father died and I had to bring up my sister? All these thoughts were going around and around my head as I walked the streets, often in the pouring rain, worrying myself sick. I just couldn't come up with an answer and resigned myself to ending up a night-watchman, because I believed that was the only thing a person with my type of disability was good for. Looking back, I suppose I was just coming to terms with what had happened and the thought of a major life change was causing me great anxiety.

"I went up to the Freeman Hospital in Newcastle, to the Artificial Limb Centre, a couple of months after the accident, initially for a meeting. I then went up again for a plaster cast to be taken of my stump and I re-visited three or four more times to get the fitting and the straps right for a prosthetic arm. I found the Centre quite reassuring actually, because there were people there with only one arm or only one leg. Some of the staff had prosthetic limbs and because we were 'all in the same boat' I didn't find it a harrowing experience, indeed, I found it reassuring.

"Soon afterwards, I travelled to Leeds for a week's course to be taught how to use my new arm and hand and the various attachments, such as a hook and a cup. I use the cup for driving, so that I can change gear. Let me tell you how the prosthetic arm fits on and how it all works.

"The false limb is placed over the stump and runs up to the elbow. Two straps go from the stump to either side of the bicep and up to a holster-like device over the left and right shoulders. This keeps the false limb in place. A separate cable at a set length runs from my left shoulder to a split hook that fits on to the prosthetic arm. When I move my left shoulder forward, the hook opens up and when I withdraw the arm the hook closes. At Leeds, I was taught to move the hook, rotate it, and to pick things up and put things down. When my fellow amputees and I went out in the evenings to the pub, I didn't feel comfortable at all because I felt extremely vulnerable in the dingy

ONE HUNDRED CIGARETTES AND TEN PINTS OF LAGER A DAY

Owen showing the prosthetic arm and accompanying straps (2012) from side and (overleaf) head-on positions.

areas we frequented. There were gangs hanging about on street corners and suspicious types eyeing us up and down. I still had my arm in a sling, even after some three months, and I felt that there was no way I

OWEN MURRAY, M.B.E., 6th DAN

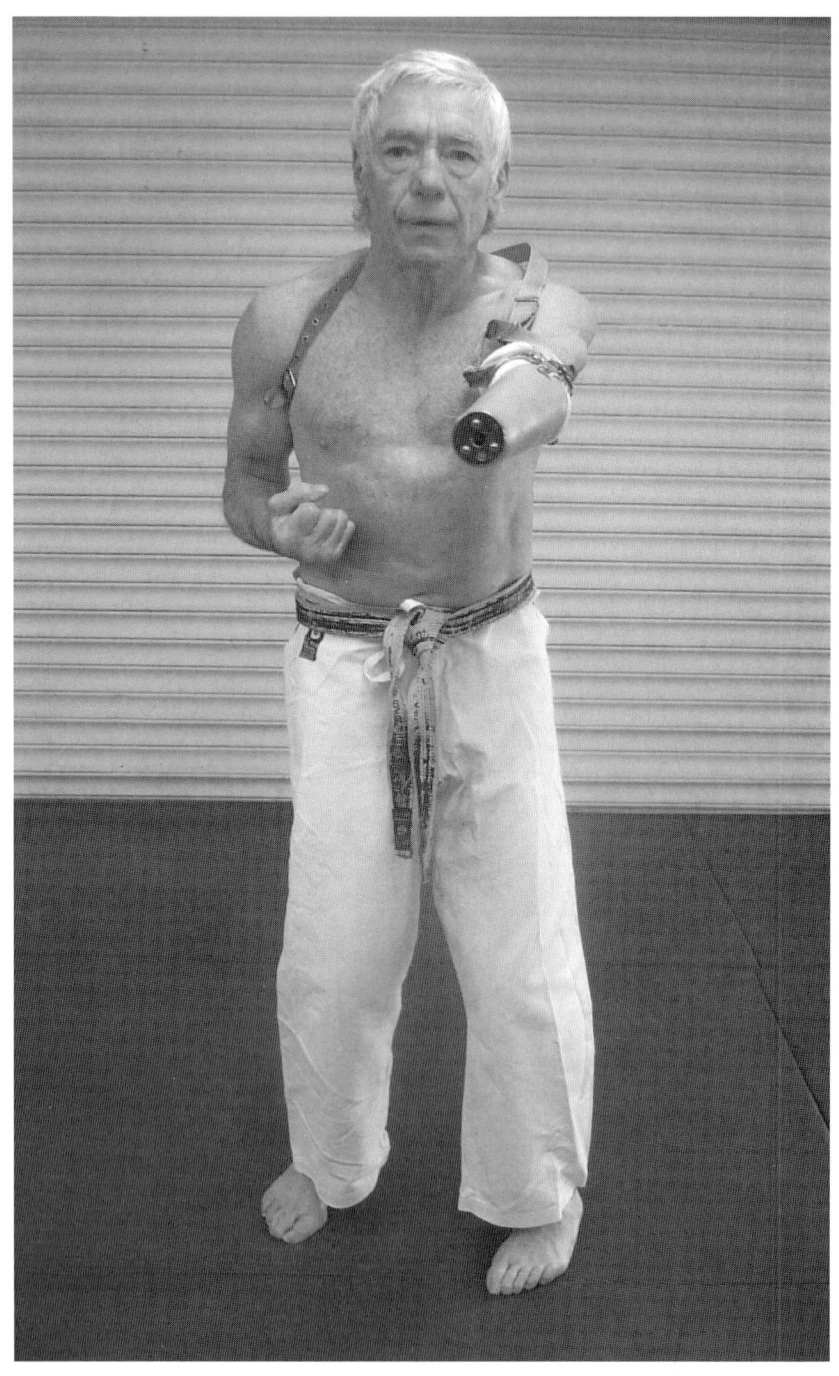

The Dragon, Janet, Joan and George – 'This I would class as my family,' Owen wrote.

could defend myself. At the back of my mind I still had the memory of a certain young lady, a ginger-haired hellion named Mary, who had beaten me up at Springwell Infant School. She was bigger than I was and, after getting me to the floor and straddling me, repeatedly punched me in the face. You don't forget things like that and here I was, now with only one hand, being checked out by some very nasty looking customers. I felt intimidated and I didn't like it.

"On my return from Leeds, I went to Joan's house to show her mum and dad what I could do. Her father's name was George and he worked as a shipwright at Austin Pickersgills, and her mother's name was Lily. I called them, affectionately, George and the Dragon, though they did not resemble the characters of the popular television series of the same name in the 1960s, starring Sid James and Peggy Mount. I remember I once went into a florist to send Lily some flowers. I wanted the card to read: 'From the One-Armed Bandit to the Dragon', but the girl refused to do it because she thought it was insulting. Well, the flowers and card arrived.

"'Why didn't you put, 'To the Dragon?'' Lily asked, and I told her what had happened. As soon as she heard the story she was on the telephone having a real moan.

"I couldn't imagine having two nicer people as future in-laws than George and Lily. I got on with them like the proverbial house on fire and far better than with my own parents. I seemed to have nothing in common with my own mum and dad, despite the fact that they were good people who tried their best. I just don't know what went wrong there, I really don't, but it's a great shame. I felt the George and Lily sort of adopted me into the Wilkinson family and I still go there, to this day, for Christmas, though George is long dead. Well, I actually go to Janet's for Christmas, Janet being Lily's other daughter and, therefore, Joan's sister.

"Anyway, when I got back from Leeds I wanted to show what I could do with my new found skills and I picked up an egg with my hook. Unfortunately, I broke it and went upstairs to the bathroom to wash the hook. Whilst there, I thought I'd go to the toilet. Well, I was still a bit uptight and pre-occupied because I'd broken the egg. I undid my zip and then, how can I put this, I experienced a sudden forceful vice-like squeezing on a certain part of my anatomy. I had rolled my shoulders inadvertently and the hook closed on me. Well, that action made me wince a bit I can tell you and had me hopping about for a while.

"My Union, SOGAT [Society of Graphical and Allied Trades], paid for Joan and I to go up to a convalescent home in Ayr, on the south-west coast of Scotland, for a week. On the train journey up – I liked to think we were going to another country – I proposed to her and she accepted. I'm not sure if the Union owned the home or not, but there were people staying with all sorts of ailments, physical and mental. Joan and I just took time out and walked along the coast overlooking the Firth of Clyde. You could see the Isle of Arran in the distance. We weren't allowed to share a room or anything like that, and I remember, at night, some of the other men and I would have a pillow fight before going to bed.

"Not long after our trip north, I went back to Vedrapak, not to work of course, but to say hello and to keep in touch. I was very apprehensive about returning and was sweating profusely and shaking all over as I walked through the doors. I didn't want to face it you see, but I knew I had to. I arrived about half-an-hour before the lunch-break and stayed for half-an-hour during lunch. My workmates were over the moon to see me. Everyone blamed George Longhurst for the accident because he was the foreman, but I didn't. George was pleased to see me, but he was a bit distant. He was worried, I think. Joan was there and she knew how I was feeling and helped me out. The noise of the factory seemed deafening, unnerving, relentless, and I suppose I had simply become used to it whilst I was there. It is the noise that I remember most about that visit. The Saragolia was lying silent and hadn't been used since the accident. It had been declared unsafe, though too late for my left hand.

"After six months of living on sick pay and reducing my meagre savings to zero, I went back to Vedrapak to work. I requested that I return to the Saragolia, which, by this time, had been refurbished and put back into operation. I made this request because I needed to prove to myself that I could still use the machine. Needless to say I was extremely wary at first. I needed to get back to work. What with the smoking, drinking and boredom, it was time for me to face my demons. I managed okay, but there was one practical thing I had trouble with and that was holding a ruler down when using a Stanley knife. My hook wasn't any good for this, so I invented something. I welded a steel ruler on to an attachment to avoid any slipping and sliding and it worked perfectly.

"When I resumed work, I still smoked and drank excessively. The drinking didn't interfere with my work though – I want to make that quite clear. What I am saying is that getting back to work didn't cure either habit. I did complete my apprenticeship with Thomas Reed's [dated 4th February 1973] and still have the indenture to prove it.

"As I've said, I had a lack of confidence before my accident and to overcome this I had tried to investigate the martial arts. I had an address for a karate club, the Wado-ryu style, run by an instructor by the name of Brian Crossley, who, I believe, was Wado-ryu's first national champion and is an 8th Dan today. Anyway, I went to the address given one evening, a school hall in Commercial Road I believe, but the place was shut up. I actually went down twice, but again there was no sign of life, so I must have got the times or venue wrong. Then I had my accident so I didn't pursue it any further.

"Like a lot of people of my generation, the cinema was the main focus for the world of moving pictures, because we didn't have a television at home and, as a child, I used to go along to Saturday Morning Club at the local cinema to watch the new releases. I remember a friend of mine, David Hills, went with me on occasion and sometimes he had free tickets. I can recall the first two lines of the song we used to sing to this day:

> 'We come along on Saturday mornings,
> Greeting everybody with a smile.'

"Later, I saw the early James Bond movies starring Sean Connery as 007, the man licensed to kill. Films like, *From Russia with Love* [1963], *Goldfinger* [1964] – who can forget Oddjob? – and, *You Only Live Twice* [1967], which was set in Japan, were hugely successful and had an impact on people joining the martial arts. On television, in the Sixties, we had *The Avengers* with Patrick Macnee and Honor Blackman, who was later replaced by Diana Rigg and, then, Linda Thornson. I didn't see the originals at the time because, as I've said, we didn't have a telly, but I saw them later. Some of these episodes had martial arts featured in them and one, in particular, was about karate.[2] However, none of these had the effect on people that Bruce Lee did and when he came along, well, everything changed.

"I must have seen *Big Boss* [1971] and *Fist of Fury* [1972] at the cinema shortly after their release. I knew it was wonderfully choreographed hokum of course, but Lee was just incredible and possibilities started to open up in my mind about what might be possible. It is very hard for people today to realise the effect that Lee had on the minds of young people, because that form of fighting is seen everywhere on the big screen and on television now. But in the early 1970s it was just not part of everyday life that it is today. It was unusual to even know someone who did a martial art, though judo was the most popular. Then, one evening after work, I was walking down Tatham Street in Sunderland and I saw a poster in a barber's shop window saying learn something called Shotokan karate. It wasn't an eye-catching advert and I don't even think it had a photograph on it. I didn't have a clue what Shotokan was as I didn't know there were different styles of karate. I think the barber's daughter, Mavis, who trained in Shotokan, must have put it up. Anyway, I took details and wondered if they'd take a disabled person. Little did I know that seeing and pursuing that advert was to change my life forever."

III

A FALSE LIMB –
'IS IT A PROBLEM FOR YOU?'

Murray continued: "The very same week I saw the advert for karate, I went to have a look with Joan and a mutual friend of ours, Patricia Hardy, who was a work colleague. Pat's younger brother, Billy Hardy, is a famous boxer who held the British bantamweight and featherweight titles, in additional to the European and Commonwealth featherweight titles. He tried for the WBO and IBF World titles, but lost to Naseem Hamed

"The Sendai Club, now based at the Crowtree Leisure Centre, was, in those days, housed at the YMCA in Toward Road, Sunderland, right by Mowbray Park. The three of us went one evening in the early part of 1972[1], after finishing at Vedrapak. I didn't have the confidence to go on my own. I was very curious about karate, though I hadn't popped along to the local library. If I had, then I would, no doubt, learned that the two 'big' Shotokan books at the time were Hidetaka Nishiyama and Richard C. Brown's, *Karate: the art of 'empty-hand' fighting* [1960], and Masatoshi Nakayama's, *Dynamic Karate* [1966]. I wasn't a great reader.

"We entered the YMCA and the receptionist directed downstairs into a room with pillars holding up the floor above. There were some school-like benches arranged around the side and we sat attentively and watched the lesson. There were about twenty people I suppose, in white suits, practising strange movements in equally strange stances, going up and down the room, forwards and backwards. I'd been used to a certain freedom at Scouts and boys clubs in the past, but this was really regimented, and that's the first thing that struck me. Jeff Barwick was in the class and wore a brown belt, 1st kyu; Colin Shubert and Barry Lawson were there too, and I remember seeing this chap, a 7th kyu, with a yellow belt wrapped around his waist and thinking to myself, 'If I can get to that stage I shall be delighted.' 7th kyu is actually quite a low grade and I soon realised that, numerically, the higher the kyu grade the lower the technical skill.

"The training went on for about two hours in those days and the technique that really impressed me was a kick, which the instructor referred to in Japanese as *mae-geri*, or front kick in English. Legs are longer than arms, so I thought that if I could become proficient in this technique, then the loss of a hand would not place me at a disadvantage. We didn't know what we were looking at of course, but we liked what we saw and at the end of the lesson I plucked up enough courage to have a word with the instructor, John Holdsworth, who wore a black belt, and asked him whether he thought I'd be able to manage the training.

"'Why not give it a go?' he said. He struck me as a very polite, relaxed, humble, yet confident individual. I liked that combination and I liked him, so I decided to take his advice."

Holdsworth recalled a similar story of their first encounter: "We used to get people looking in on the class all the time and I remember seeing Owen in the YMCA lobby, watching the training. After the class finished we had a chat. I didn't know he only had one hand and during our conversation he held up his false limb.

"'Do you reckon I can do it with this?' he said.

"'Is it a problem for you?' I replied.

"'No!' came his immediate response, so I said that it wasn't a problem for the club either. After that, there was no looking back."

Barwick recalled: "We used to get a fair number of people coming to watch us training at the YMCA and some who did decided to join the club. One day a young man with a false arm came along and he started the following week. When I got home, I told my wife about our new member and she asked his name. When I told her, she instantly remembered him from when he was brought into the hospital after his accident when she looked after him. She said he was a tough, brave man. It's a small world, isn't it?"

Murray continued: "The three of us turned up the next week in loose clothing, as we had been advised to, and just did what we were told and followed everyone else. It was only after beginning training that I realised the effect that all that smoking and drinking had had on my health. To be honest, after only a relatively small number of movements I was out of breath. I could only do three or four press-ups and less than ten sit-ups. The pain doing press-ups on my stump was quite severe.

"The fitness level at Sendai was high and the stretching exercises were really difficult for me too. I thought I'd never be able to last to the end of that first lesson. There seemed to be natural athletes all around me. What's more, the straps supporting my prosthetic arm chaffed quite badly around my armpits and shoulders. I applied vaseline, but it didn't really work and I resigned myself to the fact that the skin would just have to suffer and harden if I wanted to continue.

"I liked the training very much, it gave me a special feeling, and I had to make a decision – continue karate or continue smoking; it simply wasn't going to be possible to engage in both. I suppose the training gave me an adrenaline rush and I felt less pain when practising. I decided to pack up smoking there and then and I can truthfully say that I haven't smoked a cigarette for forty years, though I must confess to the very rare cigar, but I haven't had one of those for seven years.

"Sendai was a club that was registered with the Karate Union of Great Britain, which in turn was registered with the Japan Karate Association. The KUGB had been formed in 1966 largely from clubs that had broken away from the first karate organisation in Britain, the British Karate Federation, which had been founded by Vernon Bell in 1957.[2] In 1966, not long before the KUGB was formed, the Sunderland Karate Club[3] joined the BKF and both John Holdsworth[4] and Jeff Barwick[5] had actually been members and had attended a course given by JKA Grand Champion, *Sense*i [teacher] Hirokazu Kanazawa[6], when he visited in [April] 1966.[7] The *dojo* had originally been founded by Harry and Alan Marr, who formed a karate section within the Sunderland Judo Academy, based in High Street East. John was actually a founder member of the KUGB, one of seven[8] who still survive within the organisation, and I don't believe there are many founder members outside it, still training. Jeff began with the KUGB in 1969 and is still a member. In 1968, Kanazawa, who had been the KUGB's Chief Instructor, went to Germany and *Sensei* [Keinosuke] Enoeda took on this important role.

"I bought myself a karate *gi*, which is the name given to the white karate suit and is lighter than a judo *gi*, and that made me feel more the part, whilst the jacket sleeves helped hide my prosthetic limb. I had no trouble tightening the string and knotting my *gi* trousers nor did I have any difficulty tying my white belt with the special knot I'd been taught.

"I trained twice a week at Sendai initially – Tuesdays and Thursdays, if memory serves. I was certainly not a natural and I felt that I had to work much harder than many other people just to get the same effect. Kicks, alas, were by far my biggest problem. I was very stiff – as stiff as the proverbial board – and had poor balance and co-ordination. I was really not very good at kicking when I started, despite my real desire to learn.

"The lessons always started with stretching the whole body and then we did basic training, *kihon*. *Kihon* is made up blocks, punches, kicks, strikes and stances. Once we had an idea of what we were doing after quite a few weeks, we learned some five-step sparring. Known as *gohon-kumite*, this was performed at both the upper level, *jodan*, and the middle level, *chudan*. Maybe we did a little one-step sparring, *ippon-kumite*, I don't recall now, and then a series of moves in a set sequence, performed without a partner, which was known as *kata*. The *kata* for the first grading was *Heian Shodan* in those days and it was some years later that *Kihon Kata* [*Taikyoku Shodan*] replaced it, at least in the KUGB.

"Sendai had some very sociable members and after training a group would go down the pub and have a drink. I was asked if I'd like to go and so I did. We had to replenish the liquid we'd lost of course and the alcohol, at least for me, helped reduce the adrenaline that was still pumping through my veins. I'd drink Newcastle Brown Ale or Double Maxim. However, when I started training, the bottles of beer weren't cold enough – we were sweating buckets after all – and lager was just coming on the scene, so we moved to lagers. At home, I'd drink whisky. I didn't need it and sometimes I'd give up all types of alcohol for months at a time. I like Scottish whisky and my favourites are Laphroaig, because it's peaty, Glenmorangie and Glenfiddich because they're single malt and that's what I prefer. The finest I've ever had is a Bells Blue Label, which was over one hundred and fifty pounds a bottle.

"I trained regularly and took my first karate grading, 9th kyu, on the 5th June 1972, under Andy Sherry, and passed. Needless to say, I was absolutely delighted. Andy had come over from Liverpool where he was the Chief Instructor of the famous Liverpool Red Triangle Club and was the senior British KUGB grade, at 3rd Dan [awarded in 1970]. I believe he was also the most senior Shotokan *karateka* in Britain, other than Japanese. When I first saw him in his normal clothes, before training, I was not impressed to be honest. He was in his late twenties and so quiet and unassuming. I thought, 'What's all the fuss about?' But when he started to move in the *dojo*, well, the speed, the power and the determination were just unbelievable. Never could someone have been so wrong in summing somebody up. His teaching style was good too – he kept tight control of the class but made us feel relaxed at the same time. Andy had a similar build to me, so I could relate to him and I watched him very carefully."

Sherry had joined the BKF in 1961 as a founder member of the Liverpool Karate Club[9] and had trained under both Vernon Bell and Tetsuji Murakami.[10] He became the first Shotokan *karateka*, along with fellow Liverpudlian, Joe Chialton, to attain *Dan*, black belt, status in Britain, in February 1966. He took the KUGB *kata* titles in 1967 and 1969, and became Grand Champion (winning both the *kata* and *kumite* titles) in 1968 and 1970. He was captain of the Liverpool Red Triangle team that had won the KUGB National Championships for five successive years. He had also been a European freestyle champion. By the time he came over to Sunderland he had largely given up competitive karate to focus on being the KUGB team coach. Sherry's story is told elsewhere.[11]

Murray continued: "Even though I passed my 9th kyu, I still wore the white belt. Then I took and passed my 8th kyu [27th August 1972] under Ken Smith and still wore the white belt. My attempt at 7th kyu [19th November 1972], again under Smith, was successful and then I changed my belt colour to yellow. So, I'd made the grade I originally set myself as a target by the end of that year. But I was gaining confidence and I could now see myself going further and had no intention of giving up – anyway, I loved it! I saw no reason why I shouldn't progress, it was up to me. What I found interesting was that those natural athletes who had been around me when I started were now all gone; they'd had the athleticism to continue you see, but not the willpower and I liked that because it set karate apart.

"As a boy, as I've said, I'd been in the Scouts and responded well to working for the various badges. The idea of karate gradings appealed to me in a similar vein. The expectations for the gradings were clear and it was up to me to practise to ensure that I didn't make mistakes. I liked that mind set because it gave me something to aim for.

"Ken Smith[12] had been a BKF member too and a founder member of the KUGB. He ran a Shotokan *dojo* in High Street West, Sunderland, and that's where the gradings I took under him were held. He was a nice chap, tall, raw-boned, strong and direct. He was solid. His stances were strong and his techniques powerful. I believe that he was the first Shotokan *karateka* to be graded to a JKA black belt from the North-East [in 1969 {Holdsworth was the second}]. He was nearing fifty years of age at the time, I should imagine. Another former BKF member who was training with Smith at this point was Robert Bewley[13], who lived over near Consett, County Durham.

"As a yellow-belt, I was still training at Sendai twice a week, but by now I was practising by myself every day as well. During 1973 I didn't miss a grading and was successful on four occasions. For 6th kyu [green belt], I was graded by Andy [11th March 1973].

"By the time I was a 6th kyu, my confidence had grown to such an extent that I entered a local *kumite* competition. I actually got to the final where I met a *karateka* now serving ten years in prison. My opponent was senior to me and I lost, but I kicked this chap's elbow and broke the toe next to my big toe on my right foot. A certain friend thought he was a nurse and decided to pull the joint apart and let it slip back into position, naturally. Unfortunately, the bone was already broken. That toe has given me jip – that's pain – for years and I've got to have it amputated [which Murray did in January 2013].

"I was graded to 5th kyu [purple belt] by *Sensei* Hideo Tomita [25th May 1973] and for 4th kyu [purple belt with white stripe] by Andy [2nd September 1973]. But before I give details of my 3rd kyu let me tell you a little story because I remember taking my 4th kyu with a broken hand which I'd sustained as a result of a fight at work. Let me explain.

"Tom Youlden had sacked this guy who was a real bully, a nasty bit of work. Prior to being told that his services were no longer required, this chap said that he was going to 'fill Tom in'. Tom took this bully-boy, who was being very noisy, to the foyer and I followed them on the pretext of going to the toilet because I knew what this chap had in mind. I heard shouting and before I could do anything, Tom had been hit and was about to be hit again. So I rushed over and dragged this yob off of him. In those days I would have been about eleven stone and this chap was, maybe, fourteen stone. We stood up to each other and I launched a punch with my right hand but he dropped his head at the same time as he came in for me and, on impact, my hand broke – the first of many times! Then we grappled. I resorted to a head butt and we eventually fell outside, where this lad got on top of me and I had my false arm, which had become detached, wrapped around my neck and was hitting him with my bare stump. It must have been quite a surreal experience for the staff to witness, as they had just been let out. So, I effectively took that grading with no hands.

"For 3rd kyu – quite an important step – I was graded by Tomita [25th November 1973] again. So, now I was a brown-belt it was actually possible to have the prestigious black belt in my sights. Okay, it was still a long way off, but with a great deal of effort and dedication I thought it could be done.

"Tomita was the first Japanese *karateka* I'd seen and I was mightily impressed by his technique – I think he was a 4th Dan. I thought his kicks were particularly noteworthy. He'd come to this country in 1972 as *Sensei* Enoeda's assistant [after Katsutaro Takahashi left] and lived down in Twickenham, London. He stayed in Britain for ten years before returning to Japan to work in the family's ceramic business. He was replaced by Yoshinobu Ohta. Tomita always had a smile on his face and I took him to be my kind of person. I believe that he was universally respected in this country and I have yet to meet anyone with a bad word to say against him."

Holdsworth recalled: "Owen really took to karate. I don't know, but maybe he'd found something through which he could prove himself. He trained really hard – and I mean *really* hard. He developed unbelievable fighting spirit and just wouldn't quit. I saw him get floored – knocked temporarily unconscious – come round, say to his opponent, 'That was a good 'un' and carry on fighting as if nothing had happened. A very strong-minded individual, a determined man and by the time he'd reached the brown belt grade I was beginning to gain a lot of respect for his attitude."

John Thompson, who joined the KUGB four years before Murray and trained at the South Tyneside *dojo*, recalled: "I once caught Owen with a punch during a competition in Sunderland. His legs went wobbly and he went down. Then, to my amazement, he got back up and carried on. Not only that, but he went on to beat me. Where this determination comes from I just don't know. He would come for you and never give up. He was, and still is, a very formidable fighter."

Holdsworth continued: "The policy we adopted at the club was to train through injuries, which we often had in those days. We wanted real commitment. Owen took to this attitude immediately and has trained with that approach ever since I first met him. If anyone quit after being injured in a competition, we used to give them grief. After every session he could have wrung his *gi* out. I don't think anyone could have put more effort into their training.

"No one saw Owen as being disabled because no allowance was made for it. That's what he wanted and that's what he got. Anyway, he was starting to beat some very good people with all their limbs intact and so whether he was disabled or not wasn't our chief concern! He used to wear a leather sleeve with some cushioning and a steel ring around the end to protect the stump where his hand was missing. He used the stump to good effect and often hit people with it. We often suffered self-injury from the sleeve over his stump as it was very hard and if you caught it with a kick or punch it caused some damage.

"Occasionally I'd say to Owen without thinking, 'Give us a hand,' when I needed help with something and he'd whip his false hand off and give it to me with a big smile on his face. That was, and still is, Owen. He never took offence at friendly banter either. We called him the 'One-Armed Swordsman' after the [1967] Chinese film showing at that time and he approved of that. Owen was born with two hands and now he had one – so what, he'd had an accident; end of story. He ignored his disability and so did the rest of us. He used to accept his nickname without any problem and never took it as a negative comment. We never hid from his disability and he appreciated the fact that we treated him like everyone else. In fact, the banter between the club members was continual, often very funny, always respectful, but never down-putting. We would probably be criticised for our approach today by the over-sensitive attitude of the politically correct brigade, but it worked. Yes, I think many of these people could have learned a lot by watching all of us interacting in those days."

Murray continued: "Before I lost my hand, I'd failed my driving test three times. Okay, I only had six lessons the first time, but I still failed. I reasoned that if I could pass karate gradings, which were certainly not easy, then I could pass a driving test, though I could in no way afford a car. I'd already been prosecuted and had points on my provisional licence for driving whilst not under the supervision of a qualified driver. When I was caught, I asked the policeman why he had pulled me over because I didn't think I'd done anything illegal, in an actual driving sense. He said he'd pulled me over because he was suspicious, as I was driving too carefully!

"After I started karate I wouldn't let things beat me. For example, the first time I re-took my driving test with one hand, the sweat just ran down my back – I was so anxious. I can feel it now – the trickle down the spine and then the cold. But I sweated when I trained, so I just accepted it and got on with the job in hand. Well, I did pass my driving test and within a couple of years I passed my test for driving a motor-bike as well. When I came to buy my first car, it cost me twenty-five pounds and was a Morris Minor van.

"By the end of 1973, nearly every young man had seen Bruce Lee's big film, *Enter the Dragon*, which had hit the cinemas. That same year, the thoughtful series, *Kung-fu*, starring David Carradine, playing the wandering American-Chinese Shaolin monk, Kwai Chang Caine, was shown on British television. I liked Caine's philosophy, it appealed, and the series was a lot more than just Wham, Bang, Wallop! Everywhere people wanted to take up martial arts and numbers wishing to learn karate at Sendai grew beyond all measure. Being a brown-belt amongst all these able-bodied white-belt beginners gave me, in a quiet way, a feeling of authority and I liked it.

"Because I lost a hand and part of my arm, I have been quoted as saying that I took up karate after seeing the famous film, *Bad Day at Black Rock*. This isn't actually true, though it's a great film and one I very much enjoyed. I'd seen it well before I lost my hand. The storyline was in the back of my mind of course, but I felt that the martial art sequence was just meant for celluloid and maybe the real world was something different."

For anyone who has not seen this film, and it is to be strongly recommended, the author would like to quote from Volume I of *Shotokan Dawn*: 'Without a doubt, the real cause of a surge in public interest in karate was as a result of the cinema. There had been, prior to the early sixties, a number of feature films that showed snippets of karate or karate-like techniques ... There is little doubt that during the Fifties the most famous and inspiring of encounters showing karate technique was to be found in John Sturges' 1955 classic, *Bad Day at Black Rock*. Spencer Tracy, at his subdued and thoughtful best, played the one-armed stranger, John J. MacReedy, and Ernest Borgnine memorably played local small-town thug, Coley Trimble. *Bad Day* ... was notable also, in a martial arts sense, for its economy of word and action. Tracy's performance, as a man looking for his Japanese friend, Kamoko Smith, was good enough to rate an Academy Award nomination for Best Actor, as indeed was John Sturges' direction and Millard Kaufman's script. Many critics regarded it as a milestone film in the history of the cinema. The much respected film critic, Leslie Halliwell, for example, wrote, 'The moments of violence, long awaited, are electrifying.' Indeed, the fight sequence is, given the context of time, probably the finest of its kind ever filmed.

'Tracy enters the town café/saloon to be shortly followed by Borgnine, who is accompanied by his boss, Robert Ryan. Borgnine tries to goad Tracy into a fight and Tracy attempts to leave, but Borgnine spins him around and issues insults, whereupon Tracy delivers a *shuto* to Borgnine's neck. The blow has such force that Borgnine crashes into a wall gasping for breath. Recovering, Borgnine throws a circular punch, but before contact is made Tracy strikes him in the stomach, and follows this up with a *shuto* to the back of the neck and a convincing upward knee strike to the face. Again Borgnine crashes into the wall. Borgnine then delivers another circular punch which Tracy side-steps and delivers a *shuto* to the back of the neck and then another *shuto* to the lower back, which sends Borgnine crashing through the establishment's front door. Recovering slowly, Borgnine swings a final punch, which is side-stepped, and Tracy catches the arm and throws his adversary, who screams. Throughout the fight there are no words spoken. Ryan, and other heavy, Lee Marvin, are taken aback. The scene ends with the town doctor, played by Walter Brennan, standing over Borgnine's body exclaiming, 'Man, man, oh man!' as Tracy leaves the café. The whole scene lasts for five minutes and thirty-four seconds of which the actual fight sequence lasts one minute and five seconds. It is a brilliantly handled piece of filming in terms of camera work, editing, timing and choreography. Ironically, Borgnine got his own back though, at least in real-life, for it was he who pipped Tracy at the post for the Academy Award of Best Actor that year for his role in the film *Marty* – though the two shared the Cannes Film Festival prize.'[14]

Murray continued: "My compensation claim for my accident ran for two years and it finally ended up in court in London. I travelled down with my union representative to a hearing in Fleet Street, then, still the home of the British Newspaper industry, before they all moved down to Wapping and Canary Wharf. I was asked questions and then requested to partially undress and dress myself. I promptly demonstrated that I could do these things by loosening my tie and shirt buttons and undoing my shoe laces and then refastening them. I really tried hard to prove I could do them. In doing so, of course, the compensation was, perhaps, not as good as it might have been. The union representative also said I would have a job within the printing industry for life, which I thought was a wrong move. Nevertheless, I was awarded seven thousand five hundred pounds, which was a lot of money at that time and was made up of claims for pain and injury suffered and loss of earnings. With that money – well, seven thousand two hundred pounds of it – I bought a middle of the range two bedroom bungalow with a garage and small garden in Arundel Gardens, a private estate in East Herrington, south of Sunderland, just off the Durham Road. Joan and I also bought a portable black and white television and a telephone.

"Joan and I were married at St. Michael's and All Angels church, Bishopwearmouth, which is now known as Sunderland Minster, on the 24th February 1973. Although virtually nothing now remains of the original church, people have been married on that site for over one thousand years.

"An hour before the wedding I sat in the Dun Cow pub – a wonderful, Grade II listed Edwardian gin palace, in High Street West,

A FALSE LIMB – 'IS IT A PROBLEM FOR YOU?'

Owen and Joan on their wedding day (1973)

across the road, right next to the Sunderland Empire, where the Beatles played and where the actor Sid James was to have his fatal heart-attack on stage three years hence. I met up with my best man, Ted Whelan and his father, a seaman, who plied me with dark rum. I remember looking out of the pub's first floor window and watching people walking to my wedding. I also recall that Ted left me at the altar answering a desperate call of nature.

"After the wedding, the reception was held at the Farringdon Social Club. If I remember correctly, Sunderland Association Football Club was playing and the match was being televised and all the lads went into the bar to watch. Interestingly, Sunderland AFC's badge now has significance for me, because the top left-hand section shows the Penshaw Monument that I've mentioned before, and the bottom right-hand section shows the Wearmouth Bridge, where I'd sat in traffic in the ambulance. The badge changed [in 1977] to show these symbols today. I'm not into football, though I did get swept along with the fervour of the F.A. Cup in 1973. I watched a few games and actually went to the Cup Final at Wembley, when Sunderland, then a Second Division team under manager Bob Stokoe, beat Leeds United 1–0, when Ian Porterfield scored in the thirtieth minute.

"On our wedding day, my Aunt Margaret couldn't attend due to illness – she died the following year, aged fifty-three – so Joan, still in her wedding dress, and I, visited her and had photographs taken at the front door of her house.

"My greatest fear has always been to stand up when other people are sitting and be the centre of attention. The mere thought of making a speech would turn me into a nervous wreck, so you can imagine how I was feeling when I actually had to make one that day. I have turned down being best man a number of times because of this problem. I just find it too stressful. On my wedding day I got a bit flustered and said, "Maybe Joan would like to say a few words?" I still don't like being the focus of attention and had to have a couple of whiskies prior to saying a few words at our daughter's wedding a few years ago.

"I remember when a mate of mine, Lance Spensley, asked me to be his best man and I refused, so he asked me to be a witness which I agreed to, not realising that, in some peoples' minds it was the same thing. When we went back to his house, I was told I had to make a speech and I said that there wasn't one and there wasn't going to be one. I made a quick bunk out of the back door and went to the nearest working man's club. I'm not a gambler, but I was bored because I was by myself and I decided to work the slot machines. I won a total of one hundred and twenty pounds, which was a lot of money in the 70's. Committee members took the money away to count it for me, so in the meantime I tried my hand at dominoes. You played dominoes for half a dollar – two shillings and sixpence – and the fellows from the wedding came over to find me. I was out first round and they laughed. I told them that I wasn't bothered because I'd just won over one hundred quid on the one armed bandits.

"'Oh Yeah,' one of them mocked, 'as if that's likely!'

"You should have seen their faces when a committee member handed me a wad of cash. I actually ended up with about forty pounds after I'd given Joan and the Dragon, and a few other people, some of my winnings and bought a few celebratory rounds.

"On our wedding night, Joan and I booked into the Mowbray Hotel, Sunderland. I love seafood and, as it was a special occasion, ordered lobster thermidor, as I'd heard of this French dish, but had never eaten it, nor, indeed, seen it, come to that. I thought to myself, 'I'll leave the lobster in the centre of the plate until last and eat all the surrounding goodies first.' When I'd finished the surrounding food, I lifted the lobster up and realised it was just a shell and I'd been eating its flesh all along. I now understand that the flesh of the lobster, mixed with egg yolk and brandy, should indeed be placed in the lobster's shell, so, despite my naivety, as luck would have it, I wasn't wrong. It was gorgeous anyway!

"We had our week-long honeymoon in London and I remember visiting the Imperial War Museum with Joan and seeing the violent western, *Soldier Blue*, on my own. Joan and I returned to live with her parents for a week because we still had to finish off some decorating in the bungalow.

"I suppose you could say that the loss of my hand had allowed me to upgrade my social and financial status a little, but I never thought of it like that, because people are people no matter where they live. Karate has taught me to respect people. You couldn't buy council houses in those days and they certainly didn't have garages. We lived in that bungalow for about seven years. Anyway, back to the karate!

"The year 1974 saw me grade twice and I passed my 2nd kyu [brown belt] under Tomita [10th March] and my 1st kyu under Andy [26th June]. Now I was a brown-belt with a white stripe. I liked freestyle and I was in the Sendai B Team at this time, along with a former school friend, Allan Turner, who now lives in Australia, and a chap named Dave Charlton, who is a highly successful hairdresser in the Philippines and who is on television over there. The Sendai A Squad was made up of John Holdsworth, Jeff Barwick, Jeff Westgarth, Jeff Candleash and Jim Caney [spelling for the last two individuals is uncertain]. We fought in the North-East Karate League, which covered participating karate clubs of differing styles from afar a field as East Kilbride and Motherwell in Scotland to the North, down to Rainworth, near Nottingham, in the South. It was run by Brian Crosley, who I've mentioned. These matches could be bruising affairs, but it was very good experience for me."

Allan Turner recalled: "I joined Sendai about a year after Owen – he was a green-belt when I started. As brown-belts, we were both picked for the B Team and fought together. Even in those days you couldn't relax when pairing-up with him. He was an intense fighter and would come in straight at you. He liked to punch, but he would also kick occasionally, especially with a fast *mae-geri*. He was an aggressive fighter, full on, but he was never a bully. I remember one fight he had at Crystal Palace in a preliminary round against a black-belt from another KUGB club. It was a pretty bruising affair. First one of them would get a bloody nose and then the other one would receive the same injury. Then one would receive a split lip and, before you could say anything, the other one had the injury too. It was a real ding-

The Sendai A Team: left to right, back row – Jeff Candelish, Jeff Westgarth, unknown; front row – Jeff Barwick, John Holdsworth, Jim Caney (*c.* 1974).

dong of a match. That was Owen – he would never give in – even when fighting a higher grade – and he took the fight."

Barwick recalled: "Owen had progressed with diligence and by the time he became a brown-belt he was quite a handful at *kumite* and when he reached 1st kyu he was a formidable, indeed ferocious fighter. John Holdsworth had brought him through. Owen could give it and he could take it, and he didn't mind taking it and that made him fearless. I remember one Northern League competition that we attended and we

The Sendai B Team: left to right, back row – all unknown; front row – Owen Murray, Alan Turner, David Charlton (*c.* 1974).

were up against another KUGB club run by a hard man, a coal miner. I recall this chap turned to me after watching Owen in action.

" 'I'm not fighting *that* until I hear it speak,' he exclaimed."

Murray continued: "They seemed to have some strange rules in some of the competitions I went in for. On one occasion I was fighting in Middlesbrough and I punched my opponent *chudan* that badly that he couldn't continue and the referee and judges gave me an *ippon*, a full-point, and I won. The following fight I controlled a punch to the head and was disqualified. So, I was declared winner and allowed to continue when I hit someone hard, but when I just touched them I got disqualified!

"On another of those league matches I was fighting against someone who was very aggressive and my method was to go forward so you can imagine the carnage that ensued. I beat this chap and he wasn't happy and told me he wanted to finish the fight off outside. Never one to back down, I agreed and off I went to the car park. This chap was a local lad, I was 'on his turf', so I asked a good pal of mine, to watch my back. I waited, but the chap never turned up, so that was fine. I suppose he'd cooled down. However, only about five or six weeks ago I went to a competition in Middlesbrough which my son was taking part in and the organiser was the same person who hadn't shown up all those years before. I walked across to him putting my prosthetic limb behind my back so he didn't realise I only had the one hand.

" 'Do you remember Owen Murray?' I asked him.

" 'Yeah,' came his reply. 'He used to be one of the fighters in the karate league.'

" 'I'm Owen Murray,' I said.

" 'Oh! That's great!' he exclaimed and we shook hands and that was that.

"I also started entering the individual *kumite* category in the KUGB National Championships down at Crystal Palace around this time and got through a few rounds. I remember, on one occasion, I was fighting and my opponent and I clashed. When we withdrew, the right sleeve of my *gi* had been ripped so violently that when I straightened my arm the sleeve fell off. It was a funny moment appreciated by all.

"That reminds me of another story that happened in a fight. Later, when I was a 3rd Dan, owing to encouragement from John Holdsworth, I became a judge [1977] and referee [1979] after attending KUGB courses in Manchester and Coventry, respectively. Andy Sherry, Charles Naylor[15] and Derek Langham[16] signed my certificates. I passed along with Colin Schubert, now at Gateshead. I am not particularly interested in officiating to be honest, but whilst refereeing in a competition I had to stop a bout because of excessive contact. The injured competitor was on the ground lying on his side and when I turned him over his eye was missing. The eye wasn't anywhere to be found and it didn't look as though it had been pushed back into its socket. I shouted to the St John's ambulance people to come over immediately. The injured fighter was really groggy after the

Owen during a break in a *kumite* encounter where the sleeve of his *gi* was ripped off. The referee is international competitor, Bob Rhodes (1974/75).

punch he'd received and it was quite a while before he could explain that he'd taken his false eye out before the fight! I didn't know about this and hadn't picked it up because I was standing on the side of his only eye. We all had a good laugh afterwards.

"We always had a good time when we went down to the KUGB Nationals. I remember, one year, a member of the Sendai team got a bit carried away and punched a hole through the wall of the hotel room. When we looked through the hole, there, in the other room, was a man sitting reading a magazine. He just sat there looking at us looking at him. It was really funny. We reported the incident to one of the KUGB Executive, who was, as you can imagine, not too pleased with us and told us so in no uncertain terms. The following year we had t-shirts made up with a picture on the front of a *karateka* punching a large collapsing wall. We called ourselves, 'The Hole in the Wall Gang!'

Julie Nicholson, who went on to take numerous National, European and World titles, recalled her first encounter with Murray: "I remember really wanting to train in karate when I was ten years old and there was a four month waiting list at Sendai at the time. Eventually, I got the green light to go along. Amongst the trainees was a 1st kyu with only one hand. My father, who had accompanied me, whispered in my ear, 'Don't say anything,' as any child might. I was mightily impressed with the way this man trained – he left a marked impression – as he was just practising so hard and was covered in sweat with his hair dripping wet. I'd never seen anything like it before."

Christine Pullan – who was successful in a good number of KUGB competitions in the years to follow and started on the same beginners' course at Sendai as Nicholson in 1975 – recalled: "I was twelve years old when I started training and I remember seeing Owen in the *dojo*. He trained so fiercely, with such a forceful attitude that it was a bit frightening for a child to be honest – at least it was for me. I was young and impressionable and the fact that he only had one hand just added to my fear."

Murray continued: "Because I had my black belt, *Shodan* [1st Dan], in my sights, I trained whenever there was an opportunity. Karate is a wonderful art if you want to be good at it. I'd go down to the YMCA and practise alone in the *dojo*. At home, I'd practise when Joan was out. I deliberately wouldn't change into my *gi*, but trained in jeans and trainers to mimic a real situation, because I wouldn't be wearing a loose *gi* walking along the streets, nor would I be barefooted. I had to work really hard on flexibility and I set myself the goal of touching the light bulbs hanging in the centre of the lounge with a kick known as *mawashi-geri*, or roundhouse-kick, which I eventually did. I also built myself a *makiwara*, which I set in concrete in the garden. At the top of the tapered post I fitted some dense rubber pads that I got from work, for absorption, and then wrapped rope tightly around them. I punched and struck that *makiwara* for a long time. I tore the skin on my fist quite badly – the rope turned red – but I wasn't bothered about that and carried on, just as I'd heard they did in Japan.[17] Stupid really, but it was good spirit training I suppose and it helped focus my mind as well as my techniques.

"At Vedrapak I'd stack two thousand sheets of paper at the side of my Saragolia and it would take about twenty minutes for the paper to work its way through. I would stand in the informal attention stance, *hachiji-dachi*, or *heiko-dachi*, and punch the paper, which, when compacted like that, was extremely hard, stronger than wood, with *choku-zuki* – straight punch. I'd check the machine was running smoothly every so often and then return to punching. The remarkable thing was nobody ever said anything or tried to stop me. Maybe they thought I was getting my own back on the machine that had cut my hand off, or perhaps they thought I was just plain crackers.

"Between two and two-and-a-half years after losing my hand, I left Vedrapak. This was a big decision for me, as Tony Reid, the owner's son, had promised me a job for life, so I kissed goodbye to security of employment. I left to become a foreman and, later, production manager in-charge of goods coming in and going out of the factory, and, also, responsible for the factory floor, at Remploy, on the Pallion Trading Estate, engaged as an able-bodied employee. There was an overall manager in charge of the office and sales and his name was Chris Greenwell. My salary went up by a small amount. Remploy was a government body established at the end of World War II under the Disabled Persons Act of 1944, with the intention of providing job opportunities for disabled people whose ranks had increased because of injuries received in the war. We had people with a broad spectrum of disabilities, from amputees to epileptics, from the blind to schizophrenics. I found communicating with deaf people the hardest challenge and I even learned some sign language from a chap named Tom Finnigan. Whilst the factory had to compete in the market place just like any other, it actually ran at a loss because the workforce was not as fast as able-bodied workers and the factory was more labour intensive than our competitors, but that was the reason why Remploy was set-up originally. Any deficit was made up by the Department of Employment. I worked in a factory dealing with plain and printed, corrugated and solid board cartons and boxes, so I knew the set-up well. I left Vedrapak because I felt the chance of promotion would have been zero, as both Dave and Graham were excellent at their jobs and they were senior to me. Strangely, later in life, I believe Remploy was planning to take over Vedrapack which would have meant I may have been Dave and Graham's manager! Anyway, I loved it at Remploy and I stayed there for about twenty years. During my lunch hour, I'd go into the warehouse and practise karate techniques on a punch bag that I'd hang up.

"I trained so hard for my *Shodan* and got as fit as I could. I hated running, but I used to run to Remploy, seven or eight miles each morning, come sweltering heat, thunderstorm or snow. However, the main reason for running was for mental attitude. I knew I would have to freestyle two people as part of the black belt grading and I intended blaming my opponents for putting me through this hell to get the grade and taking it out on them on the day. I was fanatical.

"I'd go at things single-mindedly, like Tom Hanks's character in the film, *Forrest Gump*, and, later, I ran the Great North Run – that's a half-marathon – three times. I used to train very hard for a non runner and involved the karate club. One of the black-belts (who was Remploy's manager) ran with me all the way on the first occasion and I did a time of one hour and thirty-seven minutes, but I had to queue up four minutes behind the start position – this being, apparently, the world's most popular half-marathon – so my real time was one hour and thirty-three minutes.

"The following year I went on holiday to Majorca and trained every day. It's a small world because when I was running, someone from Sunderland stopped me to ask for my autograph. On the way back home, I had half a bottle of whisky, then six pints in the pub. The Great North Run was the next day and my intention was to complete it in a time less than one hour and thirty minutes. I lined up at Newcastle and ran with a policeman named Les Hodgekinson who had the same goal. He realised after a few miles that I wasn't going to make the time. I actually beat Les to the finish and you may think, 'Well done me,' but I arrived in an ambulance! I lasted eleven miles and was dragged to one side because I would not give in! I was barely with it, mentally, but I do remember being wrapped up like a papoose on the side of the road.

"'Look that's Owen,' people would say as they passed by.

"I recall all too clearly being in the ambulance thinking, 'What's happened? Have I had a stroke or a heart attack?' I finished back at the hospital tent. I was placed on a bed and had to wait for a doctor. After a while I came to my senses and rolled off the bed and slid under the tent and left. The last year I did the run I decided to take it easier. Upon reaching the eleven mile mark, I was greeted by members of Sendai who had made a massive banner which read, 'Murray's Last Stand' and they followed me for a couple of miles into South Shields. The amazing thing was that both the banner and I were filmed, televised, and broadcast over the entire country! I think I took one hour and forty-five minutes that time. Anyway, back to my *Shodan* grading.

"The big day finally arrived – 2nd February 1975. I'd been training under three years, but really intensively. I went down to London with John Holdsworth and his first wife, another Joan, who was also taking her black belt grading. I wanted that grading so much.

Owen finishing the Great North Run

"It was the first time I'd seen *Sensei* Enoeda and needless to say I was very impressed by him. He was a former All-Japan JKA *kumite* champion [1963] and they don't come much better than that. He had also been captain of the famous Takushoku University karate club during the 1950s, before completing the JKA Instructors' Course. He was one of the four JKA instructors [the others being Taiji Kase, Hirokazu Kanazawa, Hiroshi Shirai] who visited England on their world tour in 1965. Kanazawa resided here and Enoeda went to South Africa before coming back and taking up residence in Liverpool. After a stay in the USA, he became Chief Instructor of the KUGB after Kanazawa went to Germany and had been so for about seven years. All the senior grades spoke about Enoeda with great respect, awe in fact. He was nearly forty years of age at the time and a real powerhouse.

"The grading started with *kihon* and then moved to *kumite*. The running paid off, because as soon as the referee called, '*Hajime*!' I was off like a bat out of hell. I showed control of course, but I beat up the opposition quite badly and the referee had to intervene. For the *kata* component, which I felt was my weakest section, I chose *Bassai-dai*.

"At the end of the grading, we were called up in a line and given the result. That was a nerve-racking moment I can tell you. I passed and, afterwards, wanted to go out and celebrate, but John's wife failed and she was, quite understandably, very disappointed, so that put a

Owen's *Shodan* certificate (1975)

damper on things.

"It was in 1974 that some friends who owned a nightclub called Boy Meets Girl, in Sunderland, approached me and asked if I'd like to be a doorman in the evenings to earn some extra money. I had never worked a door before and didn't have a clue what to do, but it sounded quite appealing and I said that I would give it a go. A doorman named Eric, who became a close friend, took me under his wing. I worked the doors in the city for the next twenty years. I had some heavy trouble with drug dealers during the later stages and I'll talk about that later.

"Joan and I split up around 1975. It was my fault entirely and I'm not going to make up any excuses, for I'd been seeing another woman. Joan went to Canada for a year to work as a nanny. Joan had been my first and only girlfriend really and I suppose I just hadn't really been ready for marriage because I hadn't sown any wild oats in my youth. I just wanted freedom; I didn't want any restrictions. I wanted the life of O'Reilly. I continued living in East Herrington for a while and then sold it and went to live in a bedsit in Athol Road, in the Hendon district of Sunderland. It was pretty rough actually.

"It was whilst living in Athol Road that I had a nasty encounter. I got back to my flat one day to discover that I'd been broken into. It turned out to be the lad next door and he'd done a bunk with my money and some of my possessions. What was particularly disappointing was that I'd helped this guy out in the past. Anyway, after six months I heard through the grapevine that he had come back and so I went to have a chat with him, if I can put it like that. Shortly afterwards, I had four angry bikers and a barking alsatian trying to break my door down – apparently this guy had mates. The door was made of wood and panelled and they smashed one of these panels out. I rushed to put my settee up against the door. I was standing there just in my underpants getting ready to go out and do a karate demonstration, but I had the sense to put my crash helmet on once I realised what was going down.

"I could see them outside through the hole they'd made and they were cursing and yelling about what they were going to do to me. Suddenly, a broom handle was thrust through where the panel had been and the end caught me above an eye and gave me a nasty cut – I didn't have the helmet's visor down. Then a large hunting knife was thrown into the room which, luckily, landed flat on my bare chest and bounced off.

"It was obvious that they were going to get in eventually, so I threw something, a chair maybe, through my back window. It didn't break all the glass and I used my false limb, which was attached, to punch out as much as I could. These bikers were nearly in, so I clambered out on to the window ledge and jumped down from the second floor on to the roof of my neighbour's outhouse. Luckily, I didn't go through the slate and slid down into his garden. Once I was there I realised to my horror that I was boxed in by walls. Trying to scale a wall with one hand is impossible, so I jumped up as high as I could in my desperation and caught the top of one wall under my armpits. The rough edges of the bricks tore into my skin causing cuts but I managed to scramble over, jump down and run along a cobbled alley. I was covered in blood by this stage because I hadn't managed to clamber out of the window unscathed, for the broken glass that still protruded from the window frame had cut deep. A lorry was turning just up the road and I jumped on the foot rest up to the driver's cabin. You can imagine the look of surprise and horror on his face when he saw this man covered in blood and with a prosthetic limb dressed only in underpants and a crash helmet suddenly beside him!

"The police and ambulance were called and I was taken to the local hospital where, waiting to get stitched up, was the lad who'd stolen from me. I went for him in Accident and Emergency, but was pulled away. I needed about a dozen stitches in all.

"Well, they weren't going to get off after that. I asked a mate of mine to go along with me to the gang house. He lifted me over a high wall, behind which gang members kept their beloved motorbikes. It was my intention to do as much damage to their bikes as I possibly could. After I landed and looked about me, I discovered there were no motorbikes, just a three wheeled Reliant Robin, like Del Boy drives in *Only Fools and Horses*. I wasn't going to hang around and climbed up on something and scrambled back over that wall as quickly as I could.

"I'm not a grass, but I did press charges against those bikers. I subsequently received threats and when I got to court, bikers were lined on either side of the courtroom. It was a frightening experience and you could just feel an atmosphere of menace and hate. One of the accused brothers had told me that if his brother got more than one year in prison, he was going to cut off my other arm. Well, he got three years.

"When this biker got out of clink, he sent word that he wanted to see me at a certain pub. Now, I had a choice – either I wouldn't go and he'd come after me with his pals which meant that I'd have to be on guard all the time, or I could go and face him on to his own turf. I decided on the latter option. I tried to get some of my mates to come along with me as back up, but I found they all had prior engagements they couldn't break. However, one of their girlfriends who was pregnant said she would come along – how about that! I thought that she wouldn't be able to do anything, but at least she could be a witness.

"When I got to the pub I walked in and there was this chap at the bar with about fifteen of his cronies. This young lady and I walked in together. My God, she had more balls than all my 'mates' put together. This was one of the most frightening encounters I have ever had. I walked up to this bloke and as I did so his mates encircled me and I was expecting to feel the cold steel of a knife blade in my back at any moment. I just had to brave it out. That was all I could do.

"'Come here!' the biker grunted.

"I tried to put a brave face on and walked straight up to him. Then he did something I just wasn't expecting – he held his hand out and I shook it. Looking back, putting a hand out like that, in such circumstances, is a wonderful way to immobilise a one-handed man – and let's face it, he'd had plenty of time to think it up – but it didn't dawn on me at the time. That, thank goodness, was the end of that episode, and I wouldn't want to repeat it."

Christine Pullan recalled: "I remember Owen telling a group of us in the bar after training one evening about his encounter with bikers and how in a state of undress and all cut up he had tried to get a lorry to stop for him. Owen is good at telling stories and he had me in fits because I had this image in my mind of him running down the road in his underpants trying to flag down this lorry expecting the driver to stop. Owen was being deadly serious and he not only couldn't understand why this chap wouldn't stop but, also, why we were all laughing.

"As a bouncer, Owen had lots of tales to tell. I remember there was the time he was in a punch up in a pub or nightclub. He saw a friend of his go down in the melée and people were going for him whilst on the floor, so Owen dived on top of his friend to protect him. This meant that Owen got a good kicking instead.

"'Get off! I'm alright,' the friend shouted at Owen. So Owen had taken a pasting for nothing. But it goes to show what sort of man he is."

Murray continued: "Deep down I was still coming to terms with the loss of my hand and this could become acute in social settings. I used to wear a black glove on my false hand and I remember crossing High Street West in Sunderland with some friends. When we reached the pavement on the other side of the road I realised my left arm felt lighter and I looked down and saw my hand had fallen off. I turned around and there it was in the middle of the High Street. Fortunately, it hadn't been run over, so I hurried back to collect it. I found that a really embarrassing moment.

"When Joan returned from Ontario, she bought a house in Farringdon. She worked for a company called Dynavox, which made headphones for aeroplanes. We got back together and on the 20th December 1977, she gave birth to our daughter, Donna. When Donna was an infant, Joan worked part-time from home for the same company. So, I was a dad and proud to be one, very proud, but it didn't stop me seeing other women.

"Less than a month after Donna's birth, Joan received a hate mail letter. There was some sick individual out there who was threatening the baby, or that's how we took it. It read as if it came from a woman, but we weren't sure. We called the police in, but they couldn't do much.[18]

"It was while living at Arundel Gardens that I met Kitty and her husband Tom, who had mental health problems. Joan and Kitty never got on very well. Kitty would swear and be quite rude and she reported us to the RSPCA for cruelty to our dogs. She thought because the dogs were left in a large run with plenty of food and water we were being cruel. Joan, being a dog lover, was furious. Kitty also thought that feeding our dogs marshmallows and chocolate biscuits was good for them, which it isn't, and she had a corgi who was obese. When Joan and I split up, Kitty would bring around homemade food for me, hot dinners and homemade soup. At the time she would do my ironing too. I would nip next door two or three times a week and have a wee dram with them. When they hit on hard times I would help them out with their bills and would slip them half a bottle of whisky which Kitty would keep on her mantle piece next to a nude photograph of herself in her younger days. This photo was her pride and joy, though her husband didn't approve. Unfortunately, Kitty had to sell her house and move to a residential home after her husband went to Cherry Knowles Mental Health Hospital. When Kitty had problems, she would phone me at work and I would nip around and sort things out and, sometimes, these were very personal. When Kitty died of cancer, in her mid sixties, she had no one and I sat with her as she passed away. That is the only time I've watched someone die. I was holding her hand and her eyes just seemed to glaze over, as if a cloud passed by. After her death, I found out that she left me everything in her will. It was then people came out of the woodwork, people I'd never seen before, such as her husband's brother. The will was contested but everyone who came forward seemed to die first! I eventually received all that was in her will. We were pals, we looked after each other in times of need, and I think of her often."

Murray's love of whisky could cause problems, as Holdsworth recalled: "Each year Sendai sent a squad to the KUGB Northern Region Championships and in 1976 it was held in Blackpool. Owen was a key member, though, as team captain, I had to prevent him bringing alcohol on to the coach, because I knew what would happen. He wasn't too happy about it, but he accepted it. Some of the team took the trip to be a 'weekend away with the lads' sort of adventure, but these were often family affairs and lads' behaviour needs to be controlled in such circumstances. Also, I naturally wanted the team to be on top form for the championship."

Nicholson continued: "I remember that Friday evening trip to Blackpool when I was eleven years of age because it was a big adventure for me. My mum, dad and elder sister, Christine, came along too on the fifty-three seater coach. Owen tried to smuggle alcohol on to the bus hidden under his coat but John caught him and asked him to hand it over.

"When we reached our guest house, some of the team members went out for a few drinks and when they came back in the early hours of the morning they were noisy. I wasn't too aware of what had happened as I slept through the noise, but they did wake my parents up."

Holdsworth continued: "I asked Owen if he'd been drinking and he said that he had, so I told him that he knew the rules and that I was dropping him from the team. Everything was done in a controlled manner and there were no raised voices. He was our best fighter, we needed him, but the club policy was no alcohol and late nights before a competition. He didn't like the decision at all and when his face went white for a moment I thought I might have a real problem. But it was okay because I think deep down he knew that I was right. He didn't fight for the team that day and although we've had a few disagreements over the decades, that was the worst one.

"My action turned out to be a one-off though and it wasn't because he gave up drinking before competitions – it was because I gave up trying to stop him! He was incorrigible – a law unto himself – and so I had to change because he was just too good to leave out."

Murray continued: "Two years after passing my *Shodan* I took my *Nidan,* or second level black belt, under *Sensei* Enoeda and passed that

Owen facing Jim Brennan (1974/75). The referee is Bob Rhodes of Leeds.

too [19th June 1977]. It was as a 2nd Dan that I won the middle-weight category at the North-East Karate League Cup in 1977[19] and 1978, both held in Washington. In 1977, I beat a chap named Doug Coulthard[20] and Sendai were League Champions, and in 1978 I overcame an opponent named Eddy Inch in the final.[21, 22] Winning these titles had some benefit. For example, I was mentioned in the local press shortly after the 1978 final and that encouraged people to support a YMCA anniversary and the money raised from that event went to help refugees.[23]

"In 1978, I took part in the North-West Open Karate Championships [held at the Atherton Leisure Centre], near Wigan, and narrowly lost in the final after extra time." A report at the time noted that the championships featured, 'a large number of entries and a high standard of competition marked the day.' The report went on to record: 'In the individual *kumite*, Owen Murray (Sunderland) got a two half-points lead on N. Gomersall (Leeds), but then Gomersall came up fast and equalised at time. In the extension, Gomersall kept up his attacks and at time got the decision and the title.'[24]

Murray continued: "From this moment onwards I started to occasionally get mentioned in the martial arts' press and, in particular, *Fighting Arts*. I took *Fighting Arts* because it was a good magazine and the KUGB and its competitions were often reported. The editor and publisher was Terry O'Neill, a famous Liverpool founder member of the KUGB, and so there were often features on Shotokan and Shotokan *karateka*.

"A fight I remember around this time was against a chap whose name I don't recall, but we called him Beefy 69 because he was well-built and looked as though he stood six feet nine inches in height. I believe he was a kung-fu champion and I fought him in an All-Styles tournament over in, I think, Birmingham. I remember facing him in his blue *gi* and thinking to myself 'Well, *jodan* is out of the question!' He scored on me with a punch and then I scored on him with a punch too and the match was declared a draw. I had a photograph taken next to him to show our differing heights. He was Afro-Caribbean and had an Afro haircut which was popular at the time. He was a really nice chap. However, not long afterwards Beefy 69 died after being kicked when competing in a competition."

The gentleman in question is, almost certainly, Jeff Douglas, who died whilst competing in the first British Full Contact Karate Championships, in October 1976, held at the Belle Vue stadium, Manchester. Douglas, who stood about six feet five inches, was rated number one in the sport. Whilst leaping to perform a jump-kick, Douglas was accidently (by virtue of the jump) kicked in the groin with a light front kick by a club-mate. Douglas collapsed and never regained consciousness. It turned out that, after a post-mortem, the kick had done no damage at all and that Douglas had been unknowingly suffering from sarcoidosis, which is likely to have placed great strain on his system when under stress. The cause of death was given as pulmonary oedema and acute myocardial failure and a verdict of death by natural causes was recorded.[25]

Murray continued: "I also came second in a semi-contact event at an All Styles Martial Arts Contest held in Bradford.[26] These competitions proved to be a very good grounding for what was to follow.

"My prosthetic arm is actually a lethal weapon. I used to wrap it in polystyrene and most of my training friends knew not to kick me on that side because I could break their toes. By the time I'd got to 2nd Dan I'd already broken three opponents' toes that way and badly bruised feet, ankles, knees and legs of countless others.[27]

"Mind you, I did get smashed up myself. I had a good relationship with the jujitsu lads in the North-East of England and they encouraged a few of us to go into a full-contact competition in Yorkshire. It was new on the scene and nobody really knew what was involved.

OWEN MURRAY, M.B.E., 6th DAN

Jeff Barwick (left) and Owen in competition (1974/75). The referee is well-known *karateka*, Bob Rhodes.

Owen fighting Bob Poynton of the Liverpool Red Triangle karate club in the 1978 KUGB National Championship semi-finals of the team *kumite* event.

A FALSE LIMB – 'IS IT A PROBLEM FOR YOU?'

" 'Yeah, we'll go down,' I said, confidently.

"When we got to the competition it was as kickboxing is today – mitts, gum shields, foot guards and a boxing ring. We had never experienced anything like this before; we felt uncomfortable and a bit out of our league. I breathed a sigh of relief when I heard there was to be a medical before being allowed to fight and being weighed. I thought they wouldn't allow me to fight because I wouldn't be able to get a boxing glove over my false limb. However, I passed the medical and they said I was okay to go on. However, just a matter of a few minutes before I was due to fight, my intended opponent pulled out, for which I was most grateful. I remember one of my team members in a full-contact bout who was getting so badly beaten that I had to throw the towel in.

"I did enter a number of semi-contact competitions though – well, supposedly semi-contact! I had nine fights in all and ended up with black eyes, a broken nose and burst lips. I remember my last team fight because my opponent and I basically just beat each other up. I didn't win a shiny 18-inch trophy or even a shiny 15-inch trophy; no, my reward for all those fights was ... wait for it ... an egg cup! However, at the end of the day I was awarded the best all-rounder trophy as I'd won the individuals, captained the team and was presented with quite a substantial trophy."

IV

EUROPEAN GOLD ... 'I WISH I COULD REMEMBER!'

Murray continued: "I'd entered the individual *kumite* event at KUGB National Championships down at the National Sports Centre, Crystal Palace, Norwood, London, for a number of years from about 1974/75 and had done quite well, getting into the quarter-finals. Then, on the 29th October 1979 – I know that because I've kept the letter – I was selected for the KUGB National Squad.[1, 2]" Murray is reported at the time as saying: 'This has been my ambition ever since I started and I can hardly believe it.'[3]

Murray continued: "Karate was giving me the confidence I'd always sought and when I, a one-armed man, was selected for the KUGB National Squad, my self-esteem received a real uplift.

"I used to travel over to the Red Triangle Club, in the Everton Road, Liverpool, where the squad training sessions were held once a month. These were gruelling sessions under *Sensei* Enoeda and Andy Sherry. The first time I went for selection I failed to get in. I was quite badly beaten up actually, but it was my own fault because my control was not that good to be honest and so maybe that was the reason. I was up against the likes of Frank Brennan and Terry O'Neill[4], so if I went for them and was lacking a bit of control, I'd pay for it. Put it this way, I soon learned to control my techniques in that rarefied environment! I remember as part of the training, squad members had to stand against a wall and defend against an attack. Firstly, the attacks would come in at you as a kick or a punch, but, later, any attack was allowed – and these were fast. There was no messing about with these boys. One session I recall, we trained for five hours with only two breaks and Andy actually sent out for water because of dehydration. My goodness me that water tasted good! This was not five hours on some karate course, but beasting, which took a special kind of person to survive it. You might compare it to SAS selection I suppose. I thought Andy was a good motivator and I responded well to his teaching. Enoeda was ... well, Enoeda, and you did what you were told.

"One squad session I was paired up with Frank. *Sensei* Enoeda had

Official notification from the KUGB Secretary, Cliff Hepburn, that Owen had been selected for the KUGB National Squad (1979).

us attacking an attack with *ushiro-geri* [back kick]. I moved in with a *gyaku-zuki* [reverse punch], and Frank kicked. Well, he brought his foot up so fast that I never saw it and he caught me smack in the solar plexus and I just went down like a lead weight. Everybody stopped and looked on, and that's saying something in KUGB squad training, I can tell you. I couldn't move. I took an intake of air but could not expel it. I honestly thought that this was the end of me. Andy put his knee in my back and pulled my arms back at the same time. *Sensei*, with a smile on his face, was giving him instructions. I recovered shortly thereafter and was told to get on with it as if nothing had happened and had to face Frank again.

"On another occasion, I went squad training after dislocating my shoulder at a jujitsu club a couple of days before. I didn't want my seniors to think I was skiving and I went along with my shoulder strapped up and my arm strapped to my side. There was no sympathy whatsoever and they showed me no leeway. All I remember was being pushed to fight Terry O'Neill!"

Terry O'Neill recalled: 'I have nothing but praise for him [Owen]; a fierce fighter who steadfastly refused to be 'disabled', and a fine man to boot – although I never did manage to do that to him, despite my very best efforts.'[5]

Barwick recalled: "Owen had told me how hard the KUGB squad training was and came back with all sorts of stories. I'll never forget one occasion when I was driving through Sunderland at night and there, in front of me, was a man staggering along the pavement, hardly able to walk. He didn't look drunk and I thought he'd been hit by a car. I stopped and got out and went up to him. To my astonishment it was Owen. He'd been to the Red Triangle that day and had got back late and was walking home. He was so shattered he couldn't walk in a straight line. He told me that training had been like the D Day landings. The squad at that time was probably the strongest it has ever been and it was dominated by Red Triangle members. Owen had to literally fight his way into the squad, with one hand. Having seen Owen that night, in that exhausted state, seeing what he was prepared to put in, just humbled me to be honest."

Nicholson recalled: "I remember when Owen, Graham Adams and I, drove over to Liverpool for squad training one Sunday in the middle of winter in Owen's car. Owen let Graham drive as, per usual, Owen used the opportunity to catch up on his sleep as he had been working on the doors the night before. The car broke down on the M62 and it was something to do with a lack of water, so Owen and Graham were trying to melt snow, but the AA had to be called in the end. Owen was really upset that he'd missed training. He said he'd be there and he couldn't be and he didn't like the thought that *Sensei* Enoeda and *Sensei* Sherry might think he hadn't made the effort."

Adams (see later) recalled the incident: "Owen may be a brilliant *karateka,* but he is a useless mechanic. I remember when his car broke down through lack of water and he thought it would be a good idea to see if we could melt snow. Well, it didn't work. There were no mobile phones in those days and we had to walk miles to the nearest pub to use the phone. When the breakdown chap finally arrived he looked under the bonnet and re-appeared some time later to offer his diagnoses.

"'You've got two snowballs stuffed in your radiator!' he said, earnestly. I just curled up. It was so funny."

Thompson was also in the KUGB National Squad at the time. He recalled: "I used to go over to the Red Triangle with Owen sometimes. I used to stay overnight with Steve Cattle and Sandie Hopkins. I would go by train or car, with Owen. I remember he was into John Denver and would play his music in the car. Those sessions in Liverpool were tough."

Nicholson continued: "Owen was always bruised and battered. I remember when I had to go into hospital to have my sinuses done – that would have been in 1978 or 1979. The male and female wards came together at a lobby and I popped out of the female ward and bumped into Owen, wearing shorts and with a bandage wrapped around his head. I thought to myself, 'What's happened now?' But Owen had a problem with an ear and it wasn't the result of a karate injury! I remember him saying that if he'd known I was in the next ward we could have done some training together! I was only fourteen at the time, but I bet you a pound to a penny he would have had me practising.

"That bandage reminds me of a demonstration Owen did where he was going to perform wood-breaking, *tameshiwari*. Jeff Barwick usually looked after the wooden boards that were to be broken, but on this occasion Owen had taken responsibility for them. Well, he'd left them out in the rain and so they were close to being unbreakable. He intended breaking some with his forehead and others with punches. He came down with his head on the boards and he didn't go through them. He tried again and again. His head was just a mass of lumps and bumps. That was the sort of crazy thing Owen would do. He's a real character."

Murray recalled the incident: "Sendai had done a karate demonstration in Seaburn and, afterwards, I had a hospital appointment at 12 p.m. I had to be admitted for a perforated ear drum and was getting one grafted. I phoned up to say that my car had broken down and that I had an injury. I used to break wood with my head and came down repeatedly on some wood that was wet and ended up with a massive bruise. So, a bit dazed, I decided to punch through the wood and broke my knuckles. I wasn't going to be beaten though and finally smashed the wood with a *shuto*, knife-hand, with my broken hand. When I got to the hospital I was in such a state that they actually thought I'd been in a car accident!

"I was also part of the KUGB Northern Area Squad, under Bob Rhodes. The training, held over in Leeds once a month, was very hard. Those boys were a good set of lads, I liked them. I remember working on various sequences, especially foot sweeping – *ashi-barai* in Japanese.

"I was never a great kicker and so I began to specialise in punching and every day, morning and night, or, if the truth be known, any available minute I had, I'd practise *gyaku-zuki* and *kizami-zuki* [jab]. My freestyle was based on good timing initially. One strategy I developed was to suddenly shift my stance and go south paw. This would momentarily confuse my opponent and allow me to seize the initiative with my right foot and right hand – with its longer reach – forward. Another strategy was to allow an opponent to attack when I deliberately dropped my guard whilst closing the distance between my opponent and myself. If I left my head vulnerable, at that distance, a *kizami-zuki* would invariably come my way. So, what I used to do was to slide and block *nagashi-uke en route* and counter *gyaku-zuki*. If my middle section was deliberately exposed, then a *chudan gyaku-zuki* would usually be delivered by my opponent and I'd block with the downward block, *gedan-barai*, as I slid in and countered with the reverse punch. Sometimes, for a *chudan* attack, I'd step back, block a reverse downward block, *gyaku-gedan-barai*, and deliver a *kizami-zuki*.

"I learned this tactic – to counter-attack my opponent whilst he was in mid flow, as it were – from *Sensei* Enoeda. It suited my personality, for no matter how experienced my opponent was, it was my intention not to allow them to complete their technique and I drove forward into them as they advanced. This type of technique requires fighting spirit, much promoted by Enoeda and the strategy was very much taken up by me. One can get caught moving into an attack of course and I was a few times, but, generally, *ai-uchi* [simultaneous strike] was the worst scenario and an *ippon* [full point] the best. I became a quick puncher, very quick, even if I say so myself. No matter how skilful my opponents were, if I blocked them at the beginning of their technique they would never get to land it before I scored. As soon as my

Owen in *kamae* (guard) – 1979

opponent moved a leg to perform a kick, or to step or slide in, I was there – bang! I beat some good people like that. I became well-known for punching and so I became a bit predictable.

"Once I'd joined the KUGB National Squad, I had to expand my strategies and techniques because I was up against really top-level international competitive *karateka* and they weren't so easily taken in – and they were really fast too! So, I developed my *kaeshi-ippon-kumite,* where I'd attack, block the counter and attack once more – three techniques. Initially, I used hand techniques alone, but this developed into punch-kick and kick-punch combinations. These worked as well. I would often fake a *mae-geri* attack by bringing my knee up and this encouraged my opponent to slide in with a punch which I would block and counter with either a punch or a kick. I did score a few points with *mae-geri* and *mawashi-geri.* The one that really stands out for me was when I caught fellow KUGB squad member, Fred Fawcett, with a *jodan mawashi-geri* in a competition and I don't know who was more shocked – him or me!

"Sometimes I would misjudge a kick. I remember kicking an opponent in the groin with *mae-geri* and he suffered a twisted testicle. When I went to visit him in hospital, the nurse said that if the testicle didn't turn by itself by the morning then an operation would be necessary. I offered to stay overnight to keep him company and to see what would happen, but I don't think my opponent was too pleased with me.

"On another occasion, I was fighting the same chap and he kicked me *mae-geri,* but I scooped it and performed an *ashi-barai* on his supporting leg. He turned upside down and landed on his head and was carted off to hospital again, this time with concussion.

"I then introduced *okuri-zuki* into my repertoire. This required me to complete a punch whilst still moving forward. The strategy was designed to be a feint initially, but it worked quite well in its own right because opponents tended to concentrate on the trunk of the body and not the extremities. So, by using *okuri-zuki,* my punch become fully extended whilst actually moving and at a closed distance that often made the difference between winning or losing. But when my opponent did follow the advancing *okuri-zuki,* I found it disguised a *mawashi-geri* off the back leg and I caught people like that too.

"My best individual performance at the KUGB Nationals came in 1980. I used to build-up to these championships and would get really nervous about a week before them. I was working in the evenings at night clubs and I'd often not get home until 3.00 a.m., get three hours sleep and be up for work at 6.00 a.m. Then I'd run to work, work all day and go training in the evening before going to the nightclubs. It was crazy, but I did it so I was too tired to worry.

"I used to train really hard before the Nationals. I became

aggressive, short-tempered and would fight anyone. We used to have 'beasting' sessions on a Wednesday evening and those sessions were hard. Broken teeth, black eyes, fractured bones; we paid little attention to them and just carried on. A good friend of mine at the time, Barry Lawson, a real character who was in the SAS reserve, was a large, raw-boned individual who didn't seem to feel pain like other people and we'd knock the hell out of each other. He trained at Sendai and was married the same day I was. Half the club went to my wedding and the other half to his, and in the evening the two groups swapped round so everybody went to both weddings. Barry went to live in Florida and I went over to Key West to visit him."

Julie Nicholson recalled: "When I got to 2nd or 1st kyu I added to my Tuesday and Thursday training at Sendai by going along to Owen's Wednesday evening session at the YMCA. I remember well the first time I partnered him. I was terrified because I was quite timid and I'd seen the way he fought and knew of his reputation. But Owen is a very good instructor and he was gentle, kind and encouraging, which was what I needed at the time. He let me go at my own pace and left openings for me to score. I never felt uncomfortable with him and he inspired me. I have a great deal of respect for him."

Christine Pullan recalled: "Owen didn't teach me at Sendai and so I didn't have much to do with him until I joined his Wednesday night training sessions when I was about fourteen or fifteen, as a brown-belt. These classes were tough, but very good. I ended up – well, I think we all ended up – with bruises, especially to the legs and arms and occasionally you'd get a whack on the nose or near the eye. I never had any broken bones though. If you were struggling, then Owen could be quite lenient, but if Sendai had a competition coming up and you made a mistake partnering him, he'd hit you – not too hard, but harder than some of the others.

"I thought Owen was a good instructor and he'd coax the best out of you. He'd bring the aggression out and channel it in a constructive way. There was never any intimidation on his part. The better he knew you, the more he'd push you on. I felt safe with him and at ease. He'd often smile and could be funny in class and I found that reassuring.

Holdsworth added: "Owen is a first-rate instructor, a natural teacher and is excellent at building confidence. I've watched him teach and trained with him many times. He is very positive and never takes advantage of students. He is both well-liked and respected by other instructors and students alike. He is charismatic and leads by example. I've seen him get whacked a few times and he never complains; he just congratulates his opponent on a good technique. I have never seen him go after someone to show who was boss, which he could easily do. He respects strong, spirited fighters and works on the basis that if he gets hit then it was his fault. He always gives as good as he gets though and isn't beyond giving everyone a hard time. I've seen him unintentionally crack a few sternums in my time and put cockiness in its place. I have never seen him get angry or show any sign of being vindictive.

"The only problem Owen had with his lifestyle in the past was striking the balance between working on the doors and having real fights and competing in tournaments where control was required. This resulted in him having to train differently for each. Working the doors with live situations requires a completely different distance and attitude to tournaments, but Owen dealt with both very well, although we did have the odd incident when his control was a little heavy, as I've said. He was always calm under pressure and extremely good to train with.

"I'll give you an example of Owen's approach and control. We made many friends when competing in the Northern League and Owen was highly regarded as a strong fighter by all. I remember, on one occasion, there was a suggestion from some competitors that a certain fighter from another team was a bully and knocked people about and Owen insisted on facing him when we fought the team he was in. We were expecting some real fireworks, I can tell you, especially if Owen's opponent lacked control. There was no incident in the fight, which Owen won, and after the fight I asked him how it went and he simply stated that his opponent had fought him fairly with good control and respect and Owen dealt with him in the same manner. I have absolutely no doubt that if there had been any lack of control from this guy, we would have seen a very different ending to the fight – with Owen getting disqualified.

"Even in high-level competitions, if he won a fight and a technique was counted in his favour when he thought it shouldn't have been, he'd go up to his opponent afterwards and say that an error had been made – though at no time would he question the decision of the referee or judges during the match. So, he wanted fair play, but he respected the rules and the officials who he believed had made a genuine mistake.

"After I retired from competition, we used to go to the KUGB Nationals with Owen as team captain. Owen, as usual, would go out the night before the tournament and take the lads with him. On a number of occasions when the competition started, most of the team members were missing as they were still in bed from the late night out with Owen. When they did turn up they were half asleep and still under the influence of the alcohol from the night out and fought badly as a result. The late night and the drinking did not affect Owen as badly as this was normal for him and he still fought reasonably well."

Murray continued: "It was on the Saturday evening, the 3rd May, 1980, that I secured my place in the semi-finals of the KUGB Nationals and was awaiting the outcome of a fight between Terry O'Neill and George Godfrey to see who I would fight. In the meantime, Steve Cattle, the 1974 winner, who would also go on to take the title in 1981, and Frank Brennan, the reigning Grand Champion, had secured their places.

"The fight between O'Neill – who had won the title four times [1969, 1973, 1975, 1977] – and George Godfrey – who would be runner-up the following year, but was a former European Champion – was a spectacular affair, and one that has gone down in the annals of KUGB history."

An article in *Fighting Arts* magazine recorded what happened: 'Only seconds into the match, Godfrey attacked with a strong *mawashi-geri* which O'Neill blocked and then in reply he feinted with a kick of his own, jumped and spun in the air with a back fist attack and then in one continuous action he spun another 360° and caught Godfrey in the head with a strong reverse roundhouse-kick. Godfrey went down and the four judges all signalled *ippon* (full point) with their flags but the referee, Charlie Naylor, with-held a decision until Godfrey, who was unconscious, was examined. The doctor could not revive him sufficiently to stand and he was carried off the area. Mr. Naylor then disqualified O'Neill for excessive contact and Godfrey was awarded the match, although it was obvious he would not be able to fight again that day. Whether the knockout was the result of the kick making contact with the head and neck or the result of Godfrey's head hitting the floor as he fell remains unsure.'[6]

Murray continued: "So, I got a bye into the finals, though I would never have chosen it to be that way – but rules are rules. In the 'other' semi-final, Frank got a *mae-geri* on Steve for a half-point and so it was Frank and I in the final." A newspaper report of the time records Murray as saying: 'I had four fights in the National Championships, winning three, and two were against Great Britain Squad members.'[7]

Murray continued: "I'd been in the National Squad about seven months by this time and had partnered Frank a few times before and the encounter I described earlier was still very much in my mind. I did feel a bit intimidated, because Frank, who was the reigning KUGB Champion, was better than me, though I felt that if he had an off day and if I could be on top form, I might just pull it off. I had to avoid his kicks though, they were devastating, but he could really punch and back-fist too, so I just had to do my best, because I knew this was the chance of a lifetime."

Barwick recalled: "Owen had done brilliantly to get through to the finals and he came over to me and said that he thought that he'd done pretty well, but I sensed a bit of resignation in his voice. Frank Brennan was at his peak then and I knew that Owen was thinking that he didn't stand a chance.

"'You've done tremendously well,' I said, and continued, 'Frank's good, maybe too good, so why don't you just sit down now and let him have the title?'

"At that moment you could see it in Owen's face as much as to say, 'I'll show him' and boy did he give Frank a fight. Most people would have been on the back foot, but Owen went for Frank and took the fight to him."

Murray continued: "Frank and I were called up from opposite sides of the square. The near three hundred[8] original entrants had been whittled down to just us two. Crystal Palace was packed out ['a capacity filled arena'[9] and described as 'the biggest championships ever arranged in the UK'[10]] and the crowd suddenly fell silent. You could feel the atmosphere, it was electric. Frank and I bowed to each other and then we bowed to *Sensei* Enoeda, the referee, who then gave the command that everyone was waiting for, '*Hajime*!' The anticipatory silence was suddenly broken and spectators seemed to shout out in unison. We were off!

"I scored first with a fast right *gyaku-zuki*. I couldn't believe it. The crowd erupted and the noise coming from the Sendai members was deafening. Some people were standing on a heating pipe that went around the hall to get a better view and with the jumping up and down it collapsed. I heard the crash. Looking back, I think because I could hear the crowd, I came out of 'the zone'. Enoeda took us back to the centre and shot his arm down on my side to indicate that I'd scored a *wazari*. I was half a point up. If I could repeat what I'd just done, I'd be the fourteenth KUGB National *Kumite* Champion.

"Frank, unperturbed, then stepped up a gear that only he had and delivered a series of blistering attacks. I believe, though I could be wrong, he caught me with a *mawashi-geri*, but it could have been a

Owen (right) in action against Frank Brennan during the final of the men's individual *kumite* at the KUGB National Championships, 1980.

punch, it was so fast I didn't really see what happened. We were called back to the centre once more and Enoeda shot down his arm on Frank's side. So, it was a *wazari* each and all to play for and the clock was ticking. Frank launched a *mawashi-geri* that caught me. The Liverpool lads were ecstatic and I knew I'd blown it. Enoeda called us back to the centre again. His hand went down to Frank's side to show he'd scored a *wazari*, and then the hand shot up into the air, again on Frank's side, to show he'd won.

"I have no complaints; Frank won fair and square. It was an honour to face him in a KUGB National Championship final to be honest – I mean, that was his second win and he would go on to take another eight individual *kumite* titles over the next twelve years.[11] I don't think that achievement, ten titles, or his fourteen [consecutive] individual *kata* titles, will ever be beaten. Frank and I bowed, shook hands and went off in our separate directions.

"Jeff Barwick came up to me and said, 'You lost it. You were up and you lost it.' Harsh words maybe, but possibly true. Anyway, we all went for a much needed drink afterwards and I received lots of hearty commiserations and not a few drinks, holding my silver medal.

Frank Brennan recalled: 'The most outstanding attribute that Owen possesses is martial spirit. Since the first time I met him more than thirty-five years ago, I have always been impressed by his mental strength and tenacity and no more so than when fighting against him ... I know that he is very well respected and a great inspiration to numerous *karateka*. Even today, when I see him training, he has the same determination and spirited attitude that he displayed in his younger years.'

Murray continued: "That very same evening, before the drinks, I was given my first chance to take part in an international team match. The KUGB were up against Hideo Ochi's German team. The Germans are always good and it was going to be a baptism of fire for me. This was an eleven-man a side contest. Even though I fought, I must be honest and say that, despite it being my first international, I cannot recall anything about it, other than the fact that England won [albeit narrowly, on the last fight, thanks to Cattle]."

A brief report of the time confirms that Murray was in the eleven-man team along with: Terry O'Neill, Bob Poynton, Steve Cattle, Billy Higgins, Jimmy Brennan, Frank Brennan, George Godfrey, Joe Farley, Fred Fawcett and Mike Sinclair[12], though another report of the event[13] excludes Murray, Fawcett and Sinclair and includes Gabriel Operanta. A newspaper report noted that Murray was 'narrowly defeated by one point in his international debut, but the selectors were impressed by his performance. He [Owen] said: 'My opponent scored an early point against me then kept out of range for the rest of the contest.'[14] A ladies team *kata* competition between the two countries also took place which Germany won. The ladies team comprised of Sandie Hopkins, June Vann and Wai Yin 'Winnie' Hatton.

Murray continued: "The women trained as hard as the men in squad sessions. They would train with us and then split to practise *kata* with Andy or *Sensei* Enoeda. Winnie, I'd known for years, as she trained at Sendai. I think she studied at Durham University. Her skills lay in *kata* and her ability to compete in competitions at the highest level. Sandie obviously trained with Steve Cattle as they were a couple and she was a *kata* specialist [winning ten consecutive KUGB National Championships *kata* titles {1973-1982}]. June was good at both freestyle and *kata*.

"I remember the KUGB Squad came up to give a course at Sendai[15] and then, a few months later [30th and 31st August 1980], I was selected to be in the English KUGB Squad to attend the 3rd IAKF

[International Amateur Karate Federation] World Championships, in Bremen, northern Germany. The local press got wind of it and did a number of nice write-ups on me."[16, 17] One newspaper report quoted Murray as saying: 'I am really looking forward to going. It's always been my ambition to represent my country'[18], whilst another quotes Barwick as saying, 'It is an incredible achievement for him. When you see him fight he is a formidable character ... he is our guiding light in freestyle ... no one from the Northern Area has ever got into the British Squad before, so it's a hell of an honour for him.'[19]

Murray continued: "This was my first time abroad, despite being twenty-nine, and I had to get a passport. There were eight in the male squad: Terry O'Neill, Bob Poynton, Billy Higgins, Frank Brennan, Steve Cattle, George Godfrey, Joe Farley and me. The women competitors were Hopkins, Vann and Hatton. *Sensei* Enoeda, *Sensei* Kawasoe[20] – I was in awe of this man, his smooth technique was perfect, but I couldn't relate to him because I didn't have the body – and Andy Sherry attended as coaches and Charlie Naylor and Derek Langham acted as officials.[21, 22]

"If I remember correctly, we flew out of Heathrow – my first flight on an aeroplane – and I recall feeling immensely proud in my smart, new official uniform with a British badge on the breast pocket of my blazer. I knew that, with the tremendous experience and depth of the largely established team, I'd only be likely to get a fight if someone else was badly injured, and, as it turned out, I didn't fight. Being the 'new boy' as it were, certain people took delight in playing jokes on me. I remember just before going to bed that first night.

"'Remember, Enoeda wants us ready at 6.00 a.m. for early morning training, so don't be late', a fellow squad member said. I thanked him because I hadn't known.

"At 6.00 a.m. I was down in the foyer in my *gi*, waiting, and no one came down. I waited for half-an-hour and then I went for a run. When I got back, the rest of the team were eating breakfast and it transpired that this individual had been winding me up. Ha, ha! I was not amused.

"The next morning, I was woken up just after 6.00 a.m. with another squad member standing beside my bed telling me to get down to the foyer in my *gi* without delay. I uttered a few expletives and rolled back over.

"'Get up!' this chap insisted. 'Don't you get it – Enoeda's waiting for you!' So, thinking that I was being wound up again, I reluctantly went downstairs and there was Enoeda, glaring at me.

"'You get up!" he exclaimed, forcefully. 'Now for squad training!'

"What could I say? I'm not a grass.

"I remember that, at the beginning of the World Championships, all the teams had to line up and follow their flags. Then the national anthems were played. When it came to 'God Save the Queen', standing there in my official uniform, I was chuffed to bits.

"Those championships were a most memorable occasion, not least because one of the great moments of British Shotokan occurred and I was privileged to see it. But first let me tell you about the team matches which were held on the first day.

"England beat Belgium, Switzerland and Iran to get into the semi-finals, where we lost to Germany. We began well enough though when Godfrey won [beating Wolf Wichman], then Higgins drew [with Hermann]. Brennan won his fight [against Wildrodt] and Poynton lost [Jurgen Hoffman], so it was up to Steve Cattle who had saved us in the friendly in exactly the same situation. This time, however, he lost [to Werner Buttgen]. So the team drew and when the points were totted up Germany won with one more *wazari*. So, England fought Egypt for third place and we won that easily [4-0]. Germany met Japan in the final and lost [the Japanese team who fought were: Hideo Yamamoto, Norimasa Hayakawa, Fujikiyo Omura, Toshihiro Mori and Masahiko Tanaka]. However, I remember reading afterwards that the JKA Chief Instructor and IAKF leader, Masatoshi Nakayama, said that he thought that although Japan had won, Great Britain and Germany were the stronger teams. As I recall, England came fourth in both the men's and ladies team *kata*."[23]

"The second day saw the individual events. Frank Brennan was on top form and did a superb *Gojushiho-dai* [for 4th place], but the part I really remember, as I'm sure everyone else who was there will do too, was the remarkable fight between Frank, the reigning European Champion and the reigning JKA Champion, Toshiro Mori.[24]

"I read an account of this encounter for a place in the quarter-finals recently that Terry O'Neill had written and it brought it all back. Terry tells it perfectly: 'Brennan attacked with a fast *mawashi-geri* which got through Mori's guard and touched his head, but the decision was that contact was made with the shin, not the foot, and therefore it was un-scorable. Unperturbed by this, Brennan attacked with the same technique – actually half a front kick, the initial part, and half a roundhouse kick, the end of the attack – and this time planted his right foot firmly in and out of Mori's mid-riff for a half point. Mori then attacked, realising that his waiting tactics just weren't going to work ... neither were ... [his new tactics] for as he came in, Brennan made a

feint with a right leg *gyaku-mawashi-geri* (reverse roundhouse kick) and then, as Mori reacted, he changed the direction of the kick and hit Mori with a clear-cut *mawashi-geri*, which won him the match and brought the whole audience to its feet.'[25]

EUROPEAN GOLD... 'I WISH I COULD REMEMBER'

The KUGB National Squad at Bremen. Left to right: Bob Poynton, Owen Murray, Andy Sherry, Frank Brennan, George Godfrey, Billy Higgins, Joe Farley and Steve Cattle.

The KUGB National Squad at the 3rd IAKF World Championships, Bremen (1980). From left to right, standing: Bob Poynton, Steve Cattle, George Godfrey, Joe Farley, Terry O'Neill, Andy Sherry, Frank Brennan, *Sensei* Enoeda, *Sensei* Kawasoe, Owen Murray, Charles Naylor, Billy Higgins; sitting, June Vann, Winni Hatton, Sandie Hopkins.

Murray continued: "Yes, that was a rare moment, a great moment. The two men shook hands and I could swear I saw a tear running down Mori's cheek. Whether that was from emotion or whether the result of a minor eye injury I cannot say. So, Frank went into the last eight but was beaten by a Yugoslavian named [Dusan] Dacic, the eventual runner-up. Ironically, due to the repercharge system, Mori fought his way back and actually became world champion, but it was a bit of a 'damp squid' for everyone knew that Frank had beaten him. At the end of the day, Nakayama presented Frank with a trophy for Most Outstanding Competitor." Brennan's account of the fight is given elsewhere.[26] In the Ladies *kata* event, June Vann came 6th and Sandie Hopkins took 8th place.

Murray continued: "I would, quite naturally, have wished to have actually fought at the World Championships, but the opportunity didn't present itself. If I'd been chosen for the last match against Egypt, even if I'd lost, we'd have still come third, so I think it's correct that the reserves get a medal too. It's the rule, after all. So I don't feel bad about it, though, as I say, I would have loved to have had the opportunity, especially after travelling all that way.

"I found our hosts, the Deutscher Karate Verband, to be very nice people and they looked after us brilliantly. We went for a meal with them and I remember this long table decked out with food. One of the dishes looked like raw sausage meat and I thought to myself, 'Surely they don't eat that?'

"Being new to this travelling abroad game, I was a bit naive. Someone wanted to take something through Customs and I said that they shouldn't, even I knew that. He insisted that he had nothing to worry about and so I thought to myself, 'Well, that's up to you mate, but if you get caught ...' Then someone else mentioned that they wanted to take something home.

"'How are you going to explain that away if you're discovered?' I asked this second chap, but he didn't seem to be worried either. Anyway, it was up to them and it had nothing to do with me. At the airport, our baggage was about to go through Customs and these two individuals looked so relaxed.

"'Aren't you worried at all?' I whispered to them in disbelief. They looked at me and smiled and then one of them whispered back.

"'Why should we be? The gear's in your bag!'

"My God! I'd been set up like a good 'un and I can tell you those next few minutes aged me, as I thought about how long I'd be serving in Durham Prison at Her Majesty's pleasure. It's a good story now

EUROPEAN GOLD ... 'I WISH I COULD REMEMBER'

perhaps, but it wasn't funny at the time I can assure you.

"When I got back to Sendai, Jeff Barwick made a big thing of the medal and I had a little bit more fame for a while, which was nice. Everyone wanted to know what had occurred."

A twenty-two year old Graham Adams from the KUGB South Tyneside *dojo* started training with Murray at this time. He recalled: "I'd been training seven years under John Thompson, a very good all-round *karateka*, but I wanted to get more freestyle sparring in and so I supplemented my usual training by going over to Owen's YMCA *dojo* about six miles away from the South Shields *dojo*. Owen had built up quite a reputation for his freestyle ability – he was the main Shotokan karate *kumite* man in the region – and I'd seen him compete locally and at Crystal Palace and so I began to attend his *kumite* class – and thirty-two years later, I'm still training with him.

"I was a 2nd Dan and very fit, but I'm telling you that Owen's classes were tough. He didn't like skivers and if you didn't give one hundred per cent commitment he'd be on you. He led by example, so there was no complaining. When you paired up with him, if you didn't keep your wits about you, he'd hit you. If you managed to catch him, which wasn't often, he respected you for it. I can recall one night sparring with him at a *dojo* above one of the pubs he worked in, Marlow's I think it was called. He had only recently had expensive dental treatment carried out and I knocked his tooth out. He never complained about it or held a grudge; he accepted it as part of training. I think he made up for it though over the years. He was a punching specialist really, but he had a very fast *mae-geri* and he caught me with that many times. He also had a short and very practical *ushiro-geri* in his armoury. Because he was a puncher and I liked to kick more than he did, I believe that we were good for each other."

Murray continued: "In September that year I entered the Shotokan Cup, which [having been established in 1975] is second in importance to the Nationals in the KUGB calendar and is a prestigious event in the organization. Two *karateka* have really affected me, personally, in my study of karate over the years and both are heroes of mine. In 1980, I beat the first of these, Steve Cattle, to get into the finals of the Shotokan Cup. Steve was the 'bee's knees' in my view and beating him did not diminish this in any way. Originally from York, he'd been a student of Gordon Thompson's[27] and a member of the BKF[28] and had moved over to Liverpool to study theology to become a teacher [at C. F. Mott College]. He ran the Kirkdale club with Sandie Hopkins, who was his girlfriend. Steve lived for karate and he had a wonderful knowledge of the subject, both technical and historical. He was tremendous at both *kata* and *kumite* and had won the KUGB National title for *kumite* twice [1974, 1981]. He was also a British All-Styles champion and a European champion, so he was top-notch. He was highly skilled in judo too, a 2nd Dan, and represented Britain at the World Student Games in Tokyo [in 1967]. He was down to earth and sociable. He'd chat away after training when we all went for a pint and that's something not all the senior KUGB instructors would do. You could ask him anything and he'd usually have an answer. He used to visit Sendai once a month and I learned a lot from him, especially body evasion – *tai-sabaki*.

"Anyway, Steve and I faced up and I caught him with a *kizami-zuki* to the head. He was the first to acknowledge the point. He always played fair, though he could be a bit heavy-handed at times and give you a real whack. But he accepted such punishment too. That was Steve."

Cattle recalled: 'I find a great friend of mine, Owen Murray, very difficult to fight. Now he is what you would call a 'hand specialist' – because he only has one hand! – but he is so good with it.'[29]

Barwick recalled: "Owen learned a lot from Steve Cattle. Owen used to stoop to the right a bit when he had his left leg forward in freestyle. This gave him a slightly hunched up appearance. Steve picked up on this and got him to stand upright because he reasoned that Owen was disadvantaged, had a momentary blind spot, which made him vulnerable to fast right-sided techniques. They worked on it together and Owen suddenly began to pick things up earlier and react earlier – only a fraction of a second, but that counts for a lot in freestyle. At this point, my strike rate against him was about one in ten. I hope people would consider me to be a competent *karateka* and so it perhaps gives you some idea of how good he was once he'd ironed-out this little problem, which, I must confess, I hadn't considered. I remember when he caught me on the nose with a punch and the lower part of my nose was knocked at a right-angle to the upper part. I went to the hospital immediately and they managed to move the cartilage back into place.

Murray continued: "I met Frank Brennan in the Shotokan Cup final – who else! I was to face the British and European Champion, who had recently beaten the JKA and World Champion. Well, I did my best, took the fight to him, but he caught me with a couple of *mawashi-geris* and that was that. But I took home silver and I still have the cup.

"I suppose my greatest fight came in the EAKF [European Amateur

Owen, placed 3rd with fellow team members, at the English Karate Board National Championships (1980).

Karate Federation] Championships that were held [6th and 7th December] at the end of 1980, at Bregenz. But before I get to those, let me tell you a couple of anecdotes I remember."

"We flew into Geneva – though Zurich is much closer – and continued by train across a very picturesque, wintery and mountainous Switzerland, to the city of Bregenz, which is situated on Lake Constance at the very western end of Austria. We arrived at the venue two days before the Junior Championships started and three days before the Senior Championships began. Enoeda decided that the day following our arrival we would have early morning training outside our hotel, in the snow and ice. I thought this was crazy to be honest. The risk of injury in the form of strains and pulled muscles was very high. I couldn't warm up by stretching properly because it was so cold – I mean, we were in the foothills of the Alps in the middle of winter! I couldn't feel my feet because they'd frozen up in my training shoes and I was sliding around on the ice. Teams from other competing countries were being kept warm and rested and they thought we were barmy training like that, and I had to agree with them. Fancy the whole team risking injury just before a European championship? Still, I suppose you could argue that it was the karate training that was the important thing, the spirit, and not the competition. Anyway, we finished the session with a snowball fight, which was good fun, but I couldn't feel my hand and fingers after that either! Joan had made me a thick skiing-type coat and I remember wearing it, walking in the snow, which was deep but not good enough for skiing, and visiting a local resort selling a type of warm wine and hot dogs.

"The prices in the hotel bar were ridiculous. I remember going up to the bar and another member of the team bought a round of six Coca Colas. You should have seen his face when the bartender asked for eighteen pounds – and that was in 1980. Eighteen pounds was close to half my weekly take home pay. I was having none of that, so I bought myself a lemonade and topped it up with some whisky I'd brought from England and that kept me warm!

"The Championships were well organised and things ran smoothly as the English team worked their way through the opposition, with Switzerland being our first opponents [then Wales]. The German team in the other side of the draw, being runners-up in the World Championships, were proving unbeatable.

Sherry recalled: 'I remember those championships for Owen Murray ... who had taken the place of an injured Frank [Brennan], and Terry [O'Neill] was injured as well. We fought our way to the final and met Germany, where Billy [Higgins] and Bob [Poynton] had won their bouts and George Godfrey had lost his. Then, it was Owen's turn to get up at number four ...'[30]

Murray continued: "I'd developed this system that worked for me, helped me get away from trivial conversation and allowed me to get focussed. Before the final began, I went off alone and faced a brick wall, concentrated on my breathing and psyched myself up, telling myself that I was going to kill the opposition and I didn't care what was going to happen to me. I went out there knowing that if I won, then we would be European Champions. I'd worked for nearly two decades for this moment and I had no intention of letting either myself or my team-mates down. I got up and faced my opponent and that, alas, is all I remember. I have absolutely no recollection of the fight that followed, as I was kicked in the head by a good *mawashi-geri* and have had to rely on what other people have told me. I went down when hit apparently, but got back up and continued [or, as Sherry described it, 'gamely fought on'[31]]. I must have been on automatic and all that hard training I'd done paid off. I scored two *wazaris* with punching techniques, won the fight, bowed, walked back to my team-mates and promptly collapsed. As I was lying there waiting for the ambulance, Enoeda apparently came over to check me out before I was put on a stretcher and I told him to f— off. I clearly wasn't myself and he never brought it up, which I'm pleased about because it would have been really embarrassing.

"My first memory after this episode is waking up in my hotel bedroom and having a fearful headache and feeling badly nauseous. I recall my team-mate, Fred Fawcett, came into my room and I asked him what was going on.

"'We're downstairs celebrating,' he replied.

"'Why?' I enquired and a big smile spread across his face.

"'Because you won your fight and we are the European Champions!' he exclaimed, and he proceeded to put my gold medal on my chest as I lay there.

"I wanted to celebrate too and tried to get out of bed, but Fred stopped me in my tracks and told me that the doctor had insisted that I had to lie down. Fred then went out of the room and locked the door behind him. I must have gone back to sleep and woke up the next morning with a blinding headache and tunnel vision. I had to take it really easy, move slowly, and it took me a full five days to get back to something resembling normality. I felt really bad, awful.

"I learned in the meantime that whilst I was awaiting the

OWEN MURRAY, M.B.E., 6th DAN

Members of the KUGB squad from the European Championships, Bregenz (1980). From left to right: Frank Brennan, Fred Fawcett, Billy Higgins, *Sensei* Enoeda, Owen Murray, Bob Poynton.

Members of the KUGB Squad from the European Championships, Bregenz (1980). From left to right, standing: Billy Higgins, unknown, Frank Brennan, unknown, Fred Fawcett, unknown, *Sensei* Enoeda, unknown, Owen Murray, unknown, Steve Cattle, Sandie Hopkins, Andy Sherry, Bob Poynton; squatting, unknown, Gary Harford.

ambulance, Steve Cattle went out after me and had his nose broken [by an *uraken*], which was unfortunate because we'd already won. We finally beat the Germans 4-1. The overall performance of the KUGB team in other events was excellent.[32]

"At Heathrow, after landing, I bumped into Glenn Foster, a well-known North-East runner and member of Sunderland Harriers. He had been competing in Holland in his first marathon and won it. We both had gold medals.

"When I got back home and went to Sendai, Jeff was very pleased and asked me what it was like to have fought, successfully, in a European Championship final. All I could say was, 'I wish I could remember!'"

Barwick recalled: "Having a member of the KUGB National team that had become European Champions in our midst was very good for the club. It brought Sendai prestige and publicity. The fact that Owen was such a champion never went to his head. If students wanted to talk about it, he would oblige, but he just carried on training diligently, as if nothing had happened. He had his head screwed on properly. For Owen it was the karate that was important, not the medals or titles.

"I remember one evening Owen couldn't get his usual *dojo* to teach his *kumite* class and so he looked for somewhere to train at the very last moment. He took his students to a multi-storey car park and trained there. Well, these were pretty intense classes he ran and what with all the *kiaiing* the police were called. I heard it said that one policeman's helmet appeared and he tentatively came out from cover, but was reluctant to approach the class."

Murray continued: "I've trained and taught in all sorts of odd places. Apart from sport centres, YMCAs and church halls, I've trained in school playgrounds, cemeteries – I remember, once, that we were moved on from outside a crematorium by a priest – beaches and warehouses, for example. I vividly recall training at Marlow's, a pub with a warehouse above, that was freezing cold. We had to wear gloves and woolly hats when training there. It didn't matter where we practised and what the temperature was, blistering heat or below zero, in true karate spirit we never missed a day's training."

Nicholson recalled this particular freezing *dojo*: "Owen was thinking about leasing a property above a pub, if memory serves me, as a *dojo*. It was the middle of winter and there was no heating. It was so cold we had to train with hats on. I remember Owen performing the *kata Enpi* where there is a jump near the end. He jumped and landed performing *shuto-uke* in *kokutsu-dachi* as he did so. The jolt of landing made his hat fall over his eyes. Owen simply adjusted the hat with his right hand and carried on as if nothing had happened.

"I remember that *dojo* – though I only trained there a few times in the late 1980's – because the floor had a large hole in it over to one side of the room, which was not conducive to training. Owen went out and bought Japanese and British flags and mounted them on the wall so they crossed, as if signifying unity between Britain and Japan through the practice of karate. This was what he wanted to do and the floor was just left in the state we found it."

Murray continued: "In 1981, *Sensei* Nakayama visited Great Britain and brought a strong JKA team with him. On the evening of the KUGB Nationals at Crystal Palace [9th May], a competition was held between the English and Japanese teams and I was selected to fight. As you can imagine, this was the big one, the really big one, and I don't think I have ever seen the venue packed out so thoroughly as it was that night. Not only were there no seats available, there was no standing room either. The atmosphere around the arena was intense.

"To be chosen to fight the Japanese was highly prestigious, no one doubted that and I was extremely nervous. I didn't want to let my country down, I didn't want to let the KUGB down, I didn't want to let Sendai down, I didn't want to let the crowd down and I didn't want to let myself down. There was a lot of pressure. Before the fight, I took myself off to face a brick wall again, alone, but with so many people around and so much noise it wasn't easy to find a place to get into the right frame of mind.

"We had a very strong team, with Terry O'Neill, Bob Poynton, George Godfrey, Steve Cattle, Frank Brennan, Ronnie Christopher and me. The Japanese – well, what can you say? Osaka was a former JKA *Kumite* Champion [1976] and reigning JKA *Kata* Champion [and for the past four years and for the following two {and past IAKF World *Kata* Champion}]; Omura was reigning JKA *Kumite* Champion and IAKF World *Kumite* Champion; Tabata, the team captain, was a close friend of Enoeda's and had been in the squad that won the World Championships in 1972, in Paris [in addition to being placed in the JKA Championships] and Kawawada would go on to [take two JKA *kata* titles {1986, 1987} and] be Grand Champion at the First Shoto World Cup. [The other Japanese team members were A. Fukami {IAKF World *Kata* team member}, E. Matsukara {a former All-Tokyo *Kumite* Champion}, T. Mizoguchi {a former All-Japan university *Kumite* Champion} and M. Tatetsu {a former All-Japan university *Kumite* Champion}]. Two rounds were planned of seven bouts each."

EUROPEAN GOLD . . . 'I WISH I COULD REMEMBER'

The KUGB National *kumite* team line up at Crystal Palace to face their Japanese opposition. From rear to front: Terry O'Neill, Bob Poynton, Steve Cattle, Frank Brennan, George Godfrey, Owen Murray, Ronnie Christopher.

A report of the event began: 'The undisputed highlight of the day was the top-level international match. The national teams of Japan – the current World Champions – and Great Britain – the current European Champions – marched on to thunderous applause, as the largest karate audience to ever grace the National Sports Centre settled back for the expected fireworks.'[33]

In the first round, Godfrey beat Fukami, Poynton lost to Omura, O'Neill beat Mizoguchi and Brennan beat Tatetsu. A detailed account of this event is given elsewhere.[33]

Murray continued: "I went up Number 5 when we were 3-1 up and faced Kawawada, a former All Japan All-Styles finalist. We had a neutral referee [German, George Piluris[3]]." In the above report it was noted that: 'O. Murray and M. Kawawada had a cautious start and then the Japanese began attacking. Murray was not to be caught easily though and was very sharp with his punching. Near the end of time, Kawawada went ahead with a counter punch and at time got the decision.'[33] A different outcome, believed incorrect, is reported in the *Echo Sunderland* where it was noted that Murray 'fought a magnificent draw against Minoru Kawada [*sic*], one of the most experienced of the Japanese squad.'[34]

OWEN MURRAY, M.B.E., 6th DAN

Murray fighting Minoru Kawawada (1981)

Christopher then lost to Osaka and Cattle drew with Tabata. At the end of the round each team had won three matches, but England had accumulated more points.

In the second round Cattle lost to Fukami, Godfrey lost to Omura, Poynton drew with Mizoguchi, O'Neill lost to Tatetsu, and Brennan beat Kawawada.

Murray continued: "I went up at Number 6 this time and we were 3-1 down. My opponent was Osaka." A report at the time noted: 'O. Murray met the stylish and very experienced Y. Osaka and the

Murray fighting Yoshiharu Osaka (1981)

Japanese fighter took the match with two good punches.'[35]

Murray continued: "The hype was high that evening and I just could not afford to be distracted. I just remember my two fights as being very explosive. I went forward and didn't back off. I don't know what either Kawawada or Osaka thought of fighting a one-handed opponent of course, though I suspect it was an unusual experience for them. Maybe they thought I was a kicking specialist and were waiting for a blistering kick at any moment. Kawawada was a bit wary at first I thought, but Osaka just expected what came."

Christopher then beat Matsukura to conclude the round. Japan won the second round 4-2. With both teams winning a round, the result was, apparently, classed as a draw. Overall, however, Japan won 7-5.

Murray continued: "The general feeling was that we had done well drawing with the World Champions and in front of our home crowd the support was fantastic, absolutely fantastic and I shall never forget the feeling. Of course I would have liked to have won my matches, but the opposition was the very best the JKA could throw at me, so I reckon I didn't do too badly."

It was reported at the time that: 'All in all, an excellently matched and well fought encounter with the only blemish on the whole proceedings coming from the adjudicating.'[35]

Murray continued: "One of the people I trained with during this time was Graham Noble, who became a well-known writer on martial arts. He was an accountant by profession and lived in East Herrington, Sunderland, and was into a number of things, including weight-lifting. He struck me as being eclectic and was not conventional and fixed in any one style. He was supple and his style relaxed. He was an excellent and powerful puncher and we'd go hell for leather at one another, sparring. I got the impression he wanted to hit things and I was one of them! Seriously though, he was good. I think he was like me and wanted to test himself. I don't really know why I like fighting to be honest, but I think it is mainly to do with testing myself against others, and I've never lost that.

Noble recalled: 'I'd known Owen for many years. I believe he was the driving force behind the Sendai competition team and he had built up a good, motivated group of fighters. I used to do weight-training at that YMCA and would often look in to watch the karate. It was pretty heavy duty training there, and one thing I liked about it was that there was very little talking – just training and hard *kumite*. Owen, of course, would do everything the class did.

'I worked out with Owen in the early 1980s. He was on the KUGB British team then and I remember him talking about team members, such as Terry O'Neill, and the trips abroad with the team. Our workouts revolved around working on fighting techniques, sparring – both non-contact and contact (with old boxing gloves) – and developing striking power on the pads. I remember being impressed by Owen's anticipation and timing and his conditioning. During these sessions we'd take turns developing techniques. For example, I remember Owen working on defending against back-kicks, anticipating the kick and either jamming it right at the start or getting inside it to counter. Naturally, he was good at this, but there was the rare occasion when the kick would get through and hit – this was realistic training and if his timing was slightly out the kick would make contact – and then he would just grunt slightly, take a deep breath, and start again immediately with the next kick. It was the same in the sparring. There was quite a bit of contact on both sides (in the 'non-contact' sparring too, actually), but Owen would never complain, and he never took advantage. He was always ready to help you develop your techniques too. I thought he was one of the best training partners ever. He never let the loss of his hand hold him back, and he never wanted to be treated differently. When we practised the contact sparring, we managed to get a boxing glove on the stump of Owen's left hand and worked with that. Of course, on the pad work Owen was limited to his right hand, but he had powerful punches; not just straight punches but boxing-like hook punches too. He told me once that he had been in a fight with a local hard case who had been causing trouble and Owen had connected with one of those hooking punches, not just knocking the man unconscious, but breaking his jaw too. Of course, Owen worked the doors in Sunderland for many years and that always gave his training a practical edge. All the training I did with him was hard, practical and down to earth. It was a good time.

'I really admire what Owen has achieved in his martial arts career. I haven't seen him for a while, but I know he'll still be training somewhere.'

Murray continued: "During this period, with all the squad training and other karate commitments, I was away for thirty-seven weekends in one year alone. This kind of life does not lend itself to being either a good husband or a good father, but, luckily, I was able to be a good son.

"I was training at the YMCA when I received a phone call around 4 p.m. from my father informing me that my mother had been taken into Sunderland Infirmary. I left straight away. My dad said she hadn't been feeling well for a few weeks and had small bruises around her body which she'd attributed to Polo Mint sweets she had kept in her dressing gown which she wore for bed. She thought she must have rolled on to them while she was sleeping. I thought that was a bit far-fetched and when I got to the hospital, she was in bed, vomiting. The colour of the vomit suggested she was bleeding internally. The nurse informed us that the specialist wanted a word early next morning. This gave me early warning signs of what was to follow. Later that night, I was out with friends and I felt something different and asked them the time. They enquired why I wanted to know; wasn't I enjoying myself? I got a bit uptight, I think they knew that something was wrong and one of them looked at his watch and said it was 11.20 p.m. I then went to Fino's night club, where they told me that I missed a phone call. I knew, then, my mother had died. I walked up to the hospital and on the way Joan pulled up in her car. Before she could even open her mouth, I said I knew. So, some seven hours from the initial phone call when I was first made aware she was ill, she was gone. And do you know what? She died at 11.20 p.m. I often wonder about that strange, to the very minute, co-incidence. Maybe we were closer than I thought?

"She was brought back home to Grindon in her coffin and laid out in a bedroom. She looked so peaceful, so relaxed, and it looked just as though she was asleep. I felt I wanted to wake her, gently. She was surrounded by the ordinary things of life that she'd chosen – the curtains and little ornaments. Joan was standing beside me. A tear ran down my cheek.

"'See, you have got emotions,' I remember her saying, because up to then I hadn't shown any. I was a bit concerned and puzzled why I hadn't shown any feelings to be honest. Had I just bottled it up tightly, or had I genuinely not felt anything? I hadn't taken any time off work and no reaction had been forthcoming, until that solitary tear. I sorted out all the funeral arrangements because, as I've said before, dad took it so very badly.

"I was pleased that my mother knew of my competitive success before she died, especially the fact that I had fought in the European Team Championship final, won my bout and taken home a gold medal. She never saw me do karate and she never said anything to me about it, but I heard, later, that she was very proud, saying things like, 'Have you seen my son? He's in the newspapers you know', to the neighbours.

"Two weeks later [12th September 1981], I travelled down to Coventry and entered the Shotokan Cup again." The Championships were very successful and the competition of a high standard, particularly noticeable in the evening finals was the excellent *kumite* ...[36]

Murray continued: "I got through to the semi-finals and met, guess who, my old nemesis, Frank Brennan, who had beaten Leeds *karateka*, Fred Fawcett, in the quarter-finals." Terry O'Neill reported on the fight: 'Murray was the aggressor right from the start, dashing in with strong punching attacks. Brennan skilfully met one attack by jumping high and scoring with a face punch and then got a second half-point from a front leg *yoko-geri* (side kick) which stopped Murray in his tracks.'[36] Frank Brennan beat his older brother, Jimmy, in the finals.

Murray continued: "So I lost out to Frank again – for the third time. That was the last time I got into the last four of either the Nationals or the Shotokan Cup. It would have been nice to have won once, got my name on a cup, but Frank was a phenomenon, a unique competitor. So, on the one hand I was unfortunate to have been competing when he was, yet, on the other hand – no pun intended – I am proud that I fought him when he was at his best. I can still kick myself for losing concentration in the 1980 National finals though, more than thirty years on!

"The next big event for which I was selected was the European

EUROPEAN GOLD... 'I WISH I COULD REMEMBER'

KUGB squad members before the 1981 European Shotokan Karate Championships, Manchester. From left to right: Sandie Hopkins, Winnie Hatton, Steve Cattle, Bob Poynton, Owen Murray, *Sensei* Enoeda, Terry O'Neill, Andy Sherry, unknown, unknown, George Godfrey, Billy Higgins, unknown, Frank Brennan, Jim Brennan, unknown, Charles Naylor, Derek Langham.

Championships held in Manchester [on the 8th November 1981] and England would be defending their title. I regret to say that I wasn't given a chance to fight this time, though England retained the European title on the last match when Cattle beat his German opponent. Frank Brennan won the individual *kumite* title again in the dying seconds of an exciting final with Repp, of Germany. An account of the championships is given elsewhere.[37] As I was in the team, I received a gold medal.

"The last time I went away with the KUGB squad was for the Ibusz Cup in [3rd April] 1982. We flew out of Manchester I think, into Budapest and the competition was held in the town hall. Hungary was still under a communist regime and the people were very poor. Most wore dark, depressingly coloured clothes, black and browns, and drove around in old, gaudy coloured cars. Even the buildings seemed to be depressing. Some local people wore jeans and tee-shirts, and I thought to myself, 'They must have watched TV and wanted to dress like Americans.' They were only interested in US dollars and British pounds and one pound went a long way out there. Let me put it this way, if I gave a waiter a pound, he was very attentive and ensured that my wine glass was never empty.

Members of the KUGB team after the 1981 European Shotokan Championships, Manchester, displaying their trophies. From left to right, standing: Charlie Naylor, unknown, Jim Brennan, Gary Harford, Mrs. Brennan, George Godfrey, Frank Brennan, Masao Kawasoe, Andy Sherry, Terry Heaton (former KUGB General Secretary), Terry O'Neill, Keinosuke Enoeda, Owen Murray (circled), unknown, Sandie Hopkins, Derek Langham, Steve Cattle; squatting/kneeling: Bob Poynton, Winnie Hatton, Billy Higgins, June Vann, unknown.

"There was also some ill-feeling towards us foreigners and I remember a man in the street said something to me in broken English that was highly derogatory. I was part of the squad and so I let it run off me like water off a duck's back and I recall Billy Higgins complimenting me on that.

"I must be truthful and say that I don't recall that much about the Ibusz Cup, so I don't think I fought this time either." Sherry recalled the event on three occasions.

Sherry noted: 'This was a high profile championship and only for team events.'[38] He wrote at the time: 'The competition was the largest ever staged in Europe, all tickets being sold out two weeks before the event, which was held in the Sportcsarnock Stadium in front of a massive thirteen thousand audience. There was continuous television coverage. The Ibusz was also one of the most prestigious ever held in Europe, due to the fact that teams from both EAKF and EKU [European Karate Union] were competing and the leaders of both world organisations, H. Nishiyama of IAKF and J. Delcourt of WUKO

EUROPEAN GOLD... 'I WISH I COULD REMEMBER'

Ibusz Cup, Budapest, 1982. From left to right: unknown, Charlie Naylor, unknown, unknown, Frank Brennan, unknown, Sandie Hopkins, Andy Sherry, unknown, *Sensei* Nishiyama, unknown, Steve Cattle, Owen Murray, unknown, Jim Brennan, *Sensei* Enoeda.

[World Union of Karate Organisations], together with officials from the International Olympic Committee, were in attendance.'[39]

Sherry continued: 'I recall that Terry, Bob and Billy, stalwarts of the KUGB's England team, were injured, and so I called upon the services of other leading KUGB members [the squad consisted of Cattle, Jim and Frank Brennan, Godfrey, Owen Murray, Ronnie Christopher, Robert Maher and Mark Healy]. In the *kumite* event, England won each match in its group [Sweden, Belgium, Lebanon] to go through to the final pool, which included France, Yugoslavia and Czechoslovakia. We beat the Yugoslavs and the Czechs [whose smallest team member was six feet four inches], but lost to France 3-2. We therefore came away in second place, because France won their other matches.'[40] Sherry wrote in his report of the event: 'The England team were very pleased with the result, for although being seriously under strength they still put up such a terrific performance.'[41] The men's and ladies' *kata* teams were placed third, and fourth, respectively.

Sherry reported two weeks after the event: 'The organisation, standard and hospitality were excellent and the event should be supported in future years.'[42]

Murray continued: "In 1983 [30th January], I took and passed my *Sandan* under Enoeda. A 3rd Dan is a sort of milestone in JKA karate and is seen as instructor level. I was delighted to have passed and, like all my other gradings, it was not easy.

"I was also selected to try for the English All-Styles Squad and went down to Crystal Palace, with Ronnie Christopher I think, to be tested. I had various fights and was successful. In one fight I floored someone with an *ashi-barai* and followed it up with a punch.

"'You can tell he's Shotokan – hard,' I remember hearing Ticky Donovan, the English Coach saying.

"Anyway, I was selected and I went to France for a competition. The Championship was held in a city hall and we had to fight in a boxing ring. Well, that was very unusual to say the least, because you were above the spectators who were sitting below. I can't say I took to it and was disqualified twice for lack of control.

"'Use you loaf; calm down,' Ticky said to me.

"After the competition we all went to a bar and Ticky joined us. He was very sociable and I liked that, and, as I've said before, not aloof like some of the senior grades I know. I remember they were discussing a nasty incident that happened in Barcelona in 1979 following revelry in a bar, when two of the English squad were shot by police. One, whose name was Stephen Ives, was hit in the back and died; the other was shot through the stomach and he was sitting next to me. I believe the two men were brothers. That was the only time I went to a competition with the English All-Styles Squad.

"I found the All-Styles Squad much more relaxed that the KUGB Squad and enjoyed the experience. The All-Styles competition required a lot of skill and control to score, whereas I was used to the school of skill and hard knocks. Because I went in too hard, I suppose I was a liability to the All-Styles team, but that's the way I trained. Some people were successful at both, could adapt, especially Billy Higgins, but it just didn't suit me. But I met some great fighters at that time, like Steve Babbs and Eugene Codrington.

"[5th May] 1984 saw my last appearance in the KUGB Squad when I took part in an international match against Sweden held at Crystal Palace on the evening of the National Championships. I don't remember much about that match, but it was fought over two rounds again and I know England won.[43] Ted Hedlund, an American *karateka* living and training in Sweden, was the Swedish team's coach.

"I was in the KUGB Squad for another few months or so and then retired. Keeping your place in the KUGB Squad is not easy because there are always new and exciting young fighters coming up vying for your place, but that is not why I 'threw the towel' in. I had developed a severe back problem which meant that I would just collapse, my legs giving way beneath me. I use to collapse in class and my classmates would train around me and even step over me. I would simply lose the use of my legs for a few minutes. It happened in Cyprus when I was teaching out there. The vertebrae in the lower back would squash down and the muscles would contract to protect my back and my legs would suddenly go numb and down I'd go. I thought, at first, it was a hamstring, but it turned out to be a problem with the sciatic nerve. I used to do a lot of running and I have always blamed that for my condition. Anyway, I wrote to Andy Sherry giving in my resignation and that was that.

"I had five years in the KUGB National Squad and that was a good run. I'd received two European gold medals, a World bronze medal and I'd fought against the Japanese JKA team, so I had nothing to complain about. It was a privilege to be alongside my team mates, to be honest – the flair of Terry O'Neill, the persistence of Steve Cattle, the technical ability of Frank Brennan, the kicks of Bob Poynton, the relaxed body movement and wonderful *tai-sabaki* of Billy Higgins, the unmoveable Bob Rhodes, the relaxed, unorthodox Fred Fawcett, the use of size to dominate in the cases of George Godfrey and Joe Farley, the *ushiro-geri* of Gary Harford, the relaxed *gyaku-zuki* of the late Randy Williams, the sudden burst of energy and extremely sharp *mawashi-geri* of George Best, the flair and unbelievable jaw-dropping techniques of Elwyn Hall – he actually did the sort of impossible things you see in films in international competitions and reminded me of Terry O'Neill in his heyday – and the aggressive, fantastic all-round ability of Ronnie Christopher; these are the attributes I remember about these *karateka*.

"There were many others too, people like John Thompson, Norman Gomersall, Jimmy Brennan, Graham Adams, Ian Roberts, Miles Draper, Steve Lamb, Jeff and George Wilkinson, Joan's brothers – all good fighters.

Andy Sherry, Chief Instructor of the KUGB noted: 'Owen was a strong, spirited and determined trainer at Squad and always gave his all. I always found him to be a fearless and courageous fighter in competition and he could always be relied upon. He is totally committed to his karate and to this day trains regularly in all aspects of the art.'

OWEN MURRAY, M.B.E., 6th DAN

KUGB National Squad: left to right, standing – Bob Poynton, Winnie Hatton, unknown, Steve Cattle, Sandie Hopkins, George Godfrey, Ronnie Christopher; kneeling – Frank Brennan, Andy Sherry, Keinosuke Enoeda, Gary Harford, Owen Murray, doctor/first aider.

Fellow KUGB team member, Bob Poynton, recalled: 'I first met Owen in Sunderland in the early 1970's and was immediately struck by his tenacity and determination. It was his tremendous spirit which enabled him to pursue a very successful competition career throughout the 1980's, in which period he gained many gold, silver and bronze medals. He has never lost these attributes in forty years of training and is an inspiration to his students and peers.'

Murray continued: "Travelling to courses and training in this country and abroad was a costly business and if it had not been for the generosity of Jeff Barwick and Sendai, who had subsidised me, I would never have been able to go. So, I shall forever be in their debt and would like to thank them, here and now, for assisting me in the way that they did. However, whilst I may not have been in the KUGB National Squad anymore, I was still captain of the Sendai team and so I continued to fight and compete. They got good mileage out of me for another six years, as we shall see!

"Attending international matches abroad with the KUGB Squad gave me a taste for travelling and, over the thirty years since, I have visited many countries [including Canada, USA, Australia, Cyprus, Mexico, Spain, France, Belgium, Switzerland, Portugal, Norway,

EUROPEAN GOLD . . . 'I WISH I COULD REMEMBER'

Owen with companion at the Pyramids, Egypt

Owen with companion at the Wailing Wall, Jerusalem

OWEN MURRAY, M.B.E., 6th DAN

Owen with a boa constrictor around his neck in the Far East

Sweden, Germany, Denmark, Luxemburg, Egypt, Israel, Greece, Turkey, United Arab Emirates, Thailand, Burma, Laos, Malaysia and Vietnam].

"I went to Canada around the time I had to resign from the KUGB Squad. A friend of mine – Terry Smith, a tall lad with a long ginger beard – lived in Regina, Saskatchewan. So I flew to Calgary, Alberta, and met up with him and travelled to Lake Louise, in Banff National Park, in Alberta's Rockies. Lake Louise is an idyllic spot. I remember the beautiful green water at the edge of a glacier. We went on a lake with Indian canoes, one paddle each side. We also went camping in the Rockies, but it was really cold. We had to be careful of bears though, and we did see them catching salmon beside the rapids. I went for a couple of runs but found it hard with the altitude being over a mile above sea level.

"I then went to Portland, Oregon, to visit friends from Sunderland. The redwoods are incredible – one tree was that big you could drive a car through the base of the trunk. Then we went down to the West coast of the USA. I have a passion for sea food, so San Francisco was great down by Fisherman's Wharf; funny enough though, I always remember the cheesecake from there. The federal prison at Alcatraz was fantastic and I walked around with headphones on listening to the stories about the inmates and their lives on The Rock. What got me was that the prisoners, one-and-a-half miles out on this island in San Francisco Bay, could hear the New Years' celebrations from the mainland, but were incarcerated for years, often life, and could not participate.

"Then it was down to Los Angeles. I recall special places on a beach were caged off so bodybuilders could pose. We met Norman Gumersol there, one of Bob Rhodes old pupils, who I've mentioned before. Then it was on to Las Vegas, Nevada. Although I don't gamble, I found the food and entertainment great, but three days in the 'Entertainment Capital of the World' was enough.

"The Grand Canyon, Arizona, was stunning, breath-taking. I didn't go into the canyon via helicopter on this occasion, but I did on another visit, later. Terry was leader of the bikers in Regina so he wanted to go to Sturgess, in the Black Hills of South Dakota, the famous bike meet, where I saw the Mount Rushmore National Memorial – the enormous sculptures of the heads of George Washington, Thomas Jefferson, Theodore Roosevelt and Abraham Lincoln. We also travelled up through Montana stopping off at Yellowstone Park.

"After the trip, the sister and mother of another friend, who we met out there, were killed by a juggernaut and his nephew was seriously injured. Not long after that, this boy's father, now a widower, took his children on holiday only to encounter an earthquake and be pulled from the rubble and was then killed by an electric cable. So the kids lost their mother and father, and also their grandmother as it so

Owen at the Grand Canyon

happened, in the space of a year. Anyway, enough of my travel ramblings and back to the karate!

"Through training on a regular basis over a five year period with some of the best Shotokan *karateka* in the world, I developed tremendous self-confidence and this became evident in my working and social life. As I've said before, I had absolutely no confidence before losing my hand, but after losing it I wouldn't even walk into a room on my own. Now I felt that I could do just about anything and not wither in the company of doctors, lawyers and other professional people. I felt that I could hold my own. Okay, I didn't have a higher education and I couldn't speak with their eloquence, but each to his own and I realised that whilst I couldn't do what they did, they couldn't do what I did either. So, when I went into a room to see a solicitor I would think to myself, 'I've fought the best *karateka* the Japanese can throw at someone, so why should I be worried by you?' I'd read that there were one hundred and seventy thousand physicians in this country, but I believe there is only one, one-armed man – at least to the best of my knowledge – who has fought for England. This kind of thinking built up my self-esteem.

Owen with Jeff Wilkinson at Mount Rushmore, USA.

"I had also lost my embarrassment about having a prosthetic arm. I had a false hand that was very lifelike, with a skin-like texture. By this time, if I wanted to have a bit of a laugh I wouldn't fix it properly into the prosthetic arm and when I shook hands with someone it would come off! I remember I went to a christening and, afterwards, when we went around the family's house for a bite to eat, all the guests suddenly heard this piercing scream – some clever clogs had put this false hand in the freezer!

"The people I associated with were so familiar with my false hand that it just became natural to them to see it lying about. As a funny example of this, I went skiing in Aviemore, in the Scottish Highlands, with some friends and in order to be able to hold the stick properly in my left hand I used a prosthetic hand that had been specially designed for use driving motorbikes. Anyway, this false hand got stuck on the stick which made things awkward so I took it off and left it to the side and carried on without it. When a female member of the group took the equipment back to the hire company, she gave my stick back with the false hand still attached!

"Because I'd given up being a member of the KUGB Squad, it didn't mean that I'd given up karate of course – far from it. Competition is only a small part of training, but it was one that I specialised in and became good at. Now it was time for me to re-consider my practice. I blamed the daily running for my back problem, as I've said, but I also blamed bad kicking technique. I decided to actually analyze what I was doing more carefully and I found a number of problems that were related, chiefly, to my supporting leg. I had been practising *mawashi-geri* and *yoko-geri* without sufficient movement on the supporting foot and this had put a lot of tension in the knee and lower back. I decided to devote more time to perfecting techniques and less time on repetition of techniques, which were incorrect in any case. Over the next few years I worked on bending and rotating the supporting foot, moving it, sometimes as much as one hundred and eighty degrees. I spent a lot of time emphasizing this to my pupils so that their bodies moved naturally and there was no jarring.

"One of the projects I took on after I'd left the KUGB Squad was a derelict terraced house in Cleveland Road, Sunderland, which I bought to refurbish. I paid around eleven thousand pounds for it and sold it for forty-five thousand pounds after a period of about four years. During this time I was looking for a derelict farm house to refurbish too. My neighbour, Bob, who was a butcher by trade and had three shops, mentioned one day that he had a pig farm for sale about four miles from the city centre in a village called South Hylton. The pig farm was well known in the area for its smell – that is the pigs generally and for the boiling of pig swill. A public path, literally four yards from the River Wear, passed the farm. Bob told me that he had applied for planning permission for a house on the land, but had been refused, so he went to the ombudsman and permission was granted. Permission had been given two-and-a-half years before, but work on the house had to start within three years or the planning permission might be rescinded. The gamble I faced if I bought the farm was whether I could complete the purchase, get plans drawn up and start building within the allotted six months. I shook hands on the deal for forty-five thousand pounds for a rundown piggery with an old diesel van.

"My immediate reaction upon signing was, 'What the hell have I done?' However, I did build a house, which was a truly horrendous experience. I was permanently walking around with a dictaphone, ordering materials for the house and organising collecting the swill

Owen's house being built

and generally keeping control on the welfare of the four hundred pigs and three farm workers in my employment. At the same time I was the production manager at Remploy with ninety people under me and running the doors in Sunderland, South Shields and Middlesbrough at nights, as well as helping to run Sendai. Things got too much when I had to go to livestock sales and when pig prices started dropping, so I decided to stop farming after three years. The farm buildings are now derelict. I flattened most of them because kids were getting in and drinking and taking drugs.

"I still live in the house and could not ask for a better home. I have countryside around me, chickens in the garden, the river running past me and, because I am on the tidal stretch, I often see seals. I have my own *dojo* and there's a pub just down the road – I mean, what else could a man ask for?

"Being a production manager, I had responsibility for people and one case I remember in particular. One of my charge hands – I won't mention his name – was a haemophiliac and because of this condition he required a blood clotting agent from the USA. Unfortunately, in the mid 1980s there was a lot of fear about Aids and the American movie star, Rock Hudson, had just died of it. Everyone was fearful of this new killer disease and many thought that it could be transmitted by breath or drinking out of the same cup, that sort of thing. It was viewed as a kind of plague – and there was no known cure. One day this chap came to me and said that he'd contracted Aids through contaminated blood.

"'Look, you're the only one who knows, apart from my wife; even my family doesn't know,' he said. He was obviously worried sick.

"It was good of him to show me such respect, but we chatted and I told him that I knew he had entrusted me with this information but I had a responsibility to the other workers and that I would have to tell the factory doctor. He understood this. The manager and one of the directors in London were also informed but it never went any further. People at the factory were constantly talking about Aids and this poor chap was sitting there feeling terrible with the condition and I knew about it and the others didn't. Eventually this chap took a turn for the worse and required a lot of time in hospital. Some of his workmates wanted to go to Newcastle with me to visit him and I couldn't really refuse them but I wasn't going to tell them what their mate really had. This was early in the Aids story and the chap died not long afterwards with what everyone was told was another condition.

"As I said earlier, two *karateka* have really affected my karate more than any others and the second of these is Dave Hazard. I'd seen Dave before, at the KUGB National Championships, and he was certainly a brilliant, fiery fighter. Dave, a Londoner, had been in the KUGB many years and had won the KUGB National title for individual *kata* in 1976. He so nearly became grand champion that year, but was denied in the *kumite* when the decision went to Bob Poynton in the final without any points being scored. Dave had been part of the KUGB National Squad, and, indeed, was part of the squad when the World Championships were held in Tokyo, when he was living out there and training at the JKA headquarters. Through a *karateka* named Caesar Andrews, I trained with Dave at Enoeda's Marshall Street *dojo*, in Soho, London, in the 1970s.

"Dave taught me to slow down, to relax, and not to go at everything at one hundred miles an hour. He taught me that kicking is not about suppleness, but 'sitting' on the supporting leg and allowing the kicking leg to be more relaxed and having the freedom to do its job. He also taught me not to travel like a train in a straight line, but learn to break, at angles.

"I decided to invite Dave up to Sendai in 1984. He'd left the KUGB by this time and was with SEKU [South England Karate Union] along with Mick Dewey. Dave later founded the Academy of Shotokan Karate. Anyway, Dave came up to the Crowtree Leisure Centre and gave a course and afterwards ran a special session at our old *dojo* at the YMCA. Sendai moved into the leisure centre [in January 1978[44]] shortly after it opened in 1976 and training was held there on Tuesday and Thursday evenings [and, later, Sundays] under John Holdsworth and Jeff Barwick. However, I kept the YMCA *dojo* going on Wednesdays, just for freestyle practise, and that continued for a good number of years before I moved the class, still held on a Wednesday, to Crowtree.

"Dave proceeded to give all the seniors a bit of a hammering – not in a brutal way, but we were, generally, out-classed. I was greatly impressed and he came up quite a few times and taught us. I felt an affinity with him and I later went down with a few of the Sendai black-belts and stayed at his home, in Hove, and visited his *dojo* at the time, in Brighton. Dave was from the East End and I asked him if we could go and have a look around because I'd heard about it but never been, to which he agreed. What followed was surreal."

Dave Hazard, who referred to Murray as 'a very tough guy and an excellent *karateka*[45]', tells what happened next in his book, *Born Fighter*: 'I took him [Murray] and his boys down the Roman Road to a little pub that I knew. It was the sort of place that had a little window in the door, with a slide across it, so the doorman could look out and see who was knocking. If he knew who you were, he let you in. If he didn't, the door remained closed. Once inside, we walked up to the bar and exchanged pleasantries with the owner, an ex-boxer, as he sorted our drinks. As we were talking, the owner noticed the glove on Owen's false hand ... [and they spoke about it and Murray showed him the false limb] ... Now, you've got to picture this little pub – small groups of men, sitting at tables, doing their deals, minding their own business. At one table, there was a larger group engaged in what looked like a very serious conversation. No one was taking any notice of us.

'Owen began talking about karate to the governor of the pub. He got so caught up in it that he demonstrated a back-fist with his false hand. But he hadn't fastened it back properly. The hand flew across the room and hit one of the guys in the large group on the back of his head. They all leaped to their feet and, the next minute, we'd got three guns pointing at us! We all put our hands up instinctively, and you can imagine how these guys stared when they saw Owen with both arms in the air but only one hand!

"I'm sorry mate,' Owen said, 'My hand just flew off.'

'It was all very serious for a few seconds, then the place was in uproar. It cost us a few drinks to get Owen's hand back, but at least he didn't get filled with lead.'[46]

V

KUGB NATIONAL CHAMPIONS

Murray continued: "Jeff Barwick is a tremendous organiser and he arranged for the European Shotokan Karate Championships to come to the Crowtree Leisure Centre in November 1986. In fact, the old European Amateur Karate Federation had been disbanded [in 1985] and a new body had been formed called the European Shotokan Karate Organisation and this became – actually during the Championships – the European Shotokan Karate Association, ESKA, that we know today.

"The KUGB did brilliantly at these championships [winning eight of the thirteen events] and England won the team *kumite* and Frank Brennan took both the individual *kumite* and *kata*. I recall that Karen Findley won the female individual *kumite* title too."

Terry O'Neill, reporting on the championships, wrote: 'In nineteen years of competing and attending karate championships, I have never seen a better organised or more efficiently run event – I've seen its equal in two of the three world championships I participated in Japan – but never its peer. The tremendous amount of work and planning that went into this event by the organisers was a great credit to them. Derek Langham was in-charge of the championship committee and he enlisted the help of Sunderland instructor Jeff Barwick. So much sterling work did this gentleman do, aided by Sunderland's Owen Murray and members of the Sendai Karate Club, that he was singled out and given a special mention (something highly unusual within the KUGB) in the championships' opening address given by ESKO President, Charles Naylor. The event was very generously sponsored by the firm of Remploy ...[1]

Murray continued: "Once I knew the championships were being held in Sunderland, I went to Remploy's divisional manager and asked if they'd like to become involved in some way. They knew I was very much into karate and I thought they might be able to help. They were happy to contribute financially and the managing director presented a prize as I recall.

"I think it was in 1987 that Tyne Tees Television visited the Sendai Club and made a *First Edition* programme about karate, entitled, *Kiai*.

It was researched by Ed Skelding, a Sendai *karateka*, and directed by a chap named David Thomasson. The Japanese featured were Kase and Enoeda, and Steve Cattle and John Holdsworth were in it too. Jeff Barwick, Julie Nicholson, Jeff Wilkinson and yours truly were interviewed and a little feature was done on the four of us, individually. A lot was crammed in actually."

The author has seen this thirty-eight minute programme. Murray is shown, variously, throughout, and is interviewed at his desk at Remploy, in Sunderland. On the factory floor, a green cutting machine very similar – though smaller and manually fed – to the one on which he lost his hand, is shown. The camera then follows Murray as a controlling doorman at a night club. Murray, Jeff Barwick, Jeff Wilkinson and Julie Nicholson (though shown with the surname 'Carter' at the time) and Christine Pullan are featured taking a grading under Enoeda. Wilkinson is shown free-styling, as are Nicholson and Pullan, together. Finally, Murray and Barwick spar and this is the best footage of Murray in action the author has seen. He is fast, straight and aggressive, delivering mostly punches, but also a *mae-geri*. Both Murray and Barwick failed their 4th Dans that day.

"Are you disappointed?" the interviewer asked Barwick, probably partially reflecting on his recent encounter with Murray (though Barwick held his own).

"No," came the reply. "[I'm] pleasantly surprised I'm still alive!"

Nicholson passed her 4th Dan, whilst Pullan failed; Wilkinson passed his 3rd Dan.

Murray continued: "The grading sequence was filmed at the Crowtree Leisure Centre that May, as were the clips of Enoeda and Kase, teaching. Jeff Barwick had organised a course that was, originally, planned to include *Sensei* Nakayama, but shortly before, Nakayama died in Japan, so Enoeda and Kase took it with another two Japanese [Ogura and Kurakoshi].[2] That was the first time I had seen Kase, though I'd heard a lot about him. He was small, rotund and nearing sixty, but he was absolutely brilliant. For someone of his body shape he was unbelievably nimble on his feet and incredibly fast. He couldn't kick much above knee height, but boy could he punch and I wouldn't have wanted to be on the end of one of those. His timing was superb, faultless, and his *tai-sabaki* was something to behold. Watching him was quite an eye-opener to be honest because Kase had overcome his body's obvious restrictions, his training was outside the box, and not dependent on the athleticism I tried so hard to compete with, and so his method and training appealed to me."

Owen (right) with Christine Pullan (left) and Gloria Middleton at a karate charity course.

Kase was born in 1929 and, having studied judo to 2nd Dan, began his study of karate as a naval cadet during World War II at the Shotokan *dojo*, situated in Zoshigaya, Toshima Ward, Tokyo. The Shotokan was the first purpose-built karate *dojo* in Japan and it is from this building that the style of karate receives its name. The *dojo* was destroyed by American bombing in the worst conventional bombing raid in history, on the 10th March 1945. Gichin Funakoshi, who is credited with introducing karate to Japan from Okinawa in 1922, and his third, and (in karate terms) highly influential son, Yoshitaka, and family, lived in the adjoining house. Kase trained under both Gichin and Yoshitaka Funakoshi, the latter of whom was to die in 1945, and Shigeru Egami, another highly significant *karateka*. Kase entered Senshu University where he was captain of the karate club and was awarded 3rd Dan in 1949. He was a judge at the first and subsequent

JKA Championships and taught at Hitotsubashi University before leading the aforementioned JKA World Tour in 1965. He instructed in South Africa before finally taking up residence in Paris. He was the senior Shotokan *karateka* in Europe and a man highly respected.

Murray continued: "One of the two lower grade Japanese did a wonderful lesson on the use of the hips in karate and actually had me out front and demonstrated upon me. This Japanese, the thinner of the two, had excellent hip flexibility, so it was a good course and I learned a great deal.

"Just because I'd failed my 4th Dan this time around didn't mean I couldn't train harder, get better and take it again. This I did, by grading successfully for *Yondan* the following year [9th September 1988] under *Sensei* Enoeda.

"So successful had the 1986 ESKA Championships been, that Jeff was asked if he'd organise the 1987 Championships as well, and so the Crowtree Leisure Centre and, indeed, Sunderland, played host once again in November 1987. I was very supportive once more and was on the organising committee, but only had a minor role[3], though Remploy did sponsor the event again and, indeed, presented a trophy for the most outstanding senior competitor. If memory serves, I was responsible for a foreign team and generally escorted them about making sure they were happy.

"I'd won two gold medals in past Europeans and it was so frustrating just sitting there watching it all happen around me. I wanted to be part of it so much. I could feel the old rush of adrenaline. One lunch-time, rather than staying at the Centre, I drove home, got changed and went for a six mile run. Unfortunately, I tore my Achilles tendon half way around and had to limp back home. Although I never miss training – I don't do that – it took eight months before that foot was working properly again.

"Anyway, the contests on this second occasion were fought over two days [7th and 8th November]. Jeff had arranged for a laser show to Vangelis's famous soundtrack from the film, *Chariots of Fire*, once the twenty nations had marched in. It was spellbinding stuff [described at the time as 'a truly magnificent visual experience'[4]]. George Best took the individual junior *kumite* title [for the second successive year] beating an Austrian [A. Kleinekathofer] and Sean Roberts came second in the senior male individual *kata* [and England came joint third in the junior male team *kumite*].[4] England did well on the second day too: Julie Nicholson got silver in the senior individual *kata* and she was part of the team that took the senior female team *kata* title [along with Winnie Hatton and Christine Pullan]. No one had got through to the last eight in the men's senior individual *kumite* event largely because Frank Brennan had an injured back and didn't compete. However, he declared himself fit for the senior men's team *kumite* final, which England had got through to. England was against Spain and I was just itching to be part of it." Ronnie Christopher lost, Randy Williams won, George Best won, Ian Roberts drew and Miles Draper won, so England took the ESKA title.[5] Grey, reporting on the event, commented: 'Alas, the championship is now over, past history, but who knows – maybe someday we will return to Sunderland again.'[5] Little did anyone know the return would be less than two-and-a-half years hence and the event would produce a great moment in British Shotokan history.

Murray continued: "Joan gave birth to our second child, Owen Patrick Murray, on the 26th June 1989. I was over the moon to have a son. I know it is only a convention, but I'd had it instilled in me from an early age that it is important to keep the family name going. Joan and I weren't living together, so Owen went to live with his mother, in Farringdon. However, I used to visit them daily, at different times, depending on my work and training schedule.

"Following on from the success of the two Sunderland ESKA Championships, Jeff Barwick brought the World Shotokan Karate Association Championships to our *dojo* in March 1990. It was wonderfully organised, as before – that's Jeff's forte. Once again, I was responsible for looking after a team and was given Bangladesh. Those poor fellows were broke and I had to take them to the cheapest places to get food. They liked pasties. They were so skint that I had to put my hand in my own pocket quite a few times. In the evenings, they weren't interested in going out really – we never went to a pub or club – and all they did was get their food and go back to their hotel. They were not adventurous at all, but, then, they could hardly afford to be.

"The World Championships were so exciting because England got through to the finals. The old adrenaline rush was still very much there. Although I am a qualified KUGB judge and referee, I didn't officiate that day as I'm not an official at international level – I'm just not interested in it. The first day was given over to individual events, of which there were four. We weren't placed in the top three in the women's *kata*, but got joint third in the *kumite* [Karen Findley]. Frank Brennan beat Masao Kagawa [reigning JKA *Kumite* Champion and 1985 JKA Grand Champion] and took silver in the individual *kata*.

"I don't like sitting and watching karate competitions to be honest,

Murray with baby Owen

KUGB NATIONAL CHAMPIONS

Team of Sendai helpers, Owen is to be seen back row, fourth left; Geoff Barwick is fifth left.

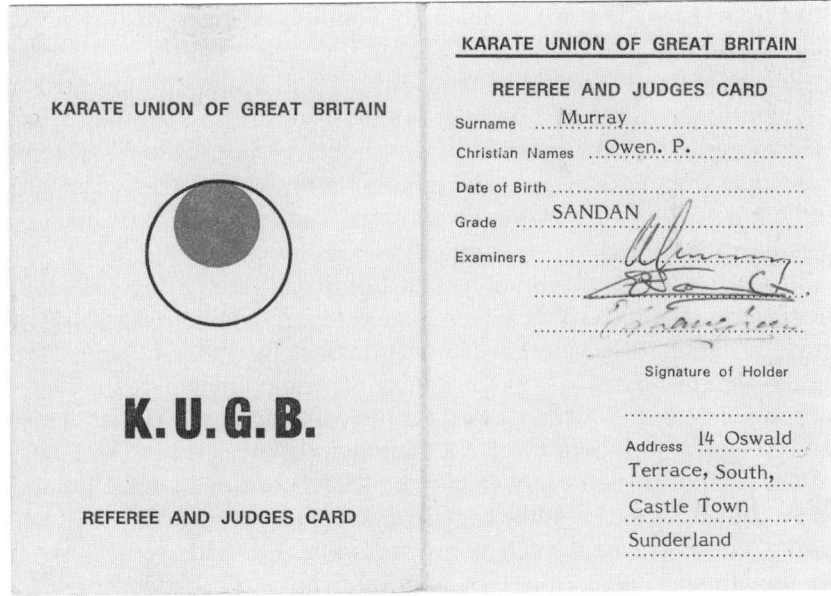

Owen's judges' licence

but the men's individual *kumite* was something special that day and Elwyn Hall was on top form – unbelievable flair – when he took his very tall Japanese opponent down with a judo throw and followed this up with punches for an *ippon*. It was absolutely brilliant and, for me, the highlight of the championships. Elwyn's team-mate, Ronnie Christopher, got through to the finals but was unable to fight Kagawa because he had been badly concussed in the previous round and could not compete, so Kagawa won the world title without fighting. What a great fight that would have been. The Japanese took all four titles that day.[6]

"The second day saw the team events. Great Britain came second in the female team *kata* and third in the male team *kata* [both being won by Japan], and that was wonderful, but the event that really had us all fired up was the team *kumite*. Britain had beaten the USA, Sweden and Denmark, in that order and met Japan in the finals. This was tremendous stuff, it really was. Elwyn Hall was up first and beat his opponent [Koike] with two punches. Then, Frank Brennan got up to face the current world champion, Imamura, and Frank spun round with an *ushiro-geri* and won by a half-point. Then a fired-up Dean Hodgkin rose to face his opponent [Noda]. Dean scored first with a *gyaku-zuki* and the rest of the time it was a case of, 'Can he keep the lead from a Japanese whose team are about to be dethroned?' On two occasions the fighters were on the floor. It was nerve-racking. Then the match ended and Britain had won. Britain had beaten the Japanese in three straight fights to take the WSKA World title. The noise was deafening. But there were still two fights to go! Britain's Ronnie Cannings fought Kagawa and lost to a kick and Gary Harford, although scoring first with a *chudan mawashi-geri*, lost to Aihara by two punches.[7]

"As I recall, the celebrations that followed that evening were long and hearty. The KUGB were standing on top of the Shotokan world, at least as far as JKA karate was concerned. It just goes to show how good Andy Sherry is as a coach. He has never really been acknowledged, in a wider sense, for his contribution to British karate and I believe he should receive a civil award.

"Sendai competed every year in the KUGB Nationals and 1990 was very special for us. I was the captain and had forged a good team. I was going through a bad patch in my personal life and went to see a hypnotist who helped me a lot with motivation. On Wednesdays I'd use what I'd learned from this chap to motivate the team in these demanding sessions. I felt we could win weeks before the championships, I really did, and now all the work we'd put in would, hopefully, reveal itself.

Adams recalled: "For about four or five months before the

KUGB NATIONAL CHAMPIONS

Owen with his Sendai team at a KUGB National Championships. Left to right: Jeff Wilkinson, Murray, Ian Jefferson, Brent McCafferty, Stuart McRoy.

A Sendai squad, left to right, back row – Graham Sparks, Jeff Wilkinson, Brent McCafferty, Dave Neil; middle row – unknown, Beverley, Brian Watson, Stew McRoy; front row – Lyne Henderson, Owen Murray, Dennis Hutchinson, George Wilkinson.

Nationals, Owen selected some twelve to fourteen lads, of whom I was one, and forged them into a real team. All we practised was *kumite* and it was hard. Owen is a very good coach and different from other instructors in my experience in that he focuses very much on *tai-sabaki*. As he was in-charge of the whole Sendai squad, he wanted to forge a strong bond between us and he insisted that every member support the other in all events. So, for example, all the men in the team would support the women's *kata*. This helped to create great support and atmosphere ..."

Pullan recalled: "It was around this time that the men's squad played a joke on Owen. The lads went to a nightclub and they all wore jeans and tee-shirts and had black gloves on their left hands. In each of their right hands they carried a coat hanger from which hung a pair of black trousers, a white shirt and a dark tie. Now Owen would always go to work in the evenings like this and change when he got there. Apparently, it took Owen thirty minutes before he cottoned on to what was happening."

Murray continued: "The club had made the quarter-finals in 1975[8]; were placed third in 1978[9], when we were beaten by the Liverpool Red Triangle [the eventual winners] and I fought Bob Poynton; and, third again in 1988 when we lost to the Red Triangle[10] once more, but it had been close, right up to the last fight. In 1990 however, Sendai made it, at last, to the finals.

"Crystal Palace was packed out as usual and our opponents were to be the old enemy, the Red Triangle. Believe me, that is a team you don't want to meet at any time, because they have won the title so often [in the previous twenty-three KUGB National Championships, the Red Triangle had won seventeen, with only Leeds winning more than once]. So, we were up against it you might say! Sendai had actually taken a couple of other KUGB National Team titles before [female team *kata*, 1985; mixed team *kata*, 1988 and 1989], but this was the first time the men had made it to the final. Julie Nicholson was a superb *kata* performer and had taken the female *kata* title five times by this time [and would take it another eleven times to 2001].

"In the team *kumite* semi-finals we had beaten a strong Birmingham team, Cocks Moors Woods, and the Red Triangle overcame Reading Apollo. In a previous round, I had beaten Ian Roberts, who had taken the men's individual *kumite* title three years before when he beat Elwyn Hall, so I felt on top form, psyched-up and ready to go."

Jeff Wilkinson recalled: "I think most coaches before a final would do a light limbering up session with their team, but not Owen. He had

KUGB NATIONAL CHAMPIONS

Owen coaching Brent McCafferty on the sidelines at the KUGB National Championships.

Owen in action in a team match on Sendai's way to take the 1990 KUGB National team *kumite* title.

us doing press-ups and sit-ups and then we practised some hard *kumite*. By the time we came to fight the opposition we were really pumped up and ready to face anyone. About five minutes before the fight started, he let us do what we wanted. Some of the lads just chatted, but I would go off by myself and pace up and down psyching myself up."

Murray continued: "Before we fought, I took the team over to the Liverpool lads and we all shook hands. It was going to be hard fought, we knew that, but it was going to be conducted in a gentlemanly manner. The atmosphere was electric. *Sensei* Enoeda was the referee, and the corner judges were Terry O'Neill, Charles Naylor, Bob Rhodes and one other, who I regret I cannot remember.

"Our first man up was Mick O'Donnell and he faced Frank Brennan. Now Frank, who was a world champion, had, less than an hour before, lost in the individual *kumite* final to Elwyn Hall, and he was fired up. In truth, it didn't matter who I sent out, for it was a case of 'sending a lamb to slaughter'. Mick, to his credit, stood his ground and put up a commendable showing, but Frank was just too good. Frank caught him with a *chudan mawashi-geri* followed by an *uraken* for a *wazari* and then performed a *chudan kekomi* off the back leg followed by a *gyaku-zuki* for another *wazari*. Okay, we were one down, but we still had four to go.

"Then Jeff Wilkinson got up to face Steve Sewell – who would later go on to take the KUGB individual title [1995]."

Wilkinson recalled: "Before I went on I turned to Owen and he slapped my face quite hard. He always did this. I felt strong. I had trained with Owen seven days a week for fourteen years by this time and he knew how to get the best out of me."

Murray continued: "I think Sewell scored first with a *kizami-zuki*, but Jeff had excellent timing and his *kizami-zuki* and *gyaku-zuki* were fast enough to get him a bronze in the individual *kumite* at the European Championships, and he took the fight with two *jodan gyaku-zukis*. So the score was one match apiece.

"Our third man was Graham Adams, a strong fighter who met Lee Williams. Williams scored first with a right *jodan gyaku-zuki* for a *wazari*, but then Graham came back and scored with a punch, I think, and then with a *chudan mawashi-geri* followed by a *jodan* punch and took the fight. So things were looking good.

"Steve Lamb had a no score draw with John O'Neill, despite two clashes, and so we were one up with one to go. As captain, I had decided to go last because I was the most experienced and might read

Owen in action against Jim Brennan in the last fight of the 1990 KUGB National team *kumite* final.

my opponent better; it might also get tactical. I got up to face Jimmy Brennan, who was a tremendous, under-rated fighter, exceptional really with feet and fists, a great stalwart who fought many times in international competitions for the KUGB. We bowed to Enoeda, then to each other, and then Enoeda called, '*Hajime!*'

"I'd worked it out that I could lose by a *wazari* and Sendai would still win on overall points, if the teams drew. Jim, who started training the same year as I did, knew he had to win by two *wazari* or an *ippon*. This promised to be a humdinger of a fight, because there was a lot at stake.

"Jim is a forceful fighter and he backed me into a corner which I broke out off. This was followed by a punching clash, but neither of us scored. Then, he attacked using a long right *jodan kizami-zuki* and scored a fraction of a second before my right *jodan kizami-zuki*. He was a *wazari* up and I couldn't afford to lose another. I knew I couldn't just back off or rely on defence as Jim was too good for that. No, I had to go for it and take the fight to him, trust in my own ability and hope he didn't score another *wazari*. I tried to *ashi-barai* his front leg with my leading right leg more as a dummy than anything else, but it did make light contact and I carried on with a right *jodan kizami-zuki*, but did not score. Time was running out for Jim now and he increased the tempo. I think we had another four clashes without scoring[11], including some grappling. Then, after the last clash we came back to our spots to start again and, as Enoeda said '*Hajime!*' the bell rang as Jim flew in with a lunge punch, a right *oi-zuki*. I stepped back and let him clip my right shoulder. It was over. [It was noted at the time that 'they both fought extremely hard'[12]]. Jim had won the bout.

"The two teams got up and faced each other. When the points were added up, Sendai had indeed won and Enoeda declared us the winners. That was a great moment that lives with me to this day. We all played our part, but Jeff and Graham had won the day for Sendai. *Sensei* Enoeda then presented us with our medals and I was given the trophy. We took our places on the rostrum and the cameras started flashing.

"We were in a state of total elation, buzzing, and unbelievable euphoria. At long last, on the 12th May 1990, a dream came true for me.

Wilkinson recalled: "After the announcement was made that Sendai had beaten the Red Triangle, we went over and shook the hands of the Liverpool team members. It was still very controlled and formalised at this stage. Then, afterwards, the scale of the achievement kicked in and we were just elated.

"We went to the pub to celebrate and members of the Liverpool, St. Helen's, Kirkdale and Leeds teams joined us. We all knew each other and there was no ill-feeling or anything like that. The Liverpool lads were gracious in defeat as we would have been if we'd lost."

Murray continued: "Needless to say, we had a few jars – we reckoned we deserved them! Then we went back to the Queen's Hotel, Crystal Palace, and we were still celebrating on the coach on the journey home. One of things I remember doing was seeing how many people we could get into the coaches tiny toilet at the same time – four!

Barwick recalled: "The team were as high as kites. I think Owen bought some bottles and they all got very merry, shall we say. Owen, who, believe me, can drink, can hold his liquor and, unlike some people who become argumentative or aggressive when they've had too

KUGB NATIONAL CHAMPIONS

Members of the winning Sendai teams at the 1990 KUGB Nationals. From left to right, standing: Owen Murray, Jeff Wilkinson, Graham Adams, Mick O'Donnell, unknown; sitting, John Holdsworth, Julie Nicholson, Christine Pullen and Mark Patel.

Sendai – winners of the KUGB National Team kumite title, 1990. Left to right: Steve Lamb, Owen Murray, Paul Dowell, *Sensei* Enoeda, unknown, Graham Adams, Brent McCafferty, Jacks (surname only).

much, Owen becomes very affable – there is no nastiness or belligerence. I think that says a lot about the man, his underlying nature and his personality in general.

"That reminds me of a story involving alcohol. *Sensei* Enoeda came up to Sendai and, after training, a grading was held. Enoeda had brought three other Japanese *senseis* with him and while the grading was proceeding, Owen took these instructors to the bar at Crowtree Leisure Centre. When the grading was over, Enoeda went upstairs to find Owen sitting there with a large smile of his face and three highly intoxicated Japs. Enoeda looked at Owen.

"'You are a bad boy – but a true samurai!' Enoeda said and laughed. The Japanese were legless so goodness knows how much whisky Owen had given them. But Owen just got up and behaved as if nothing had happened, though I bet you a pound to a penny he had drunk as much, if not more, than the Japanese."

Murray continued: "That was my last fight. I retired after that. I'd done what I'd wanted to do. I'd been fighting in competitions for eighteen years and was coming up to forty years of age. I'd had a good run and it was time to call it a day and move on.

"1990 was a good year for Sendai because Julie took the individual *kata* again and Christine Pullan came second. We also took the mixed team *kata* gold with John Holdsworth, Julie and Christine performing *Sochin*, making it a hat-trick. John was, and still is, very good at *kata* and was placed many times, and, indeed, won regional competitions."

Nicholson recalled: "Taking the National team *kumite* title that year was like winning the FA Cup Final, it really was. Sendai had worked for more than twenty years to win that trophy, so you can imagine the elation. It was a wonderful moment."

Pullan recalled: "We had a lot of supporters and the crowd were behind us because Sendai had never won before and beating the Red Triangle would be a big upset that people wanted to be witness to. Everything just erupted when we won."

Wilkinson recalled: "Winning the KUGB Nationals was the highlight of my competitive career. Owen had been my instructor since 1976 and he'd taken me to two European bronze medals, but after he ceased being coach it just wasn't the same for me anymore. I continued for another year, but then gave up competition at the age of thirty-one.

"Owen was an inspiration to me since Day One. He was a demanding teacher, very hard, but always positive and determined. He led by example and he wanted his students to give their all. If you weren't giving your best he'd be on you in a flash and he was fierce and 'in your face'. If you went down, you had to get up quickly, because he'd go for you on the floor. Feinting injury was simply not an option.

"I like to think that I was Owen's first protégé. He was my one and only teacher. The Japanese instructors were good of course but they never inspired me. Let me put it another way – I would never have followed them into battle, but I would have followed Owen."

It has been reported that Sendai were the runners-up to the Liverpool Red Triangle in the team *kumite* in the KUGB Nationals the following year. The report noted: 'Last year Sendai joined the elite number of teams to have upset Liverpool's dominance in this event. This year, however, the men from the Red Triangle were determined to avenge their defeat and, despite a very spirited attempt by last year's surfers, the final score was 4 wins to 1.'[13]

Holdsworth recalled: "Owen was the best fighter that Sendai ever had – and that's saying something. He has been wonderfully loyal to the club and the KUGB. He never missed training and never faltered in his teaching commitments despite what was happening in his private life. However, I must be honest and say that, even though he is a great friend, in my opinion his lifestyle of working late into the night – he'd always sleep on the coach and even on the side benches or floor at competitions and we'd wake him up just before his fight – and drinking the way he did, prevented him from reaching what he truly could have been – and that is one of the greats. I expect he'll disagree with me on this point, but that's how I see it. As soon as he finished competing he would go to the pub and return just as the tournament was finishing ready for the return journey. On occasions, we had to go looking for him. At this top level, a small fraction of a second really counts and the small number of hours he slept each day and the debilitating effects of alcohol must surely have worked against him.

"Owen and I have always been close when it comes to karate training but have completely different life styles and attitudes to things outside the *dojo*. Despite this fact, I have no doubt that if I had a problem and wanted his help, he would provide it instantly and without question and I would do the same for him. If I ever got myself into a live fight situation, the two people I would most like beside me would be Owen and Jeff Barwick and I can give them no greater compliment than that."

Murray continued: "1990 was the year my pal, Steve Cattle, left the KUGB after twenty-four years. He'd been a founder member of the

Union but had decided to follow Kase, who had left the JKA along with Shirai [based in France and Italy, respectively] not long after Nakayama died, to form the World Karate Shotokan Academy. There was a lot of fragmentation around this time as a consequence of Nakayama's demise. Steve thought Kase was inspirational and he came to the conclusion that there was more to Shotokan karate than the JKA had opened his eyes to. Steve was very interested in the karate of Yoshitaka, because Kase was teaching karate from that period [1940s], when, he believed, Shotokan had reached its zenith. Because Steve believed WKSA offered things that were unavailable elsewhere, he took a very bold step because he distanced himself from the KUGB and particular club instructors within it who had hired him for courses. This was Steve – karate first, income second. He did interviews[14] and wrote articles in karate magazines[15-20] to explain why he had chosen his path. I believe he wanted his freedom and through teaching in Norway and Sweden had found his wings, so to speak. I respected his decision and didn't care which association he belonged to – it was the man I was interested in – and I carried on training with him when he came up to our neck of the woods. It was strange not seeing him at the KUGB National Championships any more though.[21]

The big event of 1991 [16th–22nd September] for martial arts in the North-East was the Budo Sai, a festival of the martial arts centred in and around Durham. There were a number of martial arts featured along with karate, such as aikido, kendo, iaido, kobudo and the Brazilian art of capoeira. Aikidoka, Arthur Lockyear, organised it and Ed Skelding filmed it and produced three, half-an-hour programmes for Tyne Tees Television which Terry O'Neill presented. Classes and demonstrations of karate were given by Shotokai master, Mitsusuke Harada, Wado-ryu master, Masafumi Shiomitsu and Shotokan master Masao Kawasoe. The organisers had flown in the famous Okinawan Goju-ryu master, Morio Higaonna, from California.

"I watched some of the aikido and attended the courses given by Kawasoe and Higaonna.[22] I have spoken about my high regard for Kawasoe before, so I'll just say a few words about Higaonna. I thought he was tremendous – real karate power – whose reputation is well deserved. I noticed that most of the Japanese came out to watch his demonstration and so I think that says it all. Higaonna was partnered with George Andrews and, even though he was being filmed for television, he never, in any way, took advantage of his student. I liked that."

Barwick recalled: "Owen doesn't like loud mouths and bullies and

I can recall some wonderful put-downs that he used to get up to if someone was too full of themselves. I'll give you two examples that happened at parties, when the booze was flowing.

"Owen would say to one of these loud mouths, who was probably boasting about his karate prowess, that he'd like to test his focus, *kime*. He'd get the chap to sit down and then would sit down opposite him. He'd then produce two spoons and instructed the loud mouth to put the end of the handle of one of these in his mouth so that the bowl and most of the spoon handle were protruding. Owen would then take up the same position. He'd asked the chap to hit him over the head with the spoon whilst it was still in his mouth to test his energy release in a harmless way. Owen then received a mild tap on the head. Then it was Owen's go. Now you have to picture the situation as the two of them were closely surrounded by people, watching on. Owen got up and, just as he was about to tap the chap on the top of his head with the end of the spoon, an accomplice would come down on the loud mouth's head with the bowl end of a soup ladle – bonk! Everyone could see what was happening and only the loud mouth was ignorant of what was going on.

"Once the loud mouth had got his senses back after rubbing his head, Owen would say to him, 'You can do better than that. I hardly felt it. I thought you said you were strong!' and so the hilarious scenario was repeated. I'll always remember the way Owen did that. It was brilliant.

"The second put-down was a test of strength and he stood upright with his arms by his sides and asked the loud mouth to put his arms between Owen's arms and body and, whilst keeping his arms straight, lift Owen by the use of his forearms alone. Well, surprise, surprise, the loud mouth couldn't lift him. Now people were all around, watching, as before, and then it was Owen's turn. He put his forearms between the loud mouth's body and arms and began to lift. What the loud mouth didn't know was that Owen had two helpers standing behind the chap and they cupped Owen's good hand and prosthetic arm, one each, and lifted as Owen did. The loud mouth shot into the air and that shut him up. This is the sort of thing Owen would do and it was great to watch.

"I remember the time that Owen was put in jail after attending a party. Now you might argue that anyone with any sense wouldn't walk around Sunderland city centre in the small hours at the best of times – even rottweilers go around in pairs – but Owen was merrily walking along, alone, wearing a St. Trinian's outfit. He'd been to the party at a

OWEN MURRAY, M.B.E., 6th DAN

Owen is a great one for fancy dress. Here as a long-haired hippy and, opposite, with Donna.

pub and there had been a fight and one of his pals had apparently whacked someone. It didn't have anything to do with Owen, but someone had seen them together and well, you couldn't mistake a one-armed man dressed up as a naughty schoolgirl now could you? The police picked Owen up for questioning and I was asked to go along to help sort things out. When I got there, the policeman said that he had been down to the cells and Owen had been dancing around. Owen later told me he had been practising his *kata*!"

Murray takes up the story and gives a different account: "Every year Sendai would have a fancy dress and on one occasion I went dressed as a St. Trinian girl, in a school uniform. Joan also went as a St. Trinian, as did a few others. Between eighty and one hundred people wandered around town in fancy dress.

"I was given a spud gun, which you press on to a potato and it fires bits of spud out the barrel by means of a spring. I was in one pub and fired the gun at the barmaid for a bit of fun. Minutes later there was a punch-up and the only person this barmaid could remember was a St. Trinian with a spud gun. A group of us went on to another nightclub and the police came to arrest me looking for the St. Trinian. However,

KUGB NATIONAL CHAMPIONS

there was more than one St. Trinian, as I've said, and when I heard the police were specifically looking for me I locked myself in a cleaner's cupboard with a pint of lager. When I found out the police were going to arrest Joan, I decided to give myself up, but I knew the policemen and they said we could sort it all out at the station. Crowtree Road is a long road and I said that there was no way that I was staggering along it in my inebriated state, so they got a van for me.

"'That's very nice of them', I thought, so I climbed into the back to be greeted by a couple of man-eating alsatians! They'd put in the police dog van! I was absolutely terrified and that sobered me up quite quickly actually!

"When I got to the police station, they took my trouser belt away and the shoe laces out of my shoes and asked me if I had anything else I ought to hand over.

"'Well, I suppose you ought to have this', I said, and pulled the spud gun out from beneath my underpants. They thought that was really funny and took an old Polaroid photo of me with my skirt askew with a policeman either side. I really wished I had kept that photograph as a memento. Then I was put in a cell, where I did press-ups and sit-ups and practised *kata*. Jeff Barwick came along to find out if I was all right. In those days they wouldn't let you out of your cell until about 6 a.m., but because I knew the sergeant he helped me make my statement and they got me back to the nightclub before it closed, so I had time for a few more pints!

"It was traditional in Sunderland to go to a nightclub known as Annabel's for the fancy dress party held the weekend between Christmas and New Year. No entrance charge would be made but you had to make a donation of food for charity, so hundreds of people would parade around town with tins. One year, I went to Annabel's dressed in shirt and tie and my friends on the door refused me entry because I wasn't wearing the compulsory fancy dress. I didn't like that, so I went into the cloakroom and found an army poncho, stripped off naked and slipped into the room where the party was being held. There was a stage at one end and when I got to it I was asked by security what my fancy dress was now and, somehow, the poncho slipped off.

"'I'm a streaker!' I shouted and I never got refused entry again."

VI

A SIERRA LEONE EXPERIENCE

Murray continued: "I met a student at the Newcastle Karate Club, in Eldon Square, named Paul Jenkins, who actually lived in Sunderland. I asked him why he didn't train in the city where he lived rather than go all the way over to Newcastle. He replied that he was a social worker helping deal with troubled youngsters, adolescents, and he wanted to pursue his karate quietly, away from the potential of prying eyes. I understood this and we got on well. John Holdsworth, Jeff Barwick, Stuart McRoy and I taught at the club on a rota basis at the time. The KUGB club is now run by Ernie Payne, a 4th Dan KUGB [who began training in 1975] and I teach up there once a month, where I see Jeff. I don't go to the Sunderland Sendai any more. Jeff gave up running the club and now concentrates on his own training, so he gave the club to John James Bruce, a worthy successor and holder of three world titles and four European titles, in addition to being KUGB National Grand Champion. John is also, and this is more important than his competition successes, a really nice man.

"Anyway, one day, out of the blue, Paul told me that he was going to Sierra Leone for a year to do what I took to be charity work, helping the poor and needy. To my utter astonishment he asked me whether I'd like to go. Now, I hadn't a clue even where Sierra Leone was and when he said it was on the west coast of Africa, on the lower part of the bulge that sticks out, just north of the equator, I said he could count me in. Looking back, I was just incredibly naive and, in this case at least, ignorance was indeed a blessing. I didn't read up on the country and walked straight into a civil war.

"Paul went out to Africa first and wrote to me a few times. I had a word with the manager at Remploy about sponsorship and what have you and, to cut a long story short, they paid for my flights and agreed to continue paying my salary for the month I planned to be out there. It was the intention that I introduce the disabled people of Sierra Leone to Remploy – its ethos and practical workings and I took out some Remploy tee-shirts. I also had a word with the Boulevard Group who paid my wages as a doorman and they said that they, too, would continue to pay me whilst I was absent. I'd like to say here and now how grateful I was, and still am, to both organisations.

"After getting an arm full of inoculations, I flew out from Heathrow to Lungi International Airport that serves Freetown, Sierra Leone's capital. It is only quite a small country, less than half the size of England I'd say, and is bordered by Guinea to the north and east and Liberia to the south and south-east and the North Atlantic elsewhere. It was February 1993 and I was going out in the middle of their dry season. Paul met me off the plane and he hurried me so we could catch the bus to a ferry that left at 6.30 p.m. I didn't understand what all the rush was for, but he said, if we missed the ferry we'd be stuck overnight.

"'So? We'll go to a hotel,' I thought to myself. But Paul was insistent and he seemed genuinely worried.

"'It's dangerous to stay here,' he said, 'because there is no electricity.'

"I couldn't believe it – a nation's capital city without electricity – and it soon became evident that Sierra Leone was a very different place to good old Blighty!

"We did manage to catch the ferry and we made it to the single storey dwelling on the outskirts of the city that Paul was staying at and where I was to be based. The building, which appeared to be constructed from breeze blocks painted white with a corrugated iron roof supported by wood painted blue, housed a group of Christian Brothers, but they didn't wear collars, smocks or anything clerical. I hadn't realised it, but Paul was a priest, or monk, of this persuasion. They were caring people and they prayed each morning and I was requested to join in as well. I don't believe in God and felt a bit awkward but I went along with it out of courtesy – you know, 'when in Rome' – praying with one hand. About one-fifth of the Sierra Leoneans are Christian and about seventy per cent are Muslim, the remaining ten per cent are a bit of an assortment.

"The Brothers had their own generator which they used very sparingly because diesel was hard to come by and expensive. They would cut up fruit and store it in a fridge and you could get it during the day. In that tropical heat, I will never forget the luxury of that iced fruit. I remember when Brother Noel took half a pig out of this freezer for the following day's dinner. He placed it on the dusty floor and chopped it into bits using a large, heavy axe – and that explained why I'd found splinters of bone in my meat at past meals!

"They had an excellent cook and she'd prepare meals of pork,

The Christian Brothers' house where Owen stayed for a month (1993)

chicken and rice. Rice was their staple carbohydrate, the equivalent of our potatoes. This cook was also the cleaner and she was paid fifteen pounds a month, which was a great deal of money out there.

"My room was simple, but the view was very pleasant. Freetown is situated in a lowland part of the country and there is bush and farmland all around – the mountains are to the east, rising to over six thousand feet. I had a bed – though, regrettably, no mosquito netting – wardrobe, cupboard, fan and candle. I remember a print of a detail from Michelangelo's fresco in the Sistine Chapel, *The Creation of Adam*, where God extends a finger to Adam and Adam extends his hand too, but they don't touch, that hung on the wall. It seemed to me that print might have some deep meaning out there.

"The poverty was appalling, absolutely appalling. There were beggars everywhere. The stench of human excrement from the open sewers was awful and, with the heat and rampant disease, the whole thing was unbelievable. I was told after I landed that the life expectancy for men was only forty-two years.

"Paul, who was a 1st kyu at the time, was training in a club that had been set up, I believe, by a Midlands engineer, who was a Shotokan black-belt and this chap was happy for me to teach there. The *dojo* was located below the seating in a robbed out sports centre built by the Chinese. All the piping, fittings, glass and parquet flooring had been ripped out and only the walls remained. I suppose the *dojo* had about twenty-five students.

The slums of Freetown

"I made it clear from the outset that training was to be conducted at certain times and people couldn't just wander in and out when they felt like it. This was the difference between what they called out there, white man's time and black man's time. Their concept of time was

The slums of Freetown

different from Westerners and it was a case of 'If I don't feel like doing it today, then I'll do it tomorrow.' I held a class most mornings at 9.00 a.m. I generally taught basics, with some *ippon-kumite*. I couldn't teach at every lesson because I became ill."

Murray took about one hour and ten minutes video footage of his trip of which some seven minutes and thirty-eight seconds is of a karate class. The footage shows the students, who seem genuinely interested and spirited, performing basics, being taught by Murray. Most of the students are wearing *gis* and there are a number of different colour belts on show. Most of these *gis* were apparently handmade, but Murray believed a few were probably picked up at the local market where clothes given free in Europe, were being sold.

The basics shown include *choku-zuki, oi-zuki, sanbon-zuki, mae-geri, yoko-geri-keage, yoko-geri-kekomi* and the combinations *ude-uki/gyaku-zuki/gedan-barai, uchi-uke/kizami-zuki/gedan-bari, shuto-uke/mae-geri/nukite,* and *kizamai-zuki/mawashi-geri/gyaku-zuki/gedan-barai*. Spectators are outside the *dojo* in the open air looking in through the empty window frames, some carrying loads on their heads. There is nothing quiet or peaceful about the session as the sounds from inside and outside echo around the stripped-out gym. Nevertheless, Murray is able to conduct his lesson with dignity and with the obvious effort of his pupils.

Paul Jenkins in a borrowed cassock

Another section of this video shows Murray performing the *kata Hangetsu,* on rock, overlooking Freetown.

Murray continued: "The heat was a real killer and because there was no regular electricity the fans didn't work most of the time, so there was no cold air circulating. However, we had electricity for three

Owen with his karate class below the stadium seating

or four hours a week and this was, I was told, because some Lebanese who lived in the immediate area, paid bribes. I over-trained, under ate and had a bad dose of diarrhoea, which I didn't recover from until I got back home. I lost a stone and a half in body weight. I felt ill. Most people had worms and these parasites would not only come out of your anus, but your mouth too. I couldn't eat the food and what I did eat went straight through me. I found a baker and a shop that sold Dairylea cheese. I was in heaven after I found them. I remember buying some Danish Blue and Edam cheeses and paying five pounds and fifty pence, which was equivalent to more than two weeks pay for a teacher and that knowledge made it difficult for me to swallow my meal. Despite my condition, I ran every day, but I overdid it. I remember playing a game of tennis with Paul and a spectator collapsed and died of cerebral malaria. I met one British girl, a voluntary worker, who had turned native and drank the local water, which is unbelievable and I doubt she is still alive. I remember we pulled some bugs, using a hair grip, which had embedded themselves into this girl's skin. The bugs were everywhere and I got bitten many times, especially by mosquitoes, which, of course, can be deadly in the tropics.

"The corruption was beyond belief. We had to pay 'dash', backhanders, all the time. I even had to pay dash to get on the plane to get back home. If we walked about, you could just feel the hate of some

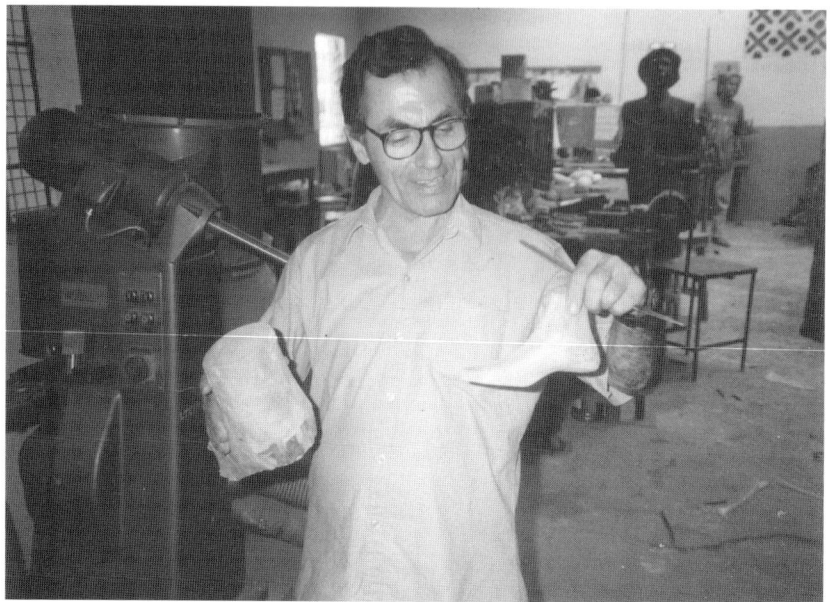

Sneider showing a chunk of wood in his right hand that would be worked into a false foot (in his left hand).

of the local people. They'd throw fish heads at you and swear in Krio. They didn't want us there and the first time this happened I thought to myself, 'What have I got myself into?' I also had sixty pounds stolen – I think I know who took it – which was equivalent to half-a-year's pay for most of them.

"I was taken to meet a German limb maker in Freetown who was known as Brother Sneider, who had spent eighteen years out there. I was told that he was the only limb maker in Sierra Leone. He also made callipers for polio victims, of which there were many. The limbs were made from local wood, the rubber from German conveyor belts and from the soles of old sandals. The day I visited he was fitting limbs to lepers, which was a bit scary. I also went to a small unit that made and repaired wheelchairs and these were very robust and, believe me, they needed to be, given the state of the roads.

"I went to Freetown Cheshire Home, which catered for victims of polio. I watched a group of teenagers playing football on crutches and swinging their wasted legs at the ball quite effectively, actually. I was asked to give a talk about Remploy and they couldn't believe that a white man could be disabled, so I was quite a novelty. I also told them

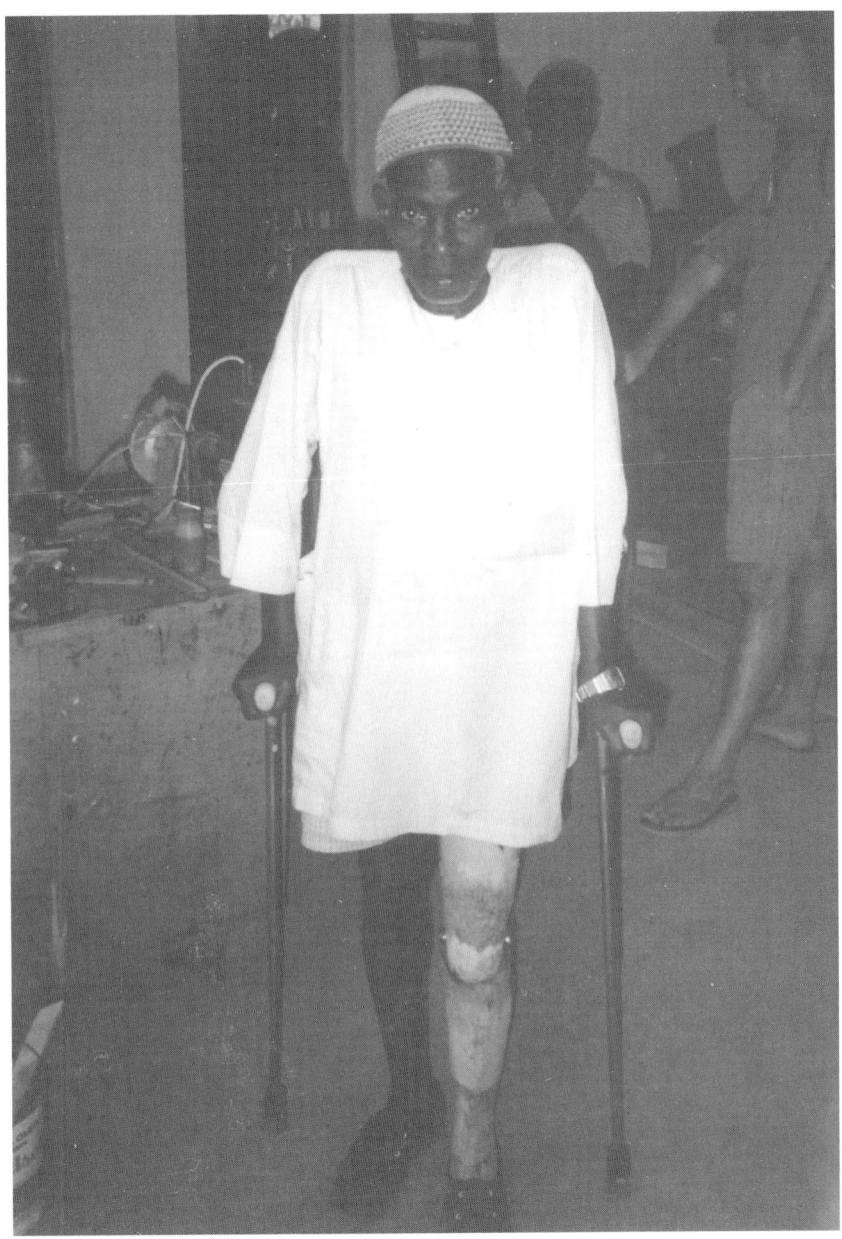
An amputee wearing one of Sneider's wooden legs

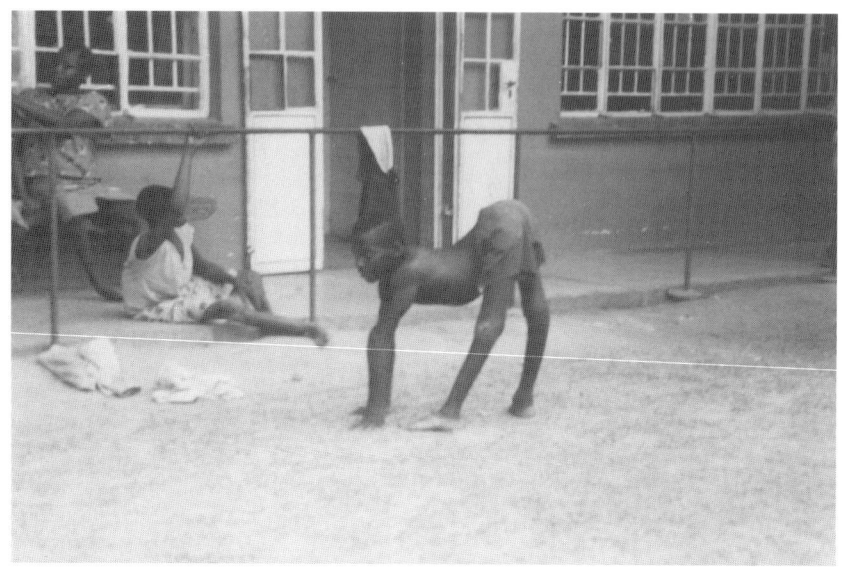

Disabled youth

Polio victim playing hand football

about karate and they were interested. The home was the only one of its kind in the capital and catered for forty-five patients – the remainder, of which there must have been many thousands, had to fend for themselves on the streets.

"I also visited the Sister Teresa Hospital. Anyone could go there, but they seemed to cater mainly for the dying. The first ward I came to was for children and that was pretty awful. I remember one child who looked about one year old I guess, but she could have been two or even three, was suffering from malnutrition. She was pitifully thin and had gone blind. I wanted to take a photograph to show people back in England the suffering, but the staff wouldn't allow it. Many of the people were blind from what they call 'river blindness'. It can take ten years for the blindness to become complete and people marry early so that their children can look after them when they go totally blind. You can see the children escorting blind adults around the city, begging. I saw a man being admitted with tuberculosis, and Aids was just appearing too. I read that one in ten infants don't reach their first birthday and was told that a quarter of all children die before the age of five. Sierra Leone has the highest maternal death rate in the world. One old chap I spoke to, a teacher who had actually been to England, remembered when Sierra Leone was a British Colony and he said that in his opinion most people wished the British were back, ruling, and, looking around me, I could see why. Sierra Leone was given its independence in 1961. As a result of colonisation, English is the official language out there, but Temme and Mende account for two-thirds of the native languages.

"Paul was responsible for seeing that money from various charities was spent on appropriate goods. One consignment he was waiting for when I was there was for twenty-four thousand bags of powered baby food that had been held up by red tape in Freetown docks. It had been there for weeks. This vital food was protected by armed guards but eight thousand bags still went missing and heaven knows how much more went astray being transported up country. The poverty, the greed, it was disgusting.

"We had a lovely little puppy in the house where I was staying and it got bitten by a rabid dog and was bleeding from everywhere. There was talk about paying someone ten pence to kill it, and I thought about doing it myself so as to do it properly. They stone rabid dogs out there for fear of the children being bitten.

"I remember the day when twenty people were killed in a motor accident. The buses were overcrowded and people just hung on. One

Owen and students in the stadium

bus was involved in a major crash with a lorry. Apart from the deaths, many people were injured and taken to the local hospital, which was a disgrace and I doubt if they coped well with the emergency.

"I was invited to Freetown University Sports Day and was accorded celebrity status. Photographs on the notice-board at the university showed a soldier beheading guerrillas and parading triumphantly with their heads. I was introduced to the captain who had done the beheading. Belief in witchcraft was strong out there and I remember this captain spoke about when he tried to shoot some witches and the bullets just bounced off them and when he beheaded them they made no noise. I just hoped they didn't think I was some kind of unholy resurrection of Bruce Lee!

"Talking of superstition, the Christian Brothers also helped with the mentally handicapped. Families who have such children are seen to be the recipients of bewitchment or a curse. The mentally handicapped are usually kept in the family compound and are rarely taken out for fear of public comment and ridicule. At the time, the Christian Brothers were trying to set up a school for these children, who were seldom educated. Even for normal children the secondary school enrolment rate was under twenty per cent, as parents preferred to have their offspring working, normally on the land or at market stalls.

"Going out into the countryside was a real eye-opener and, in retrospect, extremely dangerous. Only about five million people live in Sierra Leone, so it's sparsely populated and news travels fast. I'd often be taken out with the Brothers or accompanying VSO workers or nurses, normally to drop off milk for babies, medical supplies, sewing machines and other such useful tools. One such trip was to Mekeni, located in the Bombali District, in northern central Sierra Leone. This city had no electricity at all and we stayed with the Christian Brothers at St. Francis School. These people were Catholic missionaries. The trip was awful, as the dry and dusty road was full of large, deep potholes and the driver kept swerving from side to side. There were road checks every now and then and we usually had to pay a bribe to proceed. I was told that if these soldiers caught a guerrilla, man or boy, they would behead him on the spot and any family members accompanying him would have to clap or suffer the same fate.

"A young lad named Fatuna, who I had met in Mekeni, walked thirteen miles to the beach at Freetown and then another five miles to the stadium to see my karate class. In that heat that was real commitment. We fed him and he stayed the night and he told us his story. He was living with his sister after his mother and father were split up by the rebels. The family had been reasonably well-off, but the rebels had taken everything. When he was sixteen, he was forced to watch his friend beheaded. The following day I took Fatuna home. A swamp was nearby and this was used as a toilet. Unbelievably, water was collected from this swamp and used for washing and drinking!

"This was a deadly place for white men. Father Eno, at one mission we visited, said there had been shelling thirteen miles away and you could often hear gunfire. The hospital at the Catholic mission had treated soldiers and civilians alike. In this area priests had been killed and I was, effectively, told that if I was caught, I'd be killed. I spoke to one young man who told me a harrowing story. The guerrillas had come and everyone had fled. The soldiers arrived and found one schoolgirl in the bush, accused her of being a rebel and cut her head off. This young man had witnessed the whole affair from his hiding spot. He retrieved his classmate's head and kept it. He showed me the skull which he'd turned into a lamp. They said the guerrillas cut off both adults and children's limbs to instil fear and I didn't fancy having my other hand cut off thank you very much! I also heard that when the guerrillas were coming, so that the children were not mutilated, some parents drowned them.

"The south and east of the country – the east being where the diamond mines are – had been occupied by the Revolutionary United

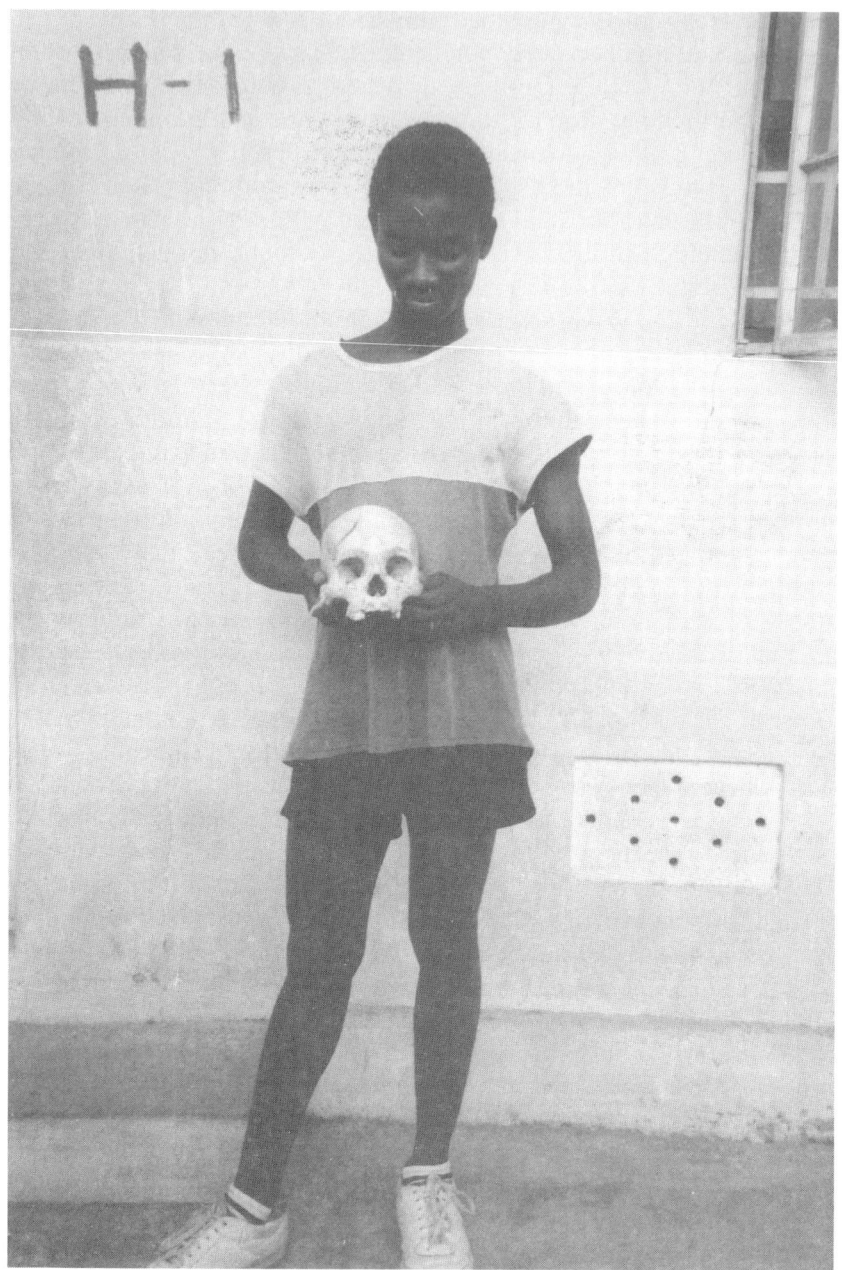

Young man with the skull of the girl he saw beheaded

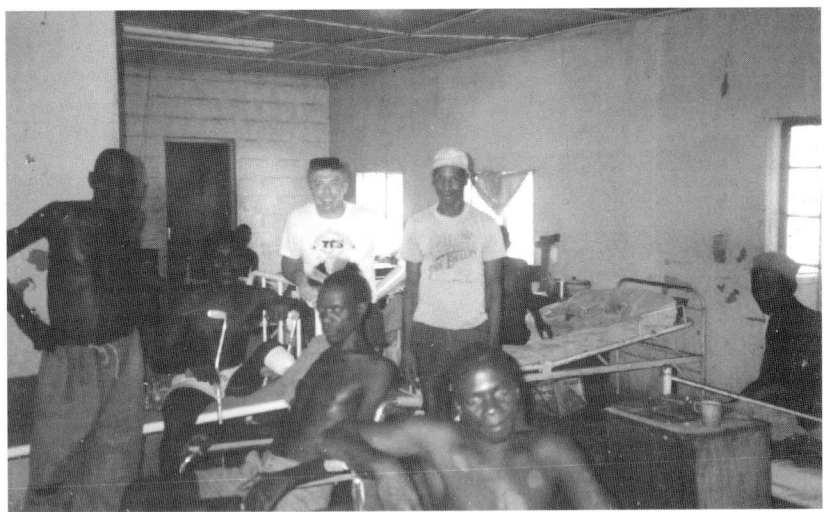

Owen at the leper's hospital

Front (RUF) and a Sierra Leone Junta named the National Provisional Ruling Party (NRPC), under Valentine Strasser, were battling them. I heard that Liberia, under Charles Taylor, was involved in some way, but politics is not my strong point.

"I was taken about twenty-five miles from Freetown up to Mesanga Hospital where I saw hundreds of lepers. I was assured the disease was not contagious after two weeks of treatment which these people had received – just as well after shaking hands with some of them, or what was left of their hands. I was told the smell was unbearable, but, luckily in this case, that is not a sense I possess. One chap I met was having his leg amputated the next day and was looking forward to it so that he didn't have to suffer the sores any longer. I also remember an albino leper, a woman, who I chatted to.

"We travelled back to Mekeni and stopped at a village en route where I could get some palm wine called porhue, or poryo, which, I was told, translated means, 'from God to man'. The liquid is tapped from the palm tree and is collected in kerosene-type cans and served in one litre jugs. I once stopped at a village and saw it being farmed. A cut is made near the top of a tree and a small pointed cane is placed at the base of the cut and a coconut-sized shell collects the 'wine' that is collected at night and then again in the morning. The porhue cost four pence a litre and the smell is, once again, appalling, so my lack of that sense saved me again, but I could have done with no sense of taste

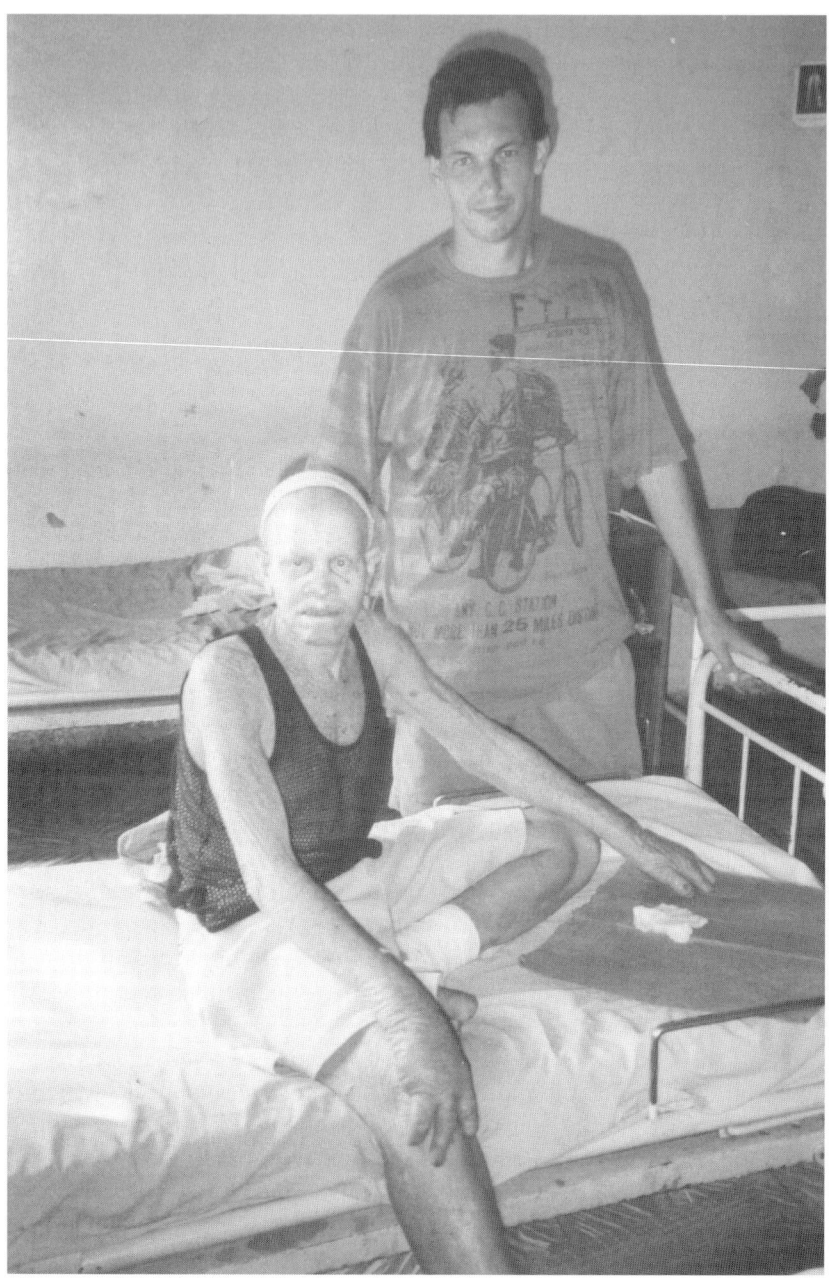

Paul Jenkins with albino leper

either, because I think they forgot to clean out the diesel from the container my porhue came from! The bar, if you can call it that, was in a tiny thatched building and cleanliness left a lot to be desired. God knows where their water came from. The outside kitchen was pots on hot stones with vultures wandering around right by it. I wonder what the Health and Safety boys would say about that! Because you couldn't drink the water, we'd often have 'jellies', which were immature coconuts which hold plenty of liquid. After the fluid is drunk, you can eat the young coconut inside, which the locals called 'jelly'.

"I would often see children with a large protrusion – sometimes as much as four inches, with a width of the same amount – where their belly buttons should have been. I was told that there were no midwives and what I was seeing was the result of an infection contracted at birth as a result of not cutting the umbilical cord cleanly.

"There wasn't much to do in the evenings after karate training other than drink and talk. It wasn't easy to go out and about because there were no lights. I remember once, on my birthday, some of the Brothers and I went into town and I met someone who offered me a bit of diamond smuggling and I must confess to having been daft enough to have been tempted.

"Despite the difficulty, I would, sometimes, walk two or three miles at night, alone, to the nearest bar and get a cold drink and a pickled egg. That was lovely, but I used to encounter fruit bats and they were massive and would suddenly just fly out of the trees. It was terrifying and it was always a toss up between risking the bats and having a cold beer.

"I also paid a visit to the British High Commission. It was like walking into an oasis in the middle of a desert. There was air conditioning and they gave me a toasted sandwich which, believe me, was luxury.

"Another trip I remember was to Bo, in Bo District, in southern central Sierra Leone, which was a five hour trip from Freetown, passing through Moyamba District. Bo is the second largest city in the country. We stopped half-way so that I could buy a pillow from a roadside stall, but we couldn't get the truck started again. The biggest dread of my life was to have no water, but, luckily after about twenty minutes we were off again – the battery had become disconnected. When we arrived, we were met by Brother Sennan, a former teacher from Birkenhead, who was recovering from cerebral malaria after two weeks in hospital. He must have had a truly strong constitution because neither the malaria nor the hospital killed him! His fellow Brother, John, was in hospital with severe dysentery and had suffered bouts of malaria. They said that dysentery is 'white man's grave' and as I was suffering from it too, I can quite believe them. The other main diseases out there were malaria, of course, but also yellow fever, cholera, lassa fever and meningitis – all killers.

"On another trip to Bo, I went to another Cheshire Home and met a lot of very friendly children with polio. I told them all about being disabled back in England and when I told them I did karate, well, I was their friend for life. They had watched cheap kung-fu/karate videos and so I was Mr. Cool.

"In Bo, I needed to see a doctor because I hadn't eaten for days and was becoming dehydrated. When I arrived, the doctor was about to lance a man's finger which was, I kid you not, twice as thick as a normal digit. The man seemed terrified. The doctor just left him sitting there and chatted to me about England, my job, and so on. After about thirty minutes he handed me some tablets, said goodbye and returned to his other patient who had moved noticeably towards the exit door. The tablets didn't do any good and I also took Dyrolite which helped a bit.

"I also went to Blama whilst Paul stayed in Bo. It was a totally black man's community and I was the odd white man. It was a bit unsettling to be truthful. I was supposed to have been picked up in the afternoon, but I eventually left in the pitch black at 9.30 p.m. It was so hot that I spent the entire day indoors, out of the sun. But back to Freetown and back to karate!

"After about two weeks I tried to get the students ready for their first grading, but they weren't up to it, not ready, so I offered them extra training on the beach for an hour in the afternoons, but only five people took up the offer. I had intended starting the grading at 4.00 p.m. sharp, but it eventually got under way at 4.30 p.m. It was a case of back to black man's time. Children from the Cheshire Home had come down by minibus to watch.

"Some students turned up late for the grading and I refused to grade them. The beginners' and 9th kyu standard was, I thought, very good, but those going for 8th kyu had a terrible attitude and I failed them all. Two people double-graded and one of these had a dwarf-like appearance. When he walked into the *dojo* initially, he was heckled. He appeared to be suffering from severe rickets. His spirit was tremendous and in stark contrast to the 'not really bothered' and laid-back athletic types, who I failed. When this chap left the *dojo,* he was

Training on the beach

clapped. In that grading he not only had overcome his disability, but also gained the respect and admiration of his fellow pupils. I graded Paul, who I called the Mad Monk, to *Shodan,* in a private grading, but he broke the toes of his right foot and hobbled home. He deserved the black belt and there was no one out there saying what I could and couldn't do.

"Two weeks later, I held another grading for those students who had failed at their first attempt and those who had missed out for various reasons. I passed seven and failed seven. I issued certificates for the examinations and they presented me with a certificate to show their gratitude. I also had to make a speech which wasn't easy for me.

"On the day of my departure back to England, some of my students arrived two hours early to see me off. Were they pleased to be seeing the back of me? No, I'm only joking, because we all got on really well. Thirty minutes out on the ferry and the captain asked me to buy him a drink. He was after my money and I had to buy him one. When I got to the airport, I wanted to buy a sandwich that cost five hundred leone – that's the currency, with one pound equalling about eight hundred leone when I was out there) – but was short by exactly the amount of money the captain's drink cost. So, I quenched the captain's thirst and

Owen, about to leave Freetown, with some of his students

Glad to be home

I had to remain hungry. Believe it or not, there was a power cut at the airport. I was glad to get out. It took seventeen-and-a-half hours of travelling to get back to Newcastle Airport at 8.30 a.m. the following day and guess what, my luggage had gone missing. I thought, with the diarrhoea and all, I'd not only left half of myself in Sierra Leone, but it appeared they were to have my belongings as well.

"When I got back home I think I was mildly depressed to be honest. I wouldn't go out in the evenings and I wouldn't spend any money, on the basis that I couldn't justify the expenditure after what I'd seen. I felt guilty if I had a beer and just thought what that money could do for an individual out in Sierra Leone. The press got to hear about my little adventure and I did get a write-up.[1] A lot of my mates thought I was crackers going out there.

"Given another chance, would I go back? Yes, I probably would, but I think I'd live to regret it."

VII

AN M.B.E AND THE DEATH OF A HERO

Murray continued: "I'd been working for Remploy for a long time and had done a lot of charity work, especially for disabled people in the area of sports. Money was raised in a variety of ways, such as the Great North Run which I've already mentioned. Some of the things I did were a bit crazy. For example, I took part in the Boxing Day dip and ran into the near freezing – or that's how it felt – North Sea dressed as an Emu. I did that dip more than once and each year there was a different dress code. Another event I was involved in was the bed push. We competed against men from HMS Arrow who had pushed a bed all the way from Portsmouth to Sunderland – that's nearly three hundred and fifty miles – and they asked teams to compete against one another at Roker, an up-market part of Sunderland. There were police, army, air cadets, *judoka*, rugby players and footballers all competing. I had no intention of being beaten by this opposition and the Sendai team won, to the great frustration of the judo club, who thought that they were going to whop us. I also took part in pulling a truck.

"Then there was the parachute jumping. I thought it was a good idea to raise money and I cajoled my team mates into doing one jump from an airfield near Sunderland which did quite regular parachute jumps in those days for people with a strong constitution, shall we say. When we got to the airfield, they wouldn't allow me to do the jump because I couldn't release the cables and I couldn't work out how I could overcome the problem. So, I watched everyone else do it. As a joke, I dropped a metal plate behind one of my colleagues just before he was about to board the plane and I pretended that it had fallen out of his parachute.

"'What was that?' he said in a concerned tone, as he turned around.

"'It's nothing to worry about mate,' I replied, 'You don't really need that bit anyway.' The poor chap was terrified when he actually stepped into the plane because he thought he only had half his parachute.

The Remploy Assault Team with the army team behind

"Another lad refused to leave the plane, so they had to threaten him until he finally let go. One chap broke his ankle on landing and my brother-in-law, Jeff Wilkinson, was nearly blown on to the A19 on his descent. So, I was glad that I didn't do it. However, after a few months I realised that if I put a hook on my hand and crossed my arms I could pull the cables, so I returned to the airfield and said, 'Look, I can pull it now.'

"'Owen, you are fairly well known in Sunderland and we'd hate to think that anything might happen to you,' an ex-SAS lad said. 'So, we'll attach a larger parachute to you and we will let you have a go, but no publicity and no advertising.'

"I climbed into the plane with twelve other people who were going to jump at sixteen thousand feet and then I was going to jump at two thousand five hundred feet. I was terrified!

"'Are you ready Owen?' this ex-soldier asked me.

"'Yep,' I replied, in a pitch higher than I would have wished and took a step forward ready to jump. Just as I was about to leap, I was dragged back in, as we were too close to the A19. I just wanted to get the business over with to be honest with you, but I had no intention of backing out as people had sponsored me and it was a matter of personal pride. Eventually, I got the all clear and I went for it. I have to say that it was one of most exhilarating experiences of my life – fantastic, absolutely fantastic. I felt I had to take a witness with me because nobody would have believed that I'd done it and so Tommy Barrass, who was my charge-hand at work, acted in that role.

"My pals and I also did an assault course every year at Catterick military base, North Yorkshire.

"On another occasion, I raised money for a *karateka* at Blythe Karate Club, who had cancer. I did three thousand seven hundred and sixty sit ups in an hour outside a pub. The worst part about this was keeping my hands behind my head – my stomach muscles were fine. Funny though, the person who sat on my legs suffered cramp!

"I just liked to push myself as part of my training and, indeed, set myself virtually impossible targets. I thought that if I was doing this sort of thing anyway, why not get people to sponsor me for a good cause along the way? In January [2013] I'm going in for my second hip replacement and I've set myself the target of being able to walk up and down the Penshaw Monument twenty times at one attempt three to four weeks after the operation. I don't know whether that's possible, or whether it's even advisable, but that's my goal.

"But, sometimes, things backfired on me and I'll give you a couple of memorable examples. I went up to Lake Windermere in the Lake District with a couple of SAS reservists and some jujitsu lads. We were going to try out surfboarding. I had to kneel on the board and hold on to a rope which was attached to a boat. The boat started off, the slack was taken up, the board jolted forward and my false hand shot off. Into the water I went and when I popped up courtesy of my life-jacket the board came crashing down on my head and dazed me. That hand is

Owen climbing near Kielder Water

still somewhere at the bottom of the lake!

"Another time, on behalf of Remploy, a colleague and I took some disabled children away to Kielder Reservoir, Northumberland, which is the largest artificial reservoir in Britain, being over five-and-a-half miles long, two miles wide, and holding an incredible two hundred billion litres of water. It is a special place for people with disabilities to learn outdoor activities. We all decided to try our hand at canoeing,

AN M.B.E. AND THE DEATH OF A HERO

Owen and Brent McCafferty at Key West

but when we got there, I discovered that one of my karate pupils was the chief canoeing instructor and I knew he was dying to get me back for all the occasions I had given him a hard time in the *dojo*. So, we went into our canoes and he knew that I was terrified of water. I've since read in *Shotokan Dawn* that Vernon Bell was afraid of water too and that fear motivated him to study judo during the war which, later, led him to introduce karate to Great Britain. Bell overcame his fear, I, alas, had not.

"I honestly don't know where my fear comes from. I'm not a bad swimmer actually – and no, with only one hand I don't swim around in circles! I was in Spain and I was caught in an undercurrent and that

Owen (right) about to go diving in Key West with Barry Lawson, a Sendai black-belt.

put the fear of God into me because I realised that I had no control over the situation. Water is just too strong and it has no conscience, there is no compassion and it will simply drown you if you let it. I feel it is something that cannot really be beaten. That incident just made me more wary. Funny enough, I can dive in, no problem, but I don't like jumping in because I find the water gets up my nose and down my throat and I have to be careful even in a shower, otherwise I panic. When my children were growing up and wanted to play in a swimming pool, or in the sea, I used to go in with them, but I didn't like them splashing me. If I dived in a pool and was splashed when I surfaced, I used to get stressed immediately.

"I went to Key West, in Florida, with a mate of mine and we knew a diving instructor out there who was also ex-SAS. He showed us what to do and how to do it in a controlled environment, but going underwater with that mask on really put the wind up me. I did my best not to show my fear and we went out in a boat for some actual real-life practice. There were mothers and children there swimming about and I just had to try it otherwise I'd never have forgiven myself. I just wasn't going to bottle out. In I went, backwards, head over heels from the side of the boat and even the disorientation caused by that had me in a real state. I went down a little bit more by accident rather than design and then I grabbed on to the rope they had hanging from the boat. Someone said that if I came up too quickly they would hang on to my legs and the thought of that just spooked me and I didn't go back in. Anyway, my pal said he'd seen a shark so that was that. Let's get back to the canoeing!

"There we all were, people with all sorts of disabilities lined up in our canoes, together, like a raft. We had to jump out of one canoe and swim to the other side of the 'raft', climb back on to the canoes and walk along from canoe to canoe and sit back in our own craft again. Even though I wore a lifejacket I was still terrified, but I didn't dare show anyone else that I suffered from hydrophobia. After that incident I decided I wasn't going to let this phobia get the better of me and I decided to learn how to canoe. Three times a week I would sneak out of Remploy and go to the local swimming baths where I was taught. It then came time to take my certificate. I was taken on to the River Wear where I was made to do an Eskimo roll, which really scared me and then had to canoe down to the coast a couple of miles away. Under normal conditions that would have been okay I suppose, paddling downstream, but that day, of all days, the weather was horrendous with waves about a metre high. It was a nightmare for me and probably the most frightening experience of my life. My instructor, Fergus, and I eventually got to the marina and I thought to myself, 'Thank God for that!' Fergus on the other hand decided to go out again in waves that must have been six feet in height. Although I did pass my first certificate – so I am qualified to a certain level – I wouldn't do it again. Still, I consider it a good achievement to learn how to canoe with one hand. And just think, I wouldn't have done any of it if I hadn't been involved in charity work!

"One day, one of the directors of Remploy informed me that I was to be nominated for a civil award and wondered if I had any objection. He said that one other person had been nominated – a doctor who came in to check the well-being of the disabled employees. I told him I didn't know anything about civil awards and had never heard of an M.B.E., which was true.

"I didn't think too much about it, but some time later I got a phone call to say that I would be receiving an award and not to tell anyone. Then I received an official letter and a booklet that confirmed that I was to become a Member of the Most Excellent Order of the British Empire. I also read that the order was founded by King George V during the First World War and that it is an order of chivalry that is split into military and civil divisions. I never in my wildest dreams thought that one day I would be so honoured. I just couldn't keep it to myself and told a few very good friends who I knew I could trust and one of these was Jeff Barwick.

Barwick takes up the story: "I remember, once, after training with Enoeda at Sendai, we were all sitting around in the bar after practice, relaxing. I was in my fifties and felt generally worn out and told Enoeda this. He seemed to sympathise and told a story about a crafty mouse that none of the young cats could catch. An older cat just sat there and watched all these youngsters rushing around trying to catch this little rodent. Then, as the mouse ran past, the old cat pounced and killed it. What Enoeda was trying to explain, of course, was that as you get older you develop different abilities. Suddenly, Owen chipped in:

"'Are you calling Jeff an old moggy then *Sensei,*' he said, and everyone laughed. For a Christmas present that year, Owen gave me a tin of Kitty Kat cat food. Owen has a mischievous side to his character and this is an example of it.

"Well I wasn't going to let him get away with that, so I waited for my moment and it came when I heard he had been justly awarded an M.B.E. I wrote an 'official' letter on headed writing paper which I had posted down in London so that it had a London postmark. It was from a Mr. McKenzie, the Secretary of Ceremonial Investiture, saying that he had been trying to contact Owen. I made it all up. I wrote the letter in a very official style saying that representative from the department would be calling at Owen's home at a specific time for a personal fitting of the investiture garment that he would be required to wear. I 'hired' a professional photographer, a chauffeur in a brand new top of the range Granada all dressed up smartly in shirt, tie and suit, and an actor in amateur theatricals who would play Mr. Farquarharson, the 'official'. These were all friends of mine who agreed to be part of it. Shortly after Owen received the letter, I got the photographer to ring him up and say that he was from the Northern Area Publicity Office and that he'd like to come along, take photographs and generally cover the event because it was newsworthy and Owen agreed.

"I'd chosen the costume from a fancy dress hire shop and it was ridiculous – an ankle length red cape that looked as though it was made from old velvet curtains. The cape had a lighter red silk lining. Over the left breast was what looked like a large heraldic badge. The cape was done up at the neck by a gold cord and there were gold epaulettes. A black hat was also included which tilted to the left and which had red, white and blue attachments.

Owen posing in his 'investiture clothes' (1994)

"Anyway, the day arrived and Mr. Faquarharson duly arrived with the chauffeur, who carried a box, with the costume inside, into Owen's house. Once Owen had seen the costume he expressed his opinion that it might be a wind-up, but a solemn Faquarharson assured him otherwise. Owen was requested to go upstairs and put a shirt and tie on and then when he came downstairs he put the costume on and photographs were taken. The party left with Mr. Farquarharson telling Owen that he would see him at the Palace, and they drove up the road where I was waiting. I slipped into the costume and persuaded the photographer to come back with me, though he wasn't keen as he thought Owen might react badly.

"I opened the door [to Murray's house] with a view to surprise Owen, but he was on the telephone talking to someone about the party that had just left. It was a classic moment; the timing was absolutely perfect. I crept in and was standing behind him.

"'It might be Barwick winding me up,' Owen said to the person on the end of the line.

"'Yes it is – and wasn't it a good 'un!' I replied.

"When Owen spun around and saw me in the investiture costume

Owen, still on the telephone, after discovering he'd been set up (1994)

he'd just taken off, his face was a picture, an absolute picture and the photographer snapped away at a safe distance. Owen was, for the first time since I have known him, speechless. It was so funny. I could even hear the person on the end of the telephone line laughing. I won't repeat what Owen came out with once he'd regained his faculties. But as I left the house I could hear the sweet words:

"'Barwick! You bastard! I'll get you back for this.'

"I must be honest and say that I watched my back for the next few months because I thought he'd try and get back at me. I went into hospital for a hip operation shortly after the prank and was about to be taken down to theatre. Then, just as I was about to go, a matron I hadn't seen before came up to me and informed me that my operation had been cancelled.

"'All right Owen, you can come out now,' I said loudly. The matron looked at me as if I was mad, because it turned out that she was genuine and the surgeon had been taken ill and had needed to go home."

Murray continued: "I could take three guests with me to Buckingham Palace to watch my investiture and I chose Joan, our daughter Donna and Joan's mother. I decided not to take my father and chose the three people I felt closest to. Remploy paid for first-class train tickets and a first-rate hotel for the four of us for two nights. They did us proud.

"I have said before that I am essentially a very shy person and when something of this magnitude presents itself I can become extremely apprehensive. Well, going down to the Palace and being presented to the Queen falls into that anxiety provoking category! I was seriously worried, just as I was when I had to give a speech at my wedding twenty years before. All the old feelings of dread re-appeared as though all the experience I'd accrued in those two decades accounted for nothing. On the journey down, all I could think about was what I was going to say to the Queen and whether I should crack a joke. Oh, it was a nightmare and that journey went on forever.

"We checked into our hotel and the big day arrived. I was just a bag of nerves. I got into my suit and popped on the top hat, both of which I'd hired. At the Palace, my guests were shepherded off in one direction and the recipients of awards in another. I found myself in this room with a lot of people in Armed Services uniforms. I thought to myself, 'What the hell am I doing here?' Everyone seemed to know each other and I just stood there like a lemon. I really felt an outsider and all I could think about was tripping over my shoe laces and making a complete fool of myself. I was well and truly out of my comfort zone. I was way out of my depth. I felt totally inadequate.

"The recipients were placed in a line of presentation and this line moved forward at a snail's pace from room to room, each room closer to the Queen. We were given instructions as to what to do, but it went in one ear and out the other. I just couldn't retain any information at all. My legs were like jelly. I remember that in the line up, two behind me, was a tall, distinguished looking Sikh with an impressive white beard and white turban. I could fight the best *karateka* that both Europe and Japan could throw at me, but in a situation like this I was next to useless.

"The presentation was, as you might imagine, held in a large, grand room with cream-coloured walls and a red carpet. I had to walk a short distance, turn to my left, bow and take two or three steps forward to the Queen. My name was called out followed by, 'Services to the disabled.' I walked forward, turned and bowed – the bow was the easy bit because I did that each and every day in the *dojo* – and took three steps to Her Majesty, who was wearing a light blue dress. She pinned the medal on to my left breast and then, to my amazement, started to speak to me about Remploy. I could answer her, but the rest is a blur. We then shook hands and at the correct moment she pushed my hand

From left to right: the Dragon, Joan, Owen and Donna, outside Buckingham Palace (1994).

towards me as if to say, 'That's it. Your time's up.' I took three steps backwards, bowed again, turned to my right and walked off.

"After the presentation I met up with my little group and we went outside. Remploy had sent a photographer and he took some pictures. We then went back to the hotel, got changed, saw a musical and had a meal and a good drink. The following day we wandered around Chinatown before returning home.

"When I got back to Sunderland, not many of my mates said anything because they didn't really understand what an M.B.E. was. People from the North-East are not, generally, easily impressed and they are prone to take the Mickey so they don't feel inferior and you don't get big-headed. A millionaire friend who was in the same class as me at school, told me he really wanted a civil award but that he couldn't buy one like he could most things. I suppose that made me feel quite good, but I found that M.B.E. could stand for a good number of three-word insults, but I liked 'Massive Bell End' the most and was happy with that because I thought, 'Now that's real status for you!'

"I used to tend to feel guilty about drinking alcohol and when I felt this way I'd usually go for a run of five, six or even ten miles dressed in normal clothes. I'd just get up and go in my shirt, tie, suit and black shoes. On one occasion, shortly after I was awarded the M.B.E, the

AN M.B.E. AND THE DEATH OF A HERO

Owen with an award presented to him by Remploy

director of Remploy came up from London to present me with a medal and certificate and I was taken out for a meal at the Seaburn Hotel, which is now the four-star Sunderland Marriott Hotel. I was allowed three guests and I took Joan, the Dragon, and Brent McCafferty, who was my best friend at the time and still is to this day and whose birthday it was. Everything was kept right, tight and correct. We shared a bottle of wine and I had a couple of pints. The director seemed quite pleased with the way things had gone and when he left we continued to drink and chat for the remainder of the day. Then we received a phone call from a friend of ours, Richie Kaigg, to say his wife had just had a son. So we all went up, took a photograph of Richie's son with my M.B.E on his chest and then went on to a nightclub, Annabell's, and continued socialising. Brent went home at about 9.00 p.m. and I continued until 1.00 a.m. when somebody asked me if I was still running.

"'Yep, no problem,' I said and got it in my mind then and there to run. So, dressed up in my smart business attire – though I took my jacket off – I ran all of the way from Annabell's up to the Penshaw Monument then around to Herrington Burn, on to Shiney Row and back to Joan's, where I collapsed. I didn't realise until the next day that I'd left my suit jacket, the M.B.E and one hundred and twenty pounds at Annabell's. Luckily, a friend owned the club and I had them returned the following day.

"On another occasion, I went to watch greyhound racing and had one too many drinks.

"'I bet you can't run now!' one of the lads said.

"'Oh yes I can!' I replied. Let's run together and see who packs up first.'

"So we ran from the dogs to the bowling alley at Seaburn, which is a few miles away, but he packed it in. I continued running and passed a nightclub, Finos, and popped in for a quick pint before continuing my run up Durham Road and back to Joan's again.

"I suppose, when I think about it now, I ran for a number of reasons. I found it necessary to get things out of my system, wear myself out so I didn't have to address them. I remember being at a European championship, disappointed, again as a spectator, so I went up into the mountains in the snow. I stripped off and ran, just ran. I don't really know why I stripped off to be honest – maybe it was the sense of freedom. I was in a world of my own and forgot how far I had run and streaked past a restaurant as naked as the day I was born! Imagine sitting having a quiet meal and seeing this nutcase with one arm, starkers, running past. But I had energy and I needed to release it. On another occasion I remember stripping down to my underpants because I didn't have any shorts and running up a mountain in Tenerife. I got to the top, in the scorching heat, and ran down again. I remember

AN M.B.E. AND THE DEATH OF A HERO

my young daughter pointing and saying, 'That's my daddy.'

"When I was awarded the M.B.E., I was mentioned in *The Times*[1] newspaper and in the local *Echo*[2, 3] where I was given write-ups and shown in photographs. I gave my medal to my father for a few weeks and I think he took it about and showed it to people. I've got the diploma hanging up at home, dated 11th June 1994, but I gave the gong to my son. Now let us move from being presented to the highest in the land to encounters with some of the very lowest.

"Working on the doors and being in-charge of security for twenty years meant that I'd met some pretty unsavoury characters to say the least – real scum with no redeeming features. The most dangerous problems I faced came from drug dealers. I wouldn't allow drugs into night clubs. I took a stand on drugs because I'd seen what it did to young people – stealing, prostitution and the like – and I didn't like it. I became well-known in the city for the stance that I took and, needless to say, the dealers weren't too happy having me around and I made some very formidable enemies.

"There was one pub where things came to a head and got really nasty. A couple of drug dealers tried it on and a fight ensued which they didn't win. About thirty minutes later somebody came down to the pub with a machete looking for the person who beat the drug dealers up. When this chap realised it was me, he put the machete away.

"'Well, what's the problem Owen?' he asked.

"'I am not allowing drugs in my pub,' I replied. That happened on the Sunday.

On the Monday I received a phone call from the dealers to ask me to go and sort this business out. I said okay. I then received information from someone else to say that, instead of meeting the dealers face to face, a gang from out-of-town had turned up packing guns and they were talking about shooting me. So, I didn't go.

"Members of this gang then came around to my place of employment and asked to see me, but someone said I wasn't there. Something else happened and the police were informed and I had an escort back to my house. Even a helicopter was involved. There were police in the car behind me and police in the car in front of me. Certain things were said. They took me home and checked the house and grounds. A direct alarm to the police was fitted and I was given advice. Once home I felt safer because I too had guns, kept legally. I had several shotguns, a .22 rifle with a telescopic sight and a 9 mm hand gun. I was a member of the Mayfair Shooting Club, in Sunderland.

Now, if the gang wanted to come calling and all else failed, I suppose you could say I was in a position to defend myself. However, I had to take other precautions too, such as making sure Joan and our offspring were prepared and safe.

"A great pal of mine, Ronnie Bestford, came to live with me during this difficult period. Ronnie first lived with me around 1982-3 after falling out with his girlfriend. I had a spare room, so he moved in for a few months, having various relationships and break-ups during this time. He would inevitably move in and out over the years and I was always happy to see him. In 1990 Ronnie worked as a pub manager for the same group for which I acted as security manager. One night, I had a phone call while working at a pub in Middlesbrough to say that Ronnie had been very seriously injured in a pub fight. I drove the forty miles or so to the hospital to find him with a head swollen like a balloon – he had an astonishing seventeen skull fractures, which resulted in bone grafts, plates and pins. These injuries were due to an incident at a bachelor party for members of a certain sporting club. Ronnie was a national judo champion in the mid 1980s and a Northern Area open champion as well and I was told that it took six or seven of these guys to get him down. He received a large payout for injuries received, I believe. After the incident Ronnie moved back in with his mother to recover.

"At the time of my trouble with the drug dealers, Ronnie would sit outside my karate *dojo* to keep an eye out when I was teaching. Ronnie is one of the hardest men I have ever met. Let me tell you a story. It might sound a bit strange, but I cannot go into specifics.

"One day, Ronnie asked me to punch him.

"'Great – that's something I've always wanted to do,' I thought. No, seriously, I didn't want to hurt him but he insisted that I hit him. He just stood there, waiting, and I lined up a good *gyaku-zuki* to his head. I struck him with force just above his left eye but he hardly moved and stood firm. I, on the other hand, broke my hand!

"'Kick me then,' he said. So I kicked him a good *mawashi-geri* to no effect. Three good kicks later he was still upright and none the worse for wear.

"'Do you want a whisky?' he smiled. What chance would anyone have in a street fight against him, that's what I would like to know?

"It was around this time that I visited the dentist on the way to the Mayfair Club. I sat in the chair in his surgery and he asked me if I was comfortable. I said that I wasn't because I had something poking into my back. I sat up and took my handgun out and put it on the table. The

AN M.B.E. AND THE DEATH OF A HERO

Left to right: Ray Stubbs, Ronnie Bestford (a British judo champion, who lived with Owen for over fifteen years) and Gary Gardin.

gun wasn't loaded – now, as if I'd carry a loaded gun around with me. I kept the ammunition at the gun club of course. The incident scared the living daylights out of the dentist and, some seventeen years on, he happened to mention it the last time I went for a check-up. All such guns had to be surrendered later, under the law.

"So, certain people carrying guns wanted to talk to me. This was for real, there was big money at stake; it was not some gangster film in production that I could just walk off the set and retire to my cosy trailer. These boys didn't mess about. I can name a few people I had the misfortune to know from this time who went down for murder and manslaughter. I also knew some of the key criminal people in Sunderland, Newcastle and Middlesbrough who profited from peddling drugs and protection rackets. One of these guys was shot and killed, another was stabbed and killed. I was on the fringe and glad to stay that way.

"I had no intention of backing down on the drugs issue though, I couldn't afford to and so I continued working in security for another six months just to show these people that I wasn't intimidated or scared of them. I cannot go into details, but the matter was quickly resolved when I finally met up with a certain drug gang leader – and broke my hand once again.

"Not long after receiving my M.B.E, I asked to be considered for redundancy from Remploy, who were centralizing the business. They didn't want to let me go and even offered me a one-year sabbatical to work with disabled people abroad, and I was tempted, but I had decided that I wanted to move on with my life because I was getting bored at work. At the same time, I decided to quit working on the doors because I'd had enough of that too. I was in my mid forties and it was simply time for a major life change.

"I got my redundancy money and went into business with an old school friend and bought a fish and chip shop in Southwick, Sunderland, which also sold pizzas and kebabs. I was advised by my solicitor not to pursue the venture and I really wish I'd listened to him, for the project turned into a nightmare and I lost a lot of money. I worked it out that, including the loss of earnings I could have had from Remploy, I lost some eighty thousand pounds over three years. It was horrendous. I was up at 6.00 a.m. each morning to get to the wholesalers and went to bed at 1.00 a.m. in the morning. I worked seven days a week. I lost weight and the pressure was enormous, mainly because we'd taken out a twenty year lease. The problem is that this sort of pressure is insidious.

"One day I had severe pains in my abdomen and chest and it was thought that I may have had a heart attack. I was taken to Accident and Emergency. The pain was terrible, but it wasn't a heart attack, it was simply acute gripes brought on, I believe, by all the stress, and once I was relieved of that, I felt okay.

"I needed a break badly and I went to Thailand with my girlfriend at the time. I'd been to Thailand before with about seven lads and had a fantastic time. I tried a hookah pipe in Pattaya, on the East coast of the Gulf of Thailand and thought it was just smoke and air. Big mistake! God knows what was in it, but it wasn't plain tobacco and I fancy something quite toxic. I was told afterwards that I'd lifted a policeman up and walked away with him! Luckily, he took it in the spirit in which it was presumably intended.

"Anyway, on this second visit we stayed on the Phi Phi Islands that were to be devastated by the 2004 tsunami, and on the boat back to the mainland, whilst sitting in the bar, I decided to close the shop down and try and sub-let it if I could.

"When I got back home and put the business on the market, a chap came along who seemed genuinely interested in taking the shop on and so I suggested that he work in the establishment for three days to see how he felt about it. I got him working with the customers and I was out the back preparing food and, unbeknown to him, on the phone to everyone I knew asking them to come around to get a free meal. The deal was that they would pay for their take-away and I would pay them back later. The idea was to give the impression that the shop was very busy. Anyway, three 'normal' customers were in the shop and three of my friends walked in. Looking up on the CCTV, I saw that a row had broken out between the two groups and before I could get out to quieten things down, a knife had been pulled by one of the 'normal' customers.

"'Oh that's great,' I thought to myself, 'now the chap's never going to buy the shop.'

"Both groups went out of the shop and carried on their argument in the street. In the meantime, I slipped out the back door with the intention of confronting the man who had pulled the knife and, in the process, almost certainly ruined my business deal.

"I met them in a side street walking towards me. They were walking ahead of my group of friends and they were still arguing and swapping insults.

"I walked straight up to the knife-puller and stood in his path.

"'What the hell do you think you are doing pulling a knife in my shop,' I said in a raised voice. I was fuming. Before he could pull the knife on me, I slapped him around the head with an open hand, spun him around and put a choke-hold on him. That put him to sleep in about eight seconds. When his mates saw how efficiently I'd dealt with their leader, they just stood there and did nothing. It took about forty-five seconds for this knife-puller to come around and when he did, I told him in a way that he couldn't possibly have misunderstand that I never wanted to see him in my shop again. He got the message all right, but it was too late and my prospective buyer didn't proceed further.

"I was sick of dealing with this scum. I'd had twenty years of it on the doors and had tried to get away from it, but it just seemed to follow me around. We even had a group come into the shop demanding protection money. One hard case came in with his mates and said he liked this and that he'd liked that but he didn't like the idea of paying for things. I made sure he paid. That thug later went down for murder I believe.

"I was walking home with Joan one evening and was passing an Indian take-away that I used to frequent. I knew the owner and he was a nice man. As we passed by I heard commotion and five or six thugs were beating him up. I charged in and dragged them off one by one and they scarpered except the ring leader and he was ready to take me on. Now, what happened next is a lesson for all *karateka* who do non-contact *kumite*. As he came at me, I kicked with a *mae-geri* but, through conditioning, controlled it. I could have floored him but instead he looked at me as if I was mad. I'd missed my chance, maybe my only chance, and then it just turned into a brawl. I hit his head against a concrete door pillar and knocked him out. So I lived to fight another day. Unfortunately, that was not the only time I messed up in that way.

"I was in a pub that had a Country and Western band playing. They were good and I was enjoying it, as were many others. Then a foul-mouthed group started heckling them and I told them to be quiet, to back off. They chose to take the dispute outside and I obliged. One of these chaps was a boxer and I struck him with a *chudan gyaku-zuki* but again, competition had taught me to control it, which I did. Within a fraction of a second I saw a right hook come my way which just glanced my head. If that had hit me square on I'd have been out like a light. Then I hit him with the steel end of my false arm and that was that. Experiences such as these have taught me to be entirely pragmatic in my training, to get real, because a lot of modern karate is make-believe.

"I'll give you another example where a kick failed me. I was in a pub with a good friend of mine, Jeff Westgarth, who is currently a 7th Dan in Dave Hazard's Association, and a fight kicked off. Chairs were being thrown all over the place. When the general melée stopped, Jeff and I checked on each other. He was okay, but my thumb was pouring blood from a pint glass that had been intended to be smashed over my head but I'd put my hand up to protect myself. A fight was still going on in a corner and we climbed some stairs to get away, but a chap came charging up at us. When he was about three steps below me I went to make a *mae-geri,* but my foot landed on his shoulder, so I ended up straddled as he grabbed hold of it. Luckily, a boxing friend of mine came up and knocked him out. I have been rescued by a boxer after I've tried a kick more than once. That night Joan and Jeff Westgarth went clubbing, while I went to hospital to get eight stitches in my thumb. But now on to something sad.

"In early 1995 [on the 21st February], news came through that Steve Cattle had died very suddenly, aboard a train, whilst returning from the Continent where he'd been training. Apparently, he'd suffered some kind of fit, which, I now understand, was brought about as a consequence of a very serious infection he'd picked up in Africa.

I was devastated; I just couldn't believe it. He was only forty-seven, an exceptional *karateka* [6th Dan] and a motivational and highly knowledgeable teacher. He never took himself too seriously and had a good sense of humour. He would talk for hours about all aspects of training – his enthusiasm seemed limitless. He didn't want a flash car or other material things, he just wanted to train and learn. I remember when we were travelling to Norway or Sweden – Malmo, I think, with Ted Hedlund – and Steve was terrified of flying, absolutely petrified, a real phobia – strange really, because he was one of the hardest men I've known, and that's why I expect he was travelling by train the day he died, alone in a carriage. Anyway, we were aboard the plane in April, 1982, waiting to take off and he was getting really uptight.

"'We're at war,' he said, suddenly and out of the blue.

"I thought that was a bit of an odd thing to say. Perhaps he'd had too much Dutch courage? Then he handed me the newspaper – we were at war with Argentina over the Falklands and that's why I remember the date!

"Steve went down well in Scandinavia and was well respected. He used to organise trips and I remember one, amongst others, when Fred Fawcett and I went with him. Fred and I stuck together. I recall certain people 'borrowed' everything they could lay their hands on, including spirits from the ship which they used as currency for petrol around Norway and Sweden. There was a chef and a butcher amongst us and they planned to steal a sheep; the butcher was going to cut it up and the chef was going to cook it. When we got to Sweden there were no sheep to be found in the fields, but they overcame this by stealing a half frozen sheep from a shop. Steve had told us about the use of mixed showers at a certain location and we were up for that, but just our luck, for the week before our arrival the Swedes had built a new shower block, so men and women were segregated.

"When competing against a Swedish team, Fred took a *mawashi-geri* to the head and he went down like a lead weight. When he didn't get up, I knew it was serious. His cheek bone was smashed, so we had to leave him in Sweden and continued to Oslo. When we got there, we found it was like Cowboy City. People were walking around wearing jeans and cowboy boots and there were fights galore. It was ridiculous. Anywhere where food was to be found, hamburgers especially, there were fights and they were far worse than anything I'd seen in Sunderland. We left there and went back to Sweden where we met up with Fred again who had been staying at Ted Hedlund's house. Fred looked okay but all of his face was swollen and the doctors had operated on his skull and pulled everything up and pinned it together. That wasn't a very good time for my pal.

"I wasn't able to attend Steve's funeral, down in York, for serious personal reasons, but I did travel to Luxembourg the following year when Kase ran a special course in Steve's memory. That was a fabulous course and the last time I saw Sandie Hopkins. Kase always impressed me and he taught over the two-day course, speaking in Japanese. He had a Frenchman present who would translate what he said into English. The particular point I remember about Kase's teaching on that occasion was that he said that *hikite* wasn't necessary. Now *hikite* refers to the opposite arm and fist that are pulled back when punching with the other fist. I listened to this intently, because, of course, I only have one fist. He used the *kata Sochin* to explain his theory.

"*Hikite* has become such an essential part of modern Shotokan that it may seem difficult to think of a time when its role was not as obvious. I'm not saying that *hikite* was not seen as very important in the past, because that is simply not true, but training has changed. Maybe the original idea of *hikite* came from grasping and opponent and pulling him towards you as you struck with the other hand or fist. In the Pre-WWII *shuto-uke*, for example, the hand that, today, comes back to act as an opposite to the blocking hand was used to augment the blocking hand and followed a similar trajectory. There are many such moves in the Shotokan *kata* set of *morote*-type techniques, both when the arms are touching, such as *morote-uke* in *Heian Sandan*, or when they are not, such as in *sokumen-awase-uke*, in *Tekki Nidan*. Just take *Heian Nidan*, with its opening block – and, remember, that was originally the first of the *Heian* to be taught before Funakoshi changed it.

"Then there are other blocks such as *juji-uke*, *kakiwake-uke* and *teisho-awase-uke* all requiring two hands to perform and therefore no *hikite*. These three blocks appear in *kata* as well. We also have the *sukui*-type blocks.

"*Gyaku-zuki* and *oi-zuki* are, by far, the most frequently practised punches and both require the use of *hikite* in *kihon*. The twisting of the wrists is important, but I cannot 'equate out' in the usual manner because I only have one wrist. With double punches such as *awase-zuki*, *yama-zuki*, *hasami-zuki* and *heiko-zuki*, *hikite* is impossible and, therefore, not required. *Kata* are a store of information passed down through the generations and all these double punches appear in the Shotokan *kata* set, with the exception of *heiko-zuki*, yet they are not

AN M.B.E. AND THE DEATH OF A HERO

widely practised today outside of the *kata* in my experience and that's a great shame. Anyway, back to Luxembourg.

"Three others went over with me in a van I had 'borrowed' from work. We caught the ferry over from Dover. It was only afterwards I realised that the van wasn't insured outside Britain. We had to rough it, sleep in the vehicle, but the worst thing for me was not being able to get my *gi* dry before training the next day. The day we returned home the weather was really atrocious. We brought some tobacco back and were stopped by Customs who thought we might be drug smuggling, but when they noticed the karate suits hanging up in the back of the van they realised that we were genuine. We still had our tickets and we managed to get back to England without any further incidents. But the weather caused many accidents.

"I remember Tony, a pal of mine from Sunderland, though he was originally from Birmingham, was moving down to St. Ives, Cornwall, and had been quoted seven hundred pounds from the removal people, which was, I suppose, the going rate at that time. I said I'd do it for him for four hundred pounds if he'd donate the money to charity. He agreed and I borrowed a van from Remploy. When we got down there, I decided to look-out the local karate club and decided to train. I was invited to teach the class and have been going down there twice a year since then, by the instructor Steve Matteson, a 4th Dan. Steve was an artist but now works maintaining a campsite. He's a really nice chap and trains hard. He used to call me *sensei* both in and out of the *dojo*.

"'You don't have to call me *sensei* outside the *dojo* – just call me Owen,' I told him. It wasn't his fault, because some instructors like to be called *sensei* outside the *dojo*. Personally, I think that's an ego trip and I'm not into that at all.

"I recall hearing about a printing machine that was for sale in St. Ives and I said to my manager that I thought I'd better go and have a look at it because Remploy could do with one – I also thought I'd have a few days off by the sea and get some training in. Well, I drove the four hundred and seventy miles down only to discover the machine was in St. Ives, Cambridgeshire, so I had drive all the way back to *that* St. Ives – three hundred fifty miles – where the company kept open specially until I got there. The machine wasn't what we were looking for and then I drove another two hundred miles back to Sunderland. That aborted break was over one thousand miles! I was the butt of quite a few jokes after that little mix-up.

"In [November] 1996, I was invited out to Australia to teach karate by my old pal, Allan Turner, who had moved out there in 1982. I flew

OWEN MURRAY, M.B.E., 6th DAN

Owen (back row, second from right) with members of the St. Ives *dojo*. To Owen's right is Steve Matteson; to Owen's left, Kim Nocol.

Owen teaching at the KUGB St. Ives *dojo*, Cornwall

AN M.B.E. AND THE DEATH OF A HERO

Carl Marriot, Owen, Don and Allan Turner

out to Manila, Philippines, and stayed for seven days with former Sendai member, David Charlton, who I've mentioned before. Out there he is famous and known as 'Mr. David'. As a celebrity hairdresser, he employs a large number of people and has salons all over the country. He is very wealthy. When I was with him, he was training for a triathlon and I went on a seven-mile run with him. Now I was a KUGB 4th Dan and very fit, but in that heat I was absolutely knackered after the distance. Heaven alone knows how anyone can run like that after swimming and cycling miles, competitively. I was mightily impressed with Mr. David's fitness level, I can tell you.

"I flew into Sydney and taught karate to members of the Karate Union of Australia, which has Carl Marriot as its Chief Instructor. Marriot reminded me a lot of Andy Sherry in build, technique, dedication and enthusiasm. I stayed two weeks teaching there."

Turner recalled: "The KUA members were impressed with Owen's pragmatic approach to karate. He was quite laid back and the Aussies liked his real-life applications. I remember he taught at the Surf Life-Saving Club on Bondi Beach itself.

"Then we flew across Australia to Perth and he was well-received there, too. At the Freemantle *dojo*, based at the Police Youth Citizens Club, I was paired-up with Owen and he demonstrated on me. In one encounter, he used *tai-sabaki* and performed a *kizami-zuki*-like

Owen in Sydney with the Opera House in the distance

technique, but instead of using a full, closed fist, he employed a single pointed forefinger. He was so close with that finger tip that he flipped my eyelid back and I had to pull it down again.

"He also taught at a *dojo* in Mullaloo, a northern coastal suburb of Perth. The session was open to all styles and clubs and once again Owen's training was well received. I was paired up with him once more, but by then, after three weeks of training, I was reduced to wearing a football shin guard on my right forearm for some protection due to the repeated blocking of Owen's left [prosthetic] forearm having bruised the bone – anyone who has trained with Owen knows what this feels like.

"We left Perth and drove for about three-and-a-half hours south to Margaret River on the south-west tip of Australia and it was scorching hot. Owen taught a two hour karate class and then another two hours straight afterwards to a class of *karateka*, doormen and biker-types dressed in jeans or shorts and tee-shirts. This lesson was more of what you'd call a self-defence class. I recall that, getting changed, a large doorman, six feet two inches tall and built like a brick wall, came over and said to Owen that he was sceptical about the use of the elbow in self-defence situations. Owen replied that *empi* was a good technique, but this chap didn't believe him.

"'Clench your teeth,' Owen said as he stood up. The doorman did just that and Owen performed a light right *yoko-empi* to the left side of this fellow's jaw. The doorman swayed a bit and then spat out two teeth.

"'You didn't clench your teeth!' Owen remarked.

"I thought a punch-up was imminent, but the doorman was okay about it, and I, for one, breathed a sigh of relief, but Owen wasn't bothered at all. I think the one-armed Pom bruised a few egos that day.

"Owen wanted to see a kangaroo whilst he was in Australia and had pestered me for a week on the subject, but we just hadn't seen one. I remember that he fell asleep on the settee in the house of *Sensei* Ken Rouw, who was putting us up, and a kangaroo hopped into the lounge whilst the French doors were open and woke Owen up by licking the stump of his left arm! We all had a good laugh over that."

Murray continued: "I have always rushed at things, whether it be karate or life in general, and I like keeping myself busy. When I was staying with Allan in Perth, he was working during the day and I just hung around for the evening classes, though I did take a couple of private lessons. It is a lovely area and Margaret River is famous for its wines and I tried quite a few. Allan's wife took me to see some tourist attractions, but I felt as though I had too much time on my hands. Maybe, if I stayed longer, I would have quietened down a bit and just entered the pace of the region, I don't know, but it's governed by the heat. The people were very nice and I have no complaints at all, but going to the pub was a forty-five minute walk – though it took an hour-and-a-half to stagger back!

"After a week in Western Australia, I flew to Thailand and spent a month on holiday with my partner at the time, Wendy Thompson, who I had arranged to meet in Bangkok. Wendy and I were together for nine years and we later had two lovely daughters – Megan Elizabeth Murray [b. 5th October 1998] and Jessica Marie Murray [b.11th October 1999]. I plan to visit Australia again in 2013 with my son.

"I graded, successfully, to *Godan* in [6th September] 1996 under *Sensei* Enoeda. I built up to this grading for two years, concentrating on *kata*. For this grading, and for the next come to that, I chose *Jiin*. I feel this form suits my style – strong and compact with only three kicks. These kicks are all *mae-geri* and so that, at least, is my favourite kick. But for my 5th Dan, *Sensei* decided that, for a second *kata*, he'd give me *Gankaku*. Now, as anyone who knows this *kata* will tell you, *Gankaku* has four *yoko-geri-keage* and one jumping-kick, *mae-tobi-geri*, plus one *fumikomi* in it and *Sensei* must have been chuckling to himself when he gave it to me. The *kata* requires good balance and suppleness, but I really surprised myself and did what he must have

Owen playing with Megan and Jessica

thought was quite a respectable form.

"In truth, I felt as though I was never really good at *kata*, although I was always strong, using the combinations with intent. Had *bunkai*, the application of *kata*, been introduced to me at an early stage in my career, I think I would have appreciated *kata* more. Initially, I thought that *kata* was for those who were scared to fight, but I was proved wrong with people like Andy Sherry, Terry O'Neill, Frank Brennan, Bob Poynton, Steve Cattle and, of course, Dave Hazard. When I got into *kata* a bit more, its mind set, I realised that there was more to a *karateka's* weaponry than *seiken* and the foot. I never used *uraken*, *shuto-uchi*, *hizagashira* or *empi*, for example, when sparring. When practising *kata* I am a lot more relaxed now and work on technique rather than how hard I can kick or punch, but I also think of the imaginary fight that I am engaged in and never lose sight of that fact as long as the *kata* lasts."

Murray did, actually, use *uraken* sometimes, as Thompson's scarred forehead proves. Thompson recalled: "Steve Cattle had brought Ted Hedlund over from Scandinavia to Britain and he ran a course at Sendai. I partnered Owen and he caught me with a back-fist using his prosthetic arm – well, it wasn't actually a back-fist because Owen's false hand wasn't fixed on, but the action was as for an *uraken* and he whacked me with what would have been his wrist. He usually covered the end of his false arm, which was metal, before fighting, but on this occasion he didn't for some reason. It was a hot session and the sweat was just pouring off me. Owen usually punched, but he caught me above the left eye with this *uraken* and the blood just poured out and ran down my face with the sweat, like a river opening up into a delta and following different channel lines. It looked impressive, but I didn't go for stitches."

Murray continued: "I was always falling asleep at competitions from working late at the night clubs and getting up early to go to work. I snore quite loudly and on one occasion it was so loud that *Sensei* Enoeda instructed Frank Brennan to wake me up. Another time I fell asleep at a competition and was woken up to be told that I was up for the individual *kata* competition and that my name had already been called. I had been set up, as I never entered *kata* competitions, but someone had entered my name. It backfired on them though, as I came in third whilst still half asleep!

"A friend of mine named Bill Forester telephoned me one day and asked if I'd be interested in doing some security work in York. A large American company were pulling down a psychiatric hospital to build a shopping mall. I said I'd like to do it and so I gathered some lads around me and off we went. There was a security company already there and we got on well with them. Our job was to keep the area free of people so that building could begin, but there was a lot of ill-feeling about the hospital going and protesters were up in the trees and down in tunnels, so the workman weren't allowed in. The site was surrounded by fencing and we had to maintain the perimeter wearing high visibility jackets. The pay was good. I began to find some of the members of the other security firm quite aggressive and, thinking that I was just another lad from the North-East, tried to dictate to me. One night we went into a pub and in walked Mick Sawyer and Tivy Gommersall. Tivy died quite recently, but at the time they were both fairly high profile *karateka*. When we walked into the pub, Tivy and Mick made a big fuss of me.

"'Well, who is this Murray?' the security staff said.

"When it was then mentioned that I used to run the doors in Sunderland and was a European karate gold medalist, they backed off quite a bit. Eventually, I took over all of the security and had one hundred per cent of my staff working there. We did the day shift and the night shift and I got the lads to walk around two at a time and then have a couple of hours break when another team took over. I would cook breakfasts, dinners and suppers. Then, at night, I'd treat the lads to a few pints. I got up to a few tricks on that job, but I'd better not talk about that!

"In the autumn of 1996, whilst contracted on the York job, I received a phone call from the police to inform me that they'd found my father, dead, at home. It was a shock and hurt me more than I thought it would. I had to tell everyone, which I found difficult, and then had to drive home for one-and-a-half hours trying to get my head around what had happened. Had it been someone who had been closer to their father than I had been, I can imagine that they would possibly have endangered themselves and others whilst driving. My father had not been obviously ill. He smoked a lot throughout his life and was very thin but he had no major problems. Apparently, he'd suffered a heart attack and had been dead a few days when they found him. But what was particularly unsavoury was that he'd collapsed in front of a lit gas fire, so I was advised not to see him, because he had, effectively, been cooked, and so we had a closed coffin. He was a caring man though and all his insurance policies and other documents had been laid out everywhere so that no one would struggle to find them.

"He had been brought up as a Catholic, but had rebelled. He did believe in a God, but not one that required you to go to church every Sunday. He believed that God is everywhere and so church attendance was unnecessary. My mother was a Protestant, Church of England, and I was baptised in an Anglican church. Neither of them had much time for conventional religion though.

"I arranged the funeral and sat there with Joan beside me. I didn't want to talk to anyone and I didn't want people to see that I was upset. My mother and father were buried together, in the same plot. I tried to get drunk that night. I just sat there, really trying to blot out the pain, but regardless of how much I drank I remained completely sober. I had bought my mother and father's council house and after he died I rented it out and sold it a few years back. It held no fond memories for me.

"I go by myself to graveyards sometimes because I like the solace, the peace. I also tend to wander around such places when I'm feeling low because it helps me to climb back up. I look around me at all the gravestones and think of those people six feet under, wishing they were standing in the sunlight next to me."

VIII

SURE SAFE

Murray continued: "Around 1996 I found myself without a job and with no real prospects. I had skills that would have been prized in other centuries, but I couldn't do much with them in Britain at the end of the Twentieth Century. Then, I became aware of an organisation called General Services, through a sign language instructor whose daughter worked at a care home. General Services deliver courses promoting the minimum use of force for care assistants, traffic wardens, housing officers and the like – people who might easily encounter difficult members of the public when working alone. This might be what *karateka* would call 'low level intervention', but I thought that this was something that I could get into and do for a living, so I signed up for their basic course – and very good it was too.

"The course was held at Cherry Knowle Mental Health Hospital and it was led by a chap named Chris Watson. The course lasted one week and I passed. Then, I decided to take their advanced course and this was of three weeks duration and held at St. Nicholas's Hospital, Newcastle. I considered myself extremely fit, and still do, but I found that course very strenuous. I suppose there must have been about fifteen of us and we were training for six to seven hours each day. The chap who took it was named Aidan Healey and he was in his late sixties, six feet two inches tall, straight as a bolt, Old School, no nonsense, who had very good technique. Someone said he was ex-SAS and he could well have been. I thought he was fantastic and he reminded me of Enoeda.

"After that course, it had been my intention to set up in business, but I was advised that I required a NVQ City and Guilds Teaching and Development Qualification Level 3, or '7306' as we called it, for further education and adult education teachers. I groaned when I heard that, but it turned out to be worthwhile and I was assessed in my karate classes. It took one or two years to complete as I recall and the award shows the date as being September 2000. I took ten units in all ranging from identifying individual learning needs and designing training and development sessions, through creating a climate conducive to

Owen celebrates his 50th Birthday (2001) as only Owen knows how!

learning and facilitating learning through demonstration and instruction, to monitoring and reviewing progress with learners, and, evaluating and developing one's own practice.

"Later, I also attended another General Services Control and Restraint Course – PMVA, the prevention and management of violence and aggression. The breakaway technique course lasted one day and the holding techniques and restraining was a four-day course. Once again, I found these programmes to be excellent.

"When I eventually set-up Sure Safe I found it very difficult to get any work and for about a year it was horrendous. Chris Watson invited me in to assist him when he was short staffed at Cherry Knowle, but that was about it. I sent out so many letters to firms that I lost count and I knocked on endless doors. It was disheartening, very disheartening, because I was enthusiastic and nobody else seemed to be. I even had a write-up in *The Northern Echo*[1] about my new consultancy, but nothing came of it in terms of clients. I didn't give up though – disappointed I may have been, but I was not disenchanted – karate has taught me never to give up.

"I had to take a job for a few years working for a pal of mine on a building site. I did the ordering of materials and their collection. I remember driving a van along the A1231 between Sunderland and Washington listening to the 911 saga unfold on the radio as the terrorist-guided planes crashed into the Twin Towers of the World Trade Centre in 2001. I also completed a CITB [Construction Industry

Training Board] construction site manager's safety course in 2003.

"Later, I became involved in Wendy's cleaning company, which was both domestic and commercial in its operations. I passed a National Vocational Qualification (NVQ) in cleaning and support services, and I attended a training course in the control of insects and rodents studying such subjects as biology, control, legislation and personal protective equipment. I succeeded in getting a good contract cleaning what we called 'void houses' – properties involving end of tenancy, after death, drug addiction occupancy (where we had to conduct needle sweeps), or the homes of just filthy people quite frankly, living a life of grime. At the beginning, my son Owen, nephew David Buckley and some of their mates worked for me. I had them collecting litter, painting fences and garage doors, stripping wallpaper, clearing out old furniture, etc. Business operations progressed to preparing houses for new tenants and clearing houses for demolition. The latter task involved removing all the copper piping and water tanks when scrap prices were high and I made a fortune.

"It was whilst working in this line of work that I met Ellen, my current partner, who, having begun as a part-time cleaner was now employed as a supervisor by Wendy. As business was doing well – at one point I was turning over seven thousand pounds a week with an outlay of only two thousand five hundred pounds – Ellen went from a suited executive-type to wearing a boiler suit and mucking in with the lads engaged in anything from moving furniture from high storey flats to cleaning up after people who had died alone and, in some cases, lain unattended for weeks. Some of these jobs were, quite literally, gut wrenching and my team would sometimes retch because of the overwhelming stench. There was one property I recall where we discovered sixty bottles of urine and eighty bags of human excrement which we had to dispose of. The occupant had even smeared the walls with his faeces and was living like that. It was at times like this that, once again, I was grateful for not having an olfactory sense. When you looked in cupboards, when you looked around corners, you never knew what you were going to find.

Ellen Grewcock recalled: 'I knew Owen when he was working on the doors and I used to see him at karate. I used to play ice hockey so our paths would cross in the Crowtree Leisure Centre. I started working for Wendy on the domestic cleaning side of her business. I was promoted and crossed over to the commercial side to work with Owen. We spent a lot of time together and it was a gradual attraction and nothing like love at first sight. However, I found him so different

Owen and Ellen at Luke's (Murray's great-grandson's) christening

from any other man I'd ever met before. I had split from my husband of thirteen years and Owen basically swept me off my feet.'

Murray continued: "David Buckley is Joan's sister, Janet's son, and he was what you'd call a troubled teenager. He was kicked out of school for being disruptive, playing truant and smoking dope. He also fell out with his mother, father and brother, Paul. He was sent to Local Housing to learn a trade for two years, but was kicked out of that as well. After twelve months, he was given two hourly sessions at 'naughty school' playing football for one hour and learning mechanics for the other, but that soon stopped. At this time he lived with Joan's mother, his grandmother, but she found it hard to cope. He briefly went back to his parents for a couple of months, but he hated everyone.

"It was suggested that David move in with me and I set about, albeit in my own way, getting him back into shape and giving his life a sense of purpose. I don't go in for the softly, softly approach. When he wouldn't get out of bed in the mornings, I'd throw a bucket of cold water over him. I wasn't going to have any nonsense. He started to respond and he finished with the drugs and began training in certain aspects of self-defence with me. Shortly after that he stopped smoking and began using the exercise bike and did sit-ups and press-ups. He trained hard and began to get a bit of self-respect, a bit of self-worth.

Owen with his son, right, and David, Owen's nephew, left

He is now involved with my self-defence classes. He is a North-East kickboxing champion too. After about five years he moved back in with his parents. He is now self employed, has a girlfriend and has turned his life around."

Buckley recalled: "I got in with the wrong crowd and became a difficult teenager, a really awkward so-and-so and was always arguing with my family and teachers. I was expelled from school at fourteen for smoking cannabis. I wasn't stealing or anything like that; I would just smoke dope and kill time because there was nothing else to do. I just didn't have any purpose and I saw no hope. My mum asked my Uncle Owen to see what he could do because no one else in the family could cope with me. Now Owen lived out in the sticks and I didn't drive so I was stuck out in the middle of nowhere at sixteen away from my mates and away from just about everything else as well. Owen got me interested in practical self-defence and I worked out regularly in his gym. He gave me a job and set me on track and today I'm a painter and decorator. He influenced me in a positive way and when I go back to where I used to live I sometimes see the guys I used to knock around with in their hoodies hanging about on street corners and that's where I would have ended up if Owen hadn't taken care of me. I've got a lot to thank him for and I know my mother feels that way too."

Murray continued: "It was on the 29th March, 2003, that I received a phone call from Jeff Barwick to say that *Sensei* Enoeda had died. That came as a really big shock because nobody even knew he was ill. I found out that he'd gone back to Japan to have an operation for stomach cancer, but complications had set in and he'd passed away. He was only sixty-seven years of age. I just couldn't believe it. I couldn't think about anything else for days. He was like a god and I thought that he'd go on forever. He never seemed to change much from year to year and he was so powerful and his fighting spirit was so strong – I mean, they nicknamed him 'Tora' [Tiger] at Takushoku University, which was known for its fanatical dedication and ferocity of training, so you can imagine what he was like. I'd trained under him once a month for five years when I was in the KUGB squad and, afterwards, whenever he came up to the North-East. I also saw him at the Nationals every year. He was an inspiration and I have always tried to emulate him. After his death, he was posthumously awarded the rank of 9th Dan by the JKA.

"The KUGB organised a memorial service for him down at Crystal Palace, where, for so many years, he had taught on the annual KUGB summer camps. I went down by train with Jeff Barwick, Ernie Payne, Terry Parkinson and Sandra Calder. We had trouble finding hotel accommodation for the night and actually ended up a fair distance away.

"An upstairs area at the end of the main arena in Crystal Palace had been laid out with tables and they were full of memorabilia. I remember a photograph album showing Enoeda with all the film stars – like Lee Marvin, Peter Sellars and Michael Caine – that he had known. Enoeda had been keen on the movie business and the people in it. He'd even appeared in a Bond movie. But there were many other photos laid out too and, having been in the KUGB team, I was in some of them. Those photos brought it all flooding back to me. Enoeda's tracksuit was displayed on a mannequin. Andy Sherry was later given that tracksuit as a memento of his teacher for thirty-seven years. There were also banners and flags on the walls.

"In a separate downstairs room, a gymnasium, a large number of people took their seats. I don't know how many people were there, but I reckon it was in the hundreds, including a fair number from Europe. Bob Poynton gave a speech on behalf of the KUGB. Enoeda's wife, Reiko, and their two children, Daisuke and Maya, were there too. Anybody who was anybody in the KUGB was in attendance. Charlie Naylor, who had been Enoeda's best man at his wedding, spoke of his teacher on a video recording. The whole thing was an emotional experience and I saw a few tears in the eyes of some very hard men that day. For many, Enoeda was a father figure and they really felt it. I thought it was a good send off. Enoeda's funeral was actually held in Japan and Andy and Frank attended on behalf of the KUGB.

"I'm not into karate politics at all, but following Enoeda's death things happened and, to cut a long story short, I suppose clubs had a choice to either stay with the KUGB under Andy or stay affiliated to the JKA, under Ohta. Some people I know went with Ohta, but I remained true to the KUGB. From that time on, I was no longer JKA and, from my understanding of what transpired after *Sensei's* death, didn't want to be.

"About eighteen months later [24th November 2004], Kase, having suffered a major heart attack back in 1999, but who continued training, was struck down by another that proved fatal. He was seventy-five years of age. In his last years he had formed Shotokan Ryu Kase Ha. I only trained under him half a dozen times, but I was always mightily impressed and I wish I had had the opportunity to study more. I shall always remember him for that lesson on the lack of need for *hikite*, which I've already spoken about. I mean, if someone comes at you with a knife or glass and you block the arm, the last thing you are going to do is bring that arm back to your hip and punch with the other. No, you grab the arm if you can and punch, but with *hikite* feeling.

"Derek Langham [6th Dan], the KUGB's Administration and Finance Officer, who was based in Nottingham, and Charlie Naylor [7th Dan], the KUGB's Vice-Chairman, who was based near Chelmsford, both died in the early part of 2007 [25th January and 14th March, respectively], so two more KUGB founder members were gone. They were both in their seventies [seventy-six and seventy-three, respectively] and were highly regarded within the KUGB and on the world scene, as international referees. Charlie's daughter, Jane, a 5th Dan, was an international competitor. I had a lot of respect for both Charlie and Derek because they were good referees and fair in their adjudications.

"The government brought in a law that said that all doormen had to undergo training. I went up to the Security Industry Authority in Birmingham and attended yet another course which, amongst other things, included building evacuation and first aid. That was a good course too, but it soon became evident that I was over-qualified, so in 2004 I attended a BIIAB [British Institute of Innkeeping Awarding Body] trainer induction programme in conflict management, and became entitled to deliver the Level 2 National Certificate for Door Supervisors, particularly Unit 2: Conflict Management for Door

Owen (left) and Graham Adams (right) after completing their 6th Dan gradings, flank Andy Sherry (2007).

Supervisors. So, I could deliver courses to doormen and things started to pick up for me in a business sense. Later, I took the NCFE [Northern Council for Further Education] Level 2 Certificate in Conflict Management and passed units in conflict management and the law and conflict management in the workplace.

"In 2007 [6th October] I took my *Rokudan* under the KUGB at a grading in Egham, Surrey. Andy Sherry and Bob Poynton were the examiners. It had been eleven years since my last grading and, to be honest with you, I wasn't sure if I wanted to put myself through it again. But then I heard that a fellow *karateka,* who is younger than me, was going for his 6th Dan and I thought to myself, 'If he can do it, why not me?' I worked for fourteen months beforehand, specifically building up to that grading. My success was reported in the local press.[2] Graham Adams from South Tyneside and Richard Poole from Rhyl and Prestatyn graded successfully with me that day for the same *dan* rank.

"So, I pulled together all my karate skills honed over thirty years and combined them with the knowledge gained from real-life encounters working on doors for two decades. Added to this were the courses I had attended and passed. Sure Safe teaches single individuals

Owen (left) and Graham Adams (right) after completing their 6th Dan gradings, flank Frank Brennan (2007).

to large groups from long-established organizations; from the very fit to the unfit, from the able bodied to the disabled.

"I like teaching disabled people how to defend themselves. I've taught the whole range really. I remember a chap by the name of Brian Finnigan, from Silsworth, who was deaf and couldn't speak either, communicating only through sign language. He used to come training with his sister, Dionne, who would act as our mutual communicator. I think a course in self-defence helped him, gave him more confidence.[3]

"Then there are the organisations we cater for. We have some very nice testimonials and letters of appreciation to choose from, such as the NHS City Hospitals Sunderland, Sunderland City Council – such as for employees working in the Regeneration and Housing Service, and the Youth Offending Team – the University of Sunderland, Durham City Council, Home Housing, Community Services, Farringdon Community Sports College, the Insolvency Service, and, Wear Valley District Council. I've instructed in all sorts of places too and the Shildon Railway Museum, County Durham, stands out.

"A number of people help me with Sure Safe. Derek Huntley is an ex-policeman, ex-teacher and a 4th Dan in Goju-ryu and Frank Harris is an ex-NHS nurse. Ellen also assists me in the paperwork and attends any talks or courses I give to groups of children in schools or female groups generally.

Ellen recalled: 'Owen is a true professional on the Sure Safe courses. Self-defence is a serious business, but he makes everything fun and enjoyable and people respond well; he is a good instructor. I find this line of work very interesting and totally different from the martial arts I was used to, by virtue of two of my sons practising karate and kick-boxing. Owen is mostly a one-man band on Sure Safe courses and I accompany him and help out generally.'

Murray continued: "In 2008, Sure Safe was invited to teach the British Embassy staff in Dubai and Abu Dhabi. Ernie Payne, who is my age, accompanied me. We flew to Dubai and were put up in a nice hotel which was a twelve minute walk from the embassy, where we gave lessons on the squash court. However, rather than walking between the hotel and embassy, we caught a taxi and the reason for this was because if we walked, our shirts would be soaked in sweat on arrival. The temperature was well into the nineties and you couldn't really do much, at least comfortably, without air conditioning. When some of the embassy staff, local Arab women, turned up, I thought we might have a problem, because self-defence requires touching and I didn't want to unintentionally break any well established courtesies or rules; I didn't want to transgress. So, I explained what was involved and they were fine grappling away and kneeing their fellow staff!

"Then it was off to Abu Dhabi by limousine. The course there was straightforward, but I remember two things in particular. Firstly, the trainees were asked to wear a tracksuit, but the ambassador's wife joined us and she came in wearing a dress. I showed her a technique and ripped the dress on the left side by her hip and I thought to myself, 'That's done it! I'm going to be in the doghouse now.' But she was okay about it and just carried on.

"Whilst taking one lesson, I was demonstrating techniques and every now and then I would hear a male voice.

"'That'll never work!' it said.

"I looked about me but couldn't place from whom it was coming. Well, it turned out not to be from anyone in the class, but from a big guy dressed in full white Arab dress who, on walking past, would offer this one liner. When I knew who it was, I confronted him and said the techniques I was showing certainly would work, upon which, he charged into the room, grabbed me by the neck and pinned me to a wall. I didn't mess about – this was bread and butter stuff for me – so I brought a knee up into his groin and he went down like a lead weight and proceeded to roll around in agony. The funny thing was that my first reaction was, 'I've killed the Sultan's son!' It turned out this chap

Owen outside the British Embassy in Dubai

was a really nice fellow and he even asked me to go out there and start a karate club.

"Oh yes, and there was an embarrassing moment as well. I took

OWEN MURRAY, M.B.E., 6th DAN

Owen and Ernie Payne, with worker at the British Embassy, Abu Dhabi

Owen and Payne in Dubai, with Embassy staff, after a Sure Safe course

Owen and Payne in Dubai, with Embassy staff, after a Sure Safe course

Owen with female members of British Embassy staff in Dubai, after a Sure Safe training session.

Owen with Lorraine (right), in Dubai

some of the embassy staff out for a meal and when I went to pay my credit card bounced!

"I'm not interested in gambling at all, it's a mug's game, but I was taken horse racing. As we were driving along, about thirty black cars passed us in a convoy which we had to make way for and I was told it was the King and his entourage. At the races the organisers had these women tied to thin wires and they looked just as though they were flying over the race course – amazing. On television they really looked as though they were flying, but because we were on-site, we could see the large cranes from which they were suspended. I'd heard it said that you can't drink alcohol out in this part of the world, but I saw more drink in tents at that race course than I've ever seen in all of Sunderland!

"Sure Safe was given a kick-start by the Business and Innovation Centre (BIC) at Sunderland Enterprise Park. It was pretty basic stuff though, like how to do business cards, letter heads and guidance on website design. My website designer is a chap named Gary Wilkie of NRG and he's really good. He came down to my *dojo* to see what was needed for my site and is now one of my self-defence pupils.

"Employers have a duty of care to their employees and Sure Safe

SURE SAFE

Owen after touchdown in Britain with two air stewardesses

provides a sound foundation for this, especially when employees work alone. If you are a social worker, a customer care officer, a rent collector, an estate agent, or work in eviction, or even just delivering handouts, you are vulnerable to attack. Being 'out and about' and away from the office may make an employee more vulnerable, but receptionists, hotel staff, shop assistants, workers in health, housing and social security, whilst office based, are still subject to potential abuse. More people are taking their employers' to court now as a consequence of stress and trauma suffered as a result of encounters at work – and this can be the product of either physical violence or psychological abuse. People have a right to protect themselves as long as they use reasonable force, often they just don't know how to, and I believe that it is the Employers' duty to ensure that, whilst at work, employees are as safe as they reasonably can be.

"Initially, it is far better not to get to the stage where counter-offensive techniques and physical restraint have to be employed. Sure Safe teaches recognition of potentially impeding violent situations by looking for warning signs that are likely to lead to an attack – such as direct extended eye contact, kicking the ground, or an individual standing tall. The intention is to make our clients aware of such signs and diffuse a situation before it gets out of hand. We also teach the next stage, which is the recognition of the danger signs of an imminent

Owen alongside the Sure Safe van

Enforcement officers from Durham Council pose with Owen after a Sure Safe course.

Security staff from Sunderland Royal Hospital after completion of a Sure Safe course.

Owen with Sure Safe students from Home Housing

attack, such as fists clenching and unclenching, lips tightening over teeth, hands rising above the waist, head dropping to protect the throat, and so on. If these can be spotted, then an escalation might still be avoided.

"Then there are varying forms of communication. For example, I teach that 7% of communication is verbal, 38% is tone and 55% is non-verbal. Making people aware of tone and non-verbal aspects is an important part of the course.

"Sure Safe offers four main courses: Personal Safety and Awareness, which lasts for three hours; Conflict Management/Resolution, which lasts one day; Breakaway Skills Training, which lasts two days; and, Control and Restraint Training, which lasts for five consecutive days. We also provide tailor-made courses for individuals and groups.

"In our Breakaway Technique Courses, trainees are encouraged to ignore, as best they might, the inherent fight or freeze dilemma, which could place them in danger and they are taught to go into the flight mode by creating distance that should prevent physical injury. So, space and distance is an important factor in all confrontational situations and we teach that intimate space is between 0-0.5 metres, normal space is between 0.5 and 1.2 metres and stranger's space should be 1.2 - 3 metres.

"The need for flight is essential, but may not be possible – for example, without any sign, an employee, let us say, is grabbed suddenly from behind by an attacker. We teach breakaway techniques for wrist holds, hair pulling, strangles from both the standing and floor positions, clothing holds and body holds. We also teach defences against punches and kicks.

"I believe it true to say that the vast majority of Sure Safe's clients are happy with the courses we provide. I like to think we are able to prepare people in their normal working lives when they come across troublesome individuals, but, at the same time, not giving them a false sense of confidence. The Sure Safe logo is a person's two hands pressed together as if holding something precious and that, to me at least, says it all."

Jeff Barwick commented on Sure Safe: "Owen has taken all his very considerable experience of working on the doors, being an international competitor, taking the self-defence that Shotokan and even some other styles offer and put them into his system for Sure Safe. He has been eclectic and I must say that he has come up with some very good, practical ideas to help people."

Jimmy Rawlins (right) of security at the University of Sunderland alongside his teacher of forty years.

Owen, Ellen and Derek Huntley (a Goju-ryu 4th Dan with over forty years experience) pose for a Sure Safe Christmas card.

Murray continued: "A few years ago I started up Self-Defence North-East as well. I have about twenty to thirty students at the moment and it caters for people who might feel awkward being part of a group where spectators or fellow trainees might goggle at them. People who are obese, very tall, disabled, badly out of condition, can feel very self-conscious and that often prevents them from taking up self-defence in a group full of toned athletic types. I teach inter-related techniques that can be used for more than one type of attack. The training builds peoples' confidence and I must confess getting a certain satisfaction watching such students flower.

"You do get some funny things happen though. I remember teaching this woman.

"'If you do the technique like that, you'll get hit in the 'three-piece', I said without thinking. Well, I suppose it was an inappropriate thing to say to a woman as she didn't possess a 'three-piece' by which I meant penis and testicles. It's the sort of thing I say to my male students who know what I'm talking about, but this woman looked at me in a vacant manner, so I assumed she didn't understand and left it at that. However, because I use that term all the time, I inadvertently said it to her again.

"'If you imagine that technique will work,' I exclaimed, 'you might as well imagine what it's going to be like being hit in the three-piece.'

"'What colour?' she asked. I must have looked at her as vacantly as she'd previously looked at me.

"'What do you mean, what colour?' I replied.

"'What colour do I have to imagine the three-piece suite to be?' Bless her. She thought I was referring to a settee and a couple of armchairs!"

"I thought to myself, 'I'm doing well here – I'm the one supposed to be teaching communications skills!'"

Adams recalled: "Owen has a reputation for being a hard man and he can be, but he is also a very caring person. He has done a lot for people he doesn't even know, let alone those he does. In 2005, my son, Luke, contracted a virulent form of meningitis and it was very much touch and go at one point. I organised a meningitis charity karate course at Brinkburn School, South Shields, and amongst the instructors who gave their time and knowledge free-of-charge, was Owen. On another occasion, I organised a disco, the proceeds from which would go to meningitis research and Owen generously supported us on that too. When I needed him he was there. He is the sort of man who can be counted upon."

Owen performing *mae-geri* (2012)

Thompson recalled: "Owen is reliable when it comes to helping people. I remember when fellow *karateka*, Steve Lamb's son, Elliott, started to suffer seizures. A group of us, including John Holdsworth, Julie Nicholson, Owen and myself, decided to raise money to send Elliott to Australia where there was a specialist working in this particular area. We taught karate courses and raised about seven or eight hundred pounds. Elliott did go out there and he is now virtually cured."

Ellen noted: 'Owen is a caring person and he loves his family to bits. He never had any real bond or love for his parents, so I think he appreciates the importance of affection. He has a very strong personality and likes doing things his way. In my opinion, Owen isn't

Owen performing *keito-uke* from the *kata Unsu* (2012)

Owen with his four children and Ellen. Children, from left to right, back: Owen Murray Jnr., Donna Murray-Allen; foreground, Megan Murray, Jessica Murray.

normal in any shape or form. He approaches everything at one hundred miles per hour, which he often doesn't need to do. He has almost a split personality. As long as things are going his way he's fine, but if something upsets him he can mope about the house for days. He is almost lazy around the house and garden and doesn't really do much, though he does do a bit of cooking. He's very untidy too and leaves everything lying around. I guess he can be quite difficult to live with at times.

'Apart from his family, Owen's two big loves in life are karate training and whisky, but he likes buying nice clothes and going on holiday – though I just wish he'd take me once in a while! I would say his two big hates are incompetent people and bad time-keeping. He likes people to be organised, to do as he says and to do it correctly. He gets down over money, lack of work and not being able to train. He's due a hip replacement soon and that will be a nightmare because he won't be able to go into the gym.'

Murray continued: "I didn't really expect to live to sixty to tell you the truth, but I'm sixty-two years of age now and calming down a bit – I mean, I'm a great-grandfather! Donna [now with the surname

Owen and Ellen with (left to right) Sam, Scott and Andi (2012)

Murray-Allen] had a little girl, Abigail, when she was quite young and Abigail gave birth to Luke recently. Sometimes I show my age and I'll give you an example. I remember when I was in the car with my two teenage daughters and they had the radio playing.

"'Turn the wireless off,' I said, and they didn't know what I meant.

"Age is no barrier to developing karate and self-defence, and this has a positive spin off effect for Sure Safe and Self-Defence North-East, because I am researching most of the time. Going in hard in karate is natural for me, but now I'm focussing on what might best described as the finer points of the art, such as specialising in refining my technique and aiming at specific, vital targets, rather than just upper-level, middle-level and lower-level. I am finding this development very interesting and rewarding both physically and intellectually. There's a lot more to karate than just *kumite* and competition."

Thompson recalled: "Owen is of the Old School and there aren't that many of us around these days. Many young people believe that karate is about winning tournaments and passing gradings as quickly as they can, but karate has nothing to with these things really. I believe the Japanese masters who promoted such competition realised, after the harm was done, what, exactly, their legacy would be and they wanted to reject it and turn back the clocks, which, of course, they

Owen receiving his KUGB 40 Year Service certificate from KUGB Chief Instructor, Andy Sherry (2012).

couldn't do. Owen is a twice European champion as part of a team and so he is qualified to speak on the subject. He was brought up properly and respects the *kyohai/sempai* relationship. Some young lads these days get a couple of *dan* gradings under their belt, win a competition and think they are at the same level as someone who may be of the same grade but who has trained thirty or forty years. Owen knows the difference. Although I am his junior in terms of rank, I started training before him and continue, so he considers me his senior. He respects me and I respect him, because we both train hard."

Murray concluded: "Last year [2012] I received a certificate from the KUGB to mark my forty years continuous membership of that organisation. It's been good. Karate has given me so much. Every day I'm in my *dojo* doing sixty straight sit-ups, twenty crunches to the left, twenty crunches to the right, forty sit-ups knees to chest and sixty press-ups. I do this routine four times a day as an absolute minimum, plus cardiovascular work. Then I do my karate and self-defence

Owen's certificate showing forty years of KUGB membership (1972-2012)

Owen with Ernie Payne, Jeff Barwick and Frank Brennan, at Sendai Karate Club.

classes. Excessive? Obsessive? Maybe, but this is my Way of life; this is what I do. Karate certainly turned me around, gave me purpose, channelled my energy when times were very difficult and I was in chronic pain and slowly killing myself. From this I came to realise the art's true value – at least for me.

"My life goes up and down just like everyone else's, good things and bad things happen, but karate is a constant that has never let me down. It is a path I follow and I have no regrets. For people who have not become seriously 'taken' with the art, it is difficult to explain the singular nature of its calling. Let me give you an example of what I mean.

"When I was having personal problems with a female partner some years ago, I was asked to attend counselling under an organization whose well-intentioned object it is to try and help couples sort out their difficulties. I didn't think they could do much for us to be honest, but I wanted to get the differences ironed out if possible and I went along a couple of times with the best of intentions. After the second session the counsellor tried to organise our next appointment, but I said I couldn't go at the allotted time. So she consulted her diary and gave me another time and I said I couldn't make that either. My partner became irritated and the counsellor quickly picked up on it. There was an awkward pause.

"'May I ask why you can't make these appointments?' the counsellor asked, quizzically. 'Isn't this important to you?'

"My reply didn't go down well with either my girlfriend or the counsellor.

"'Yes, it is important,' I replied, 'but you have to understand that I go karate training at those times.'

"From my answer, the counsellor naturally inferred that karate was more important to me than trying to sort out my relationship with my partner – and I suppose, if the truth be told, she was right."

REFERENCES & NOTES

PREFACE

1. Mills, A.D. *A Dictionary of Place-Names* (Oxford University Press, 1991).
2. Layton, C. *Andy Sherry, 9th Dan, Vol. II (1971-1983): a celebration of the KUGB as seen through the eyes of its chief instructor and other notable members* (KUGB, in press).

CHAPTER I – SEEMINGLY, JUST ANOTHER DAY AT THE FACTORY

1. Pip, Squeak and Wilfred refer to the 1914-1915 Star, British War Medal and the Victory Medal, respectively.
2. Turnbull, M. *Veteran Slams Medal Pledge* (*Sunderland Echo*, 21st December 2012, p. 5).

CHAPTER II – ONE HUNDRED CIGARETTES AND TEN PINTS OF LAGER A DAY

1. Murray achieved the following CSE grades (Grade 1, being the highest and Grade 5 the lowest) as recorded on his CSE certificate, 1967: English Language Oral – Grade 2; English Language Written, Geography, Woodwork – Grade 3; History, Mathematics, Physics – Grade 4; Technical Drawing – Grade 5.
2. The episode in question was entitled, *The Cybernauts,* when Steed and Peel investigate a series of broken necks from devastating blows.

CHAPTER III – A FALSE LIMB – 'IS IT A PROBLEM FOR YOU?'

1. A photograph and short write up appeared in the *Echo, Sunderland*, on the 19th March 1974, showing training at the Sendai Karate Club, YMCA, during an Open Week. The piece notes that the club meets four times a week.
2. Bell was born in Ilford in 1921. An account of his early life and how he established karate in Britain is given in great depth in *Shotokan Dawn, Vols. I & II* (Mona Books, 2007), *The Shotokan Dawn Supplement* (Mona Books, 2007), and, *Shotokan Horizon* (Mona books, 2007). See also: *Shotokan Dawn Over Ireland* (Aiki Pathways, 2006), *You Don't Have to Dress to Kill* (Saisho, 2007), *The Liverpool Red Triangle Karate Club* (KUGB, 2007), *Scotland's First Karate Club* (Mona Books, 2009), and Appendix I of *Ronnie Watt, 8th Dan* (National Karate Institute {Scotland}, 2009), all by the author. Bell died of cancer in 2004 and his obituary appeared in *The Times* (8th March 2004, p. 28 {page 56 of the compact edition}). He also features in *The Oxford Dictionary of National Biography*, with the entry written by the author.
3. For details of the BKF Sunderland club see, *Shotokan Dawn, Vol. II*, pages 167-168, and, *The Shotokan Dawn Supplement*, pages 110-113.
4. John Holdsworth signed his BKF membership application form on the 10th April

1966.
5. Jeff Barwick signed his BKF membership application form on the 10th April 1966.
6. Kanazawa was born in 1931 in Miyako, Iwate Prefecture. He attained 2nd Dan in judo before attending Takushoku University, where he began his study of karate in 1952. He was awarded his 1st Dan in just eighteen months and by 1955 was a 2nd Dan. Upon graduation in 1956, he joined the newly instigated JKA's instructors' programme and successfully pursued the one-year course. Entering the first JKA Championships in 1957 with a broken hand, he won the *kumite* title and the following year became the first of only six JKA Grand Champions (to date), by winning both the *kumite* and *kata* events on the same occasion. From 1961-1963 he became the JKA's representative to Hawaii, after which he returned to Tokyo. He had been an instructor at the JKA Headquarters, Musashi Industrial University, Mitsubishi Shoji Company and the Arabia Oil Company before taking up residence in Britain, as a 5th Dan, in 1965. Master Kanazawa's story, to the time he came to Britain, is told in the author's book, *Kanazawa, 10th Dan: Recollections of a Living Karate Legend – the early years (1931-1964)* {Shoto Publishing, 2001}). How it was arranged for Kanazawa to come to Britain and his year, 1965-1966, is told in detail in the author's *Shotokan Dawn, Vol: II* (Mona Books, 2007).
7. According to BKF records, on the 10th April 1966, Barwick graded to temporary 8th kyu and Holdsworth to temporary 7th kyu (*Shotokan Dawn: Vol. II*, p. 168).
8. The six other remaining founder members are: Andy Sherry (Liverpool), Terry O'Neill (Liverpool), Bob Poynton (Liverpool), Ian Maclaren (York), David Collacott (Exeter {now living in France}), and Dorothy Naylor (Chelmsford).
9. Layton, C. *The Liverpool Red Triangle Karate Club – Origins and Early Years (1959-1966) – and the Formation of the KUGB* (KUGB, 2007).
10. Murakami was born in Shizuoka in 1927 and began training in a number of martial arts at the Yoseikan *dojo*. Residing in France since 1957, having been brought over to Europe by Frenchman Henri Plee, Murakami was a 3rd Dan in Yoseikan karate, a 3rd Dan in aikido, a 2nd Dan in kendo and a 1st Dan from the JKA. Bell had trained with Murakami in Paris in 1958 and in 1959 Murakami made his first of many trips to England for the BKF. Murakami was highly influential in Europe at this time, but with the onset of the arrival of JKA instructors he lost favour in some quarters. His senior students in Britain were Terry Wingrove and Jimmy Neal. Murakami last taught for the BKF in 1964. He subsequently joined the Shotokai and was graded 5th Dan by Egami. Later moving to Spain, he continued to teach throughout Europe and North Africa. Murakami died of cancer in 1987.
11. Layton, C. *Andy Sherry, 9th Dan, Vol. I (1943-1970): a celebration of the KUGB as seen through the eyes of its chief instructor and other notable members*; *Andy Sherry, 9th Dan, Vol. II (1971-1983): a celebration of the KUGB as seen through the eyes of its chief instructor and other notable members* (KUGB, both books in press).
12. Ken Smith signed his BKF application form on the 9th April 1966, when forty-two years of age and an electric welder by occupation. According to BKF records, on the 10th April 1966, Smith graded to temporary 7th kyu (*Shotokan*

REFERENCES AND NOTES

Dawn: Vol. II, p. 168). In 1966, Smith had agreed to being BKF Area Officer for the North-East on recommendation of Alan Carr, who noted that Smith was 'a most able and conscientious chap' (*The Shotokan Dawn Supplement*, p. 112).

13. Robert Bewley signed his BKF application form on the 10th April 1966, when twenty-six years of age and a melter by occupation.
14. Layton, C. *Shotokan Dawn: Vol. I* (Mona Books, 2007), pp. 291-292.
15. Charles Naylor signed his BKF application form on the 31st August 1961, when twenty-eight years of age and a sales engineer by occupation.
16. Derek Langham signed his BKF application form on the 22nd August 1965, when thirty-five years of age and a representative by occupation.
17. For an account of such training in Japan see: Layton, C. *Kanazawa, 10th Dan: Recollections of a Living Karate Legend – the early years (1931-1964)* (Shoto Publishing, 2001), pp. 49-50.
18. The author has seen this letter – the envelope is dated 13th January 1978.
19. This is confirmed by Stout, R. *England Pick Brave Owen* (unknown newspaper article).
20. Uncredited. *Karate Cup Crunch* (unknown newspaper clipping). This information is believed to be from 1977, though the clipping has no date.
21. Uncredited. *N.E. Karate Cup Finals* (*Echo*, Sunderland, 3rd October 1978, p. 22).
22. Uncredited. *Karate Kings* (unknown newspaper article).
23. Uncredited. *Y.M. Night Will Help Refugees* (unknown newspaper article).
24. Uncredited. *The North West Open Karate Championships* (*Fighting Arts*, Vol. 3, No. 5, p. 39).
25. Uncredited. *Kung-Fu Tragedy* (*Fighting Arts*, Vol. 3, No. 2, pp. 40-41).
26. Uncredited. *Swept off their Feet* (unknown newspaper article).
27. Wardle, J. *Krunch!: kicking king Owen can get your toes in a tangle* (*Sunday Sun*, September 18th, 1977, p. 5).

CHAPTER IV – EUROPEAN GOLD ... 'I WISH I COULD REMEMBER!'

1. This fact is confirmed by Stout, R. *England Pick Brave Owen* (unknown newspaper article).
2. This fact is confirmed by an uncredited article, *Top the Chops* (unknown newspaper).
3. Uncredited. *Disabled Man's Karate Triumph* (unknown newspaper).
4. Terry O'Neill signed his BKF application form on the 21st May 1963, when sixteen years of age and a schoolboy.
5. Correspondence with the author (16th May 2012).
6. Uncredited. *The 14th National Karate Union of Great Britain Championships* (*Fighting Arts*, Vol. 4, No. 2, pp. 42-45).
7. Uncredited. *Top of the Chops!* (*Sunderland and Washington Times*, Issue 11, May 15th 1980, p. 17).
8. The actual figures are unknown, but in the 1978 KUGB National Championships there were 277 entrants in the individual male *kumite* event and in 1981, 276.
9. Uncredited. *The 14th National Karate Union of Great Britain Championships* (*Fighting Arts*, Vol. 4, No. 2, pp. 42-45).

10. *KUGB Executive Committee Minutes* (2nd November 1980).
11. Frank Brennan's KUGB record is remarkable. In the individual *kumite* category, he won ten times (1979, 1980, 1982-1986, 1988, 1991, 1992) and in individual *kata* he won fourteen times in straight succession (1979-1992). He was, therefore, KUGB Grand Champion an astonishing ten times. In addition, as part of the Liverpool Red Triangle, he won the team *kumite* title many times.
12. Uncredited. *The 14th National Karate Union of Great Britain Championships* (*Fighting Arts*, Vol. 4, No. 2, pp. 42-45). Hideo Ochi's and Horst Handel's German JKA team consisted of (and Murray would have fought one): Jurgen Willrodt, Wolf Wichman, Marijan Glad, Robert Rege, Werner Buttgen, Jurgen Hoffman, Ronald Repp, Jurgen Wolff, Burghard Rebmann, Dieter Ruh and Dieter Steinberg.
13. Uncredited. *Brennan Does it Again* (*Karate & Oriental Arts*, No. 86, Sept/Oct 1980, pp, 8-11).
14. Uncredited. *Top of the Chops!* (*Sunderland and Washington Times*, Issue 11, May 15th, 1980, p. 17).
15. This is confirmed from a newspaper cutting showing that Bob Poynton, Frank Brennan, George Godfrey, Andy Sherry, Terry O'Neill and Steve Cattle were present.
16. Uncredited. *Owen Out for Glory* (unknown newspaper clipping).
17. Uncredited. *Owen For England* (unknown newspaper clipping).
18. Uncredited. *Champion Ambition: Now it's Owen UK* (*The Journal*, 27th August 1980).
19. Smith, P. *Meet Sunderland's Karate King! Single Handed Success* (unknown newspaper article).
20. For a detailed account of Kawasoe's life to the time he came to Britain, see: Layton, C. *Masao Kawasoe, 8th Dan: Recollections of a Shotokan Karate Master – the early years (1945-1975)* (Mona Books, 2008). For a detailed account of aspects of Kawasoe's technique, see: Layton, C. *Master Masao Kawasoe: The Foundations of Shotokan Karate Technique – an explorative rendering based on an extended interview* (Mona Books, 2011).
21. *KUGB Executive Committee Minutes* (21st June 1980).
22. O'Neill, T. *The 3rd IAKF World Karate Championships* (*Fighting Arts*, Vol. 4, No. 3, pp. 47-51). Also published in: *International Amateur Karate Federation 3rd IAKF World Karate-Do Championships, Bremen, 1980* (*EAKF Official Magazine*, No. 2, Nov. 1981, pp. 20 – 27).
23. O'Neill, T. *The 3rd IAKF World Karate Championships* (*Fighting Arts*, Vol. 4, No. 3, pp. 47-51).
24. Mori graduated from the JKA instructors' class in 1975 and at the time of writing holds the rank of JKA 7th Dan.
25. O'Neill, T. *The 3rd IAKF World Karate Championships* (*Fighting Arts*, Vol. 4, No. 3, pp. 47-51).
26. Layton, C. *Andy Sherry, 9th Dan, Vol. II (1971-1983): a celebration of the KUGB as seen through the eyes of its chief instructor and other notable members* (KUGB, in press).
27. Gordon Thompson signed his BKF application form on the 25th January 1961, when thirty years of age and a coach body maker by occupation. He was a

REFERENCES AND NOTES

founder member of the KUGB and remained with the Union for more than forty years. He died in 2010, aged 79. His contribution to Shotokan in the North-East of England is highly significant. His introduction to karate under Bell and Murakami, the founding of the York BKF *dojo* and early visits by Kanazawa and Enoeda to that *dojo* are told in *Shotokan Dawn, Vols. I & II*.

28. Steve Cattle signed his BKF application form on the 2nd October 1963, when sixteen years of age and a schoolboy.
29. O'Neill, T. *Fighting Arts Interviews Karate Champion Steve Cattle* (*Fighting Arts International*, No. 30, pp.44-50).
30. Layton, C. *Andy Sherry, 9th Dan, Vol. II (1971-1983): a celebration of the KUGB as seen through the eyes of its chief instructor and other notable members (KUGB, in press).*
31. Sherry, A. *E.A.K.F. European Senior and Junior Championships* (*Fighting Arts*, Vol. 4, No. 4, p. 51).
32. In the senior events, the KUGB took first place in the men's team *kata*, second place in the individual *kata* (Poynton), second and joint third places in the individual *kumite* (Higgins and Godfrey, respectively), second place in the women's team *kata* and second in the women's individual *kata* (June Vann). In the junior event, first places in the team *kata*, team *kumite*, individual *kata* (Brennan), in addition to first place in the middleweight (Ronnie Christopher) and two third places in the individual *kumite* (G. Davison and I. Roberts, in the heavyweight and middleweight categories, respectively).
33. Uncredited. *International Japan Vs. G.B.* (*Fighting Arts*, Vol. 4, No. 5, pp. 25-27).
34. Uncredited. *Owen Earns a Draw* (*Echo Sunderland*, May 20th 1981).
35. Uncredited. *International Japan Vs. G.B.* (*Fighting Arts*, Vol. 4, No. 5, pp. 25-27).
36. O'Neill, T. *The 1981 KUGB Shotokan Cup* (*Fighting Arts*, Vol. 4, No. 6, p. 51).
37. O'Neill, T. *Another Victory for England at the 1981 E.A.K.F. European Karate Championships* (*Fighting Arts*, Vol. 4, No. 6, pp. 28-31).
38. Layton, C. *Andy Sherry, 9th Dan, Vol. II (1971-1983): a celebration of the KUGB as seen through the eyes of its chief instructor and other notable members (KUGB, in press).*
39. Sherry, A. *KUGB Competes in Hungary: the Ibusz Cup – April 3rd 1982* (*Fighting Arts*, Vol. 5, No. 1, p. 45).
40. Layton, C. *Andy Sherry, 9th Dan, Vol. II (1971-1983): a celebration of the KUGB as seen through the eyes of its chief instructor and other notable members (KUGB, in press).*
41. Sherry, A. *KUGB Competes in Hungary: the Ibusz Cup – April 3rd 1982* (*Fighting Arts*, Vol. 5, No. 1, p. 45).
42. *KUGB Executive Committee Minutes* (17th April 1982).
43. The KUGB English squad was: Jim Brennan, Frank Brennan, Ronnie Christopher, Randy Williams, Ian Roberts, Gary Harford and Murray; the Swedish squad were: L. Anderberg, K. Larson, P. Lim, B. Gynscer, L. Jenson and Anderson. See, O'Neill, T. *The 18th National Karate Union of Great Britain Championships* (*Fighting Arts*, Vol. 5, No. 5, pp. 63-67).
44. Jeff Barwick – private communication.

45. Hazard, D. & Parker, C. *Born Fighter* (John Blake Publishing, 2007), p. 156.
46. Hazard, D. & Parker, C. *Born Fighter* (John Blake Publishing, 2007), pp. 157-158.

CHAPTER V – KUGB NATIONAL CHAMPIONS

1. O'Neill, T. *The European Shotokan Karate Championships* (*Fighting Arts International*, No. 41, pp. 38-43).
2. Richards, C. *Top Japanese Karate Sensei Visit the North-East* (*Fighting Arts International*, No. 44, p. 67).
3. Murray's contribution was acknowledged. See, Grey, G. *The 1987 ESKA European Karate Championships: Part 2* (*Fighting Arts International*, No. 48, p. 54).
4. Grey, G. *The 1987 ESKA European Karate Championships: Part 1* (*Fighting Arts International*, No. 47, pp. 52-56).
5. Grey, G. *The 1987 ESKA European Karate Championships: Part 2* (*Fighting Arts International*, No. 48, pp. 48-54).
6. O'Neill, T. *Great Britain Defeats Japan ... and Everyone Else, at the JKA World Karate Championships! Sunderland, England, March 17th/18th 1990: Part 1* (*Fighting Arts International*, No. 64, pp. 4-10).
7. O'Neill, T. *The JKA World Karate Championships! Sunderland, England, March 17th/18th 1990: Part 1* (*Fighting Arts International*, No. 65, pp. 14-18).
8. Uncredited. *The 9th National Karate Union of Great Britain Championships* (*Fighting Arts*, Vol. 2, No. 4, pp. 8-10) confirms this fact.
9. Uncredited. *The 12th National Karate Union of Great Britain Championships* (*Fighting Arts*, Vol. 3, No. 5, pp. 34-35) confirms this fact.
10. Pollard, P. *The 22nd National Karate Union of Great Britain Championships: A Family Affair* (*Fighting Arts International*, No. 53, pp. 26-36).
11. This is confirmed in a film of the event.
12. O'Neill, T. *Consistency is the Key ... The 24th National Karate Union of Great Britain Championships* (*Fighting Arts International*, No. 66, pp. 44-48).
13. Uncredited. *Silver Anniversary Celebrations ... as etiquette and 'proper behaviour' take pride of place over all the kicks, punches and kiai at ... The 25th National Karate Union of Great Britain championships* (*Terry O'Neill's Fighting Arts International*, No. 70, pp. 42-48).
14. Cheetham, J. *Steve Cattle, 5th Dan: Back to the Roots* (*Shotokan Karate Magazine*, No. 23, pp. 4-8). This in-depth interview explains the reasoning behind Cattle leaving the KUGB/JKA.
15. Cattle, S. *A Meeting with Kase Sensei* (*Traditional Karate*, Vol. 2, No. 6, 1988, pp. 4-12).
16. Cattle, S. *The Tangled Web: A Short History of the Japan Karate Association, Part I: What the Afternoon Knows, the Morning Never Expected* (*Traditional Karate*, April, 1989, pp. 54-59).
17. Cattle, S. *The Tangled Web: A Short History of the Japan Karate Association, Part II: The Golden Age – 1922-1946, 'The Fearful Symmetry'* (*Traditional Karate*, May, 1989, pp. 54-61).
18. Cattle, S. *A Short History of the Japan Karate Association, Part III: The Golden*

REFERENCES AND NOTES

Age – 1946-55, 'The Law of Tooth and Claw (*Traditional Karate*, June, 1989, pp. 54-58).
19. Cattle, S. *History of the JKA, Part IV* (*Traditional Karate*, July, 1989, pp. 56-59).
20. Cattle, S. *A History of the JKA, 1966, 'The Turning of the Tide* (*Traditional Karate*, September, 1989, pp. 30-34).
21. Terry O'Neill noted in his report of the 1990 KUGB Championships that 'a notable exception this year was Cattle, who has now officially left the KUGB to join a new association' (*Fighting Arts International*, No. 66, p. 44).
22. For s short biography of Higaonna, to 1986, see: Layton, C. *Conversations with Karate Masters* (Ronin, 1988), pp. 109-128.

CHAPTER VI – A SIERRA LEONE EXPERIENCE

1. Uncredited. *Owen's Fighting Spirit* (unknown newspaper article).

CHAPTER VII – AN M.B.E AND THE DEATH OF A HERO

1. *The Times,* June 11th 1994.
2. *Echo*, December 14th 1994.
3. Uncredited. *A Kick Start in the Honours* (*The Echo Sunderland*, 1994).

CHAPTER VIII – SURE SAFE

1. Uncredited. *Consult Owen About Violence in Workplace* (*The Northern Echo*, 22nd October 2002).
2. Forster, J. *Handicap Can't Stop Karate Expert Owen* (unknown newspaper, 11th October 2007).
3. *Brian Gets to Grips with Self-Defence* (*The Sunday Post*, 23rd September 2001, p. 12).

GLOSSARY

Ai-uchi – simultaneous strike
Ashi-barai – foot sweep
Awase-zuki – U-punch
Bassai-dai – to penetrate a fortress (a Shotokan *kata*)
Bunkai – *kata* application
Choku-zuki – straight punch
Chudan – middle level
Dan – black belt rank
Dojo – training hall (literally, 'place of the Way)
Empi – elbow
Enpi – Flying Swallow (a Shotokan *kata*)
Fumikomi – stamping kick
Gankaku – crane on a rock (a Shotokan *kata*)
Gedan-barai – downward (sweep) block
Gi – (karate) suit
Godan – 5th Dan
Gohon-kumite – five-step sparring (pre-arranged)
Gojushiho-dai – 54 steps {major} (a Shotokan *kata*)
Gyaku-gedan-barai – reverse downward (sweep) block
Gyaku-mawashi-geri – reverse roundhouse-kick
Gyaku-zuki – reverse punch
Hachiji-dachi – open-leg stance
Hajime – begin
Hangetsu – half-moon (a Shotokan *kata*)
Hasami-zuki – scissors punch
Heian – Peaceful Mind, (a series of five *kata*)
Heian Nidan – Peaceful Mind, second level (a Shotokan *kata*)
Heian Sandan – Peaceful Mind, third level (a Shotokan *kata*)
Heian Shodan – Peaceful Mind, first level (a Shotokan *kata*)
Heiko-dachi – parallel stance
Heiko-zuki – parallel punch
Hikite – pulling-in fist
Hizagashira – knee
Ippon – full point
Ippon-kumite – one-step sparring (pre-arranged)
Jiin – temple grounds (a Shotokan *kata*)
Jodan – upper level
Judoka – student of judo
Juji-uke – X-block
Kaeshi-ippon-kumite – two-step-one-attack-sparring
Kakiwake-uke – wedge block
Karateka – student of karate
Kata – Form(s) (set movements in (a) set sequence(s))
Keito-uke – chicken-head-wrist block
Kihon – basic(s)

Kiai – a special kind of yell
Kihon Kata – see *Taikyoku Shodan*
Kime – focus
Kizami-zuki – jab
Kokutsu-dachi – back stance
Kumite – sparring
Kyohai – junior
Kyu – non back belt rank (ranking 9th {lowest} – 1st {most senior})
Mae-geri – front kick
Mae-tobi-geri – front jump kick
Makiwara – striking pad on a tapered post
Mawashi-geri – roundhouse-kick
Morote-uke – augmented forearm block
Nagashi-uke – sweeping block
Nidan – 2nd Dan
Nukite – spear hand
Oi-zuki – lunge punch
Okuri-zuki – sliding punch
Rokudan – 6th Dan
Sanbon-zuki – three punches
Sandan – 3rd Dan
Seiken – fore-fist
Sempai – senior
Sensei – teacher
Shodan – First (and lowest) *Dan* rank
Shuto – knife-hand
Shuto-uchi – knife-hand strike
Shuto-uke – knife-hand block
Sochin – to suppress (a Shotokan *kata*)
Sokumen-awase-uke – side two-handed block
Sukui-uke – scooping block
Taikyoku Shodan – First Cause (a Shotokan *kata*)
Tai-sabaki – body shifting
Tameshiwari – wood breaking
Teisho-awase-uke – combined palm-heel block
Tekki Nidan – horse riding second level (a Shotokan *kata*)
Uchi-uke – inside block
Ude-uke – forearm block
Unsu – to part the clouds (a Shotokan *kata*)
Uraken – back-fist
Ushiro-geri – back kick
Wazari – half-point
Yama-zuki – wide U- punch
Yoko-empi – side elbow
Yoko-geri – side kick
Yoko-geri-keage – side snap kick
Yoko-geri-kekomi – side thrust kick
Yondan – 4th Dan

ABOUT THE AUTHOR

Clive Layton was born in Hertfordshire in 1952, the son of an architect. He began his martial arts training with judo in 1960 under Terry Wingrove and started Shotokan karate in 1973 under Michael Randall and the Adamou brothers, Nick and Chris, gaining his black belt from Hirokazu Kanazawa in 1977. Originally studying environmental design, he later read for M.A and Ph.D degrees from the University of London, and is a Chartered Psychologist and teacher. Doctor Layton has appeared on both BBC television and radio in connection with his academic work. A prolific writer with over one hundred publications, including twenty-seven books on karate and numerous learned research notes, he has emerged not only as, almost certainly, the most productive (with well over one million published words), but, arguably, the finest writer on Shotokan in the world. He has co-authored with famed Okinawan Goju-ryu master, Morio Higaonna; former British manager/coach to the world champion All-Styles karate team, Kyokushinkai master, Steve Arneil; the founder of British karate, Vernon Bell; and, Michael Randall, amongst others. Doctor Layton's biographies, *Kanazawa 10th Dan*, *Masao Kawasoe 8th Dan*, *Karate Master: The Life and Times of Mitsusuke Harada*, *Reminiscences by Master Mitsusuke Harada*, and, *Ronnie Watt, 8th Dan*, along with, *Funakoshi on Okinawa*, a portrait of life on Okinawa in the 19th century, have been published to acclaim, as has his two volume work, *Shotokan Dawn*, and its Supplement, which, along with *Shotokan Dawn Over Ireland*, *Shotokan Horizon*, *You Don't Have to Dress to Kill*, *The Liverpool Red Triangle Karate Club*, and, *Scotland's First Karate Club*, chart the first ten years of Shotokan karate in the British Isles in astonishing detail. He has been the recipient of the Historian of the Year award (2004) and Writer of the Year award (2008) of the International Ryukyu Karate Research Society, and a holder of the Scottish Samurai Award of the National Karate Institute (Scotland). He was a correspondent for *Fighting Arts* magazine from 1984-1997 and has also acted for more than twenty years as a consultant reader for the journals, *Perceptual and Motor Skills*, and, *Psychological Reports*, on experimentation into the martial arts. Any spare time is taken up researching new books, pursuing his love of archaeology and world cinema, and enjoying the peace of rural life, by the sea, with his wife, daughter and labrador. A highly innovative and deep-thinking *karateka*, he graded 7th Dan in 2004.